The Joy of
TWINS

The Joy of

TWINS

Having, Raising, and Loving Babies Who Arrive in Groups

Pamela Patrick Novotny

CROWN PUBLISHERS, INC. □ NEW YORK

For Jerry, who has heard it all,
and who has the heart to keep listening

Publisher's Note: The case histories in this book are derived from actual interviews and research. The relevant facts are real, but some of the names and other identifying details have been changed to protect the privacy of the individuals. While the book discusses certain issues, situations, and choices regarding pregnancy, birth, child care, diet, and exercise, it is not intended as a substitute for professional medical advice.

Photo/Illustration Credits: Page x, purchased from Wide World Photos. Page 7, Koshi Shimizu. Pages 8, 241, Carol Hendershot. Pages 36, 57, 58, 75, Kathleen Sherman. Pages 38, 96, 178, 216, 257, Nancy Patrick. Pages 138, 151, 160, Heather Murphy. Page 230, Doug Conarroe. Page 239, Brook Anderson. Page 244, Twins Foundation. Page 247, Janet Robertson. Page 249, David Grimm. Page 266, Josephine Robertson.

Published by Crown Publishers, Inc., 201 East 50th Street, New York, New York 10022. Member of the Crown Publishing Group.

Random House, Inc. New York, Toronto, London, Sydney, Auckland

CROWN is a trademark of Crown Publishers, Inc.

Manufactured in the United States of America

Library of Congress Cataloging-in-Publication Data

Novotny, Pamela Patrick.
  The joy of twins.
  Bibliography: p.
  Includes index.
  1. Twins. 2. Child rearing. I. Title.
HQ777.35 N88   1988   649'.144   87-27281

ISBN 0-517-56819-5

10 9 8 7 6 5 4 3 2

Contents

Acknowledgments   vi

Introduction   vii

1 Who Has a Multiple Birth and Why?   1

2 Transitions   11
—Understanding yourself and doing well with your babies during their earliest days.

3 Feeding the Masses   39
—How-tos and whys of breastfeeding and bottlefeeding for twins and triplets.

4 That First Year   81
—Developing the attitudes, routines, and help so life can be more than just okay.

5 Mothercare   139
—How to take care of yourself so you can take care of them.

6 Feeling the Changes: Fathers and Families   179
—How to make the adjustment to the birth of multiples smoother and happier.

7 Going Back to Work   205
—How you can do it if you want to. Why you may not want to. How to get a paycheck without going to an office.

8 Language Ability and Brains: Is There Enough to Go Around?   227
—Why the news about development in multiples is not bad news.

9 Halves of a Whole or Complete in Themselves? How Multiples Realize Individuality   245
—Why many twins and triplets have a stronger sense of identity than the rest of us.

10 What's Good About Twins   269
—A quick-reference list.

Reader Questionnaire   273

Resources   274

Bibliography   282

Index   290

Acknowledgments

This book may never have been born if I hadn't first given birth to our twins, Anna and Claire. I am grateful to them for showing me what is, in fact, the joy of twins. And I am grateful to Rachel and Samuel, who came (one at a time) after my twins, for giving me the gift of perspective. Of course, no one can undertake—and complete—a project like this without a supportive spouse, and my husband, Jerry, is the best. My heartfelt gratitude must also go to Marilyn Low, who became a very important and loving part of my children's lives during the hours I spent in my office.

Others helped too. My thanks to Genevieve Paulson for inspiration and clarification, and to Diana Korte for reading and reading, and keeping me honest. The book would not have had the photographs it does, in such number or quality, without the organizational skills and tenacity of Doyen Mitchell, or the photographic skills of Nancy Patrick.

Some of the professionals whose comments and information kept me on track are: Kate Capage, David Hay, Robert Plomin, and Alan Ryan.

I have a special place in my heart for all the wonderful parents of twins and triplets who so willingly let me know what it is like for *them* to be a mother or father of multiples, and who sent photographs by the hundreds for consideration for the book.

And last, a special thanks must go to my editor at Crown, Barbara Grossman, and to my agent, Lynn Seligman. They both understand, as no other editor and agent could, what a blessing multiples are.

Introduction

What did they say when you told them you were expecting two babies instead of one?

Your mother-in-law might have said, "Boy will you have your hands full."

Your neighbor might have said, "I'm glad it's you and not me."

Your sister might have said, "Oh no, double (or triple) trouble."

And your husband might have just said, "Oh no!"

Chances are, one or two of the people you told of your impending multiple birth thought it was wonderful and told you so. But you may have also discovered what the majority of mothers of multiples know: There isn't much in the way of positive support for parents of multiples.

What there is for many people is a lot of worry and anxiety that may make you think:

• This job of caring for multiples will be (or is) too hard; I can't do it.

• My twins or triplets will have problems all their lives because they are multiples.

• My family, my career, and my other children will all suffer because of the birth of my multiples.

While taking care of infant multiples is not easy, and guiding twins or triplets through childhood and adolescence may have its own special concerns, *The Joy of Twins* can show you how to do more than just get by as a parent of multiples.

This book offers the kind of realistic *and* positive outlook that can help parents of multiples successfully and joyfully adjust to babies who arrive in groups. For example, until now the small amount of information available has stressed the chaos and difficulties of parenting multiples and has focused on developmental and social problems some multiples may have. But *The Joy of Twins* takes a look at the most recent research, which shows that the vast majority of twins and their families are not only healthy, happy human beings, but many of them feel that being twins and having twins has given them an *advantage* in understanding themselves and those around them.

I have two hopes for this book. The first is that it will enable you to find your own best way of caring for yourself and your family by showing you options you may not have considered. The second is that it will help demolish some of the mythology—most of it negative—that surrounds multiples and their families. You don't have to believe your children are *less* because they are twins—*less* intelligent, *less* social, *less* healthy, *less* of an individual. And you don't have to believe your ability to enjoy your own life is diminished because you had two or three babies instead of one. I hope you'll see why in these chapters.

As a mother of twins and two single born children, I would be the first to admit that caring for all of them as well as myself and my husband is not easy. That is why I've included the What's Good About Twins Quick-Reference List. A mother of one calm six-month-old may laugh at the idea of having a list posted on the refrigerator to remind her why her child is so terrific, but a mother of multiples will understand.

Mothers of multiples will also understand why this book has been designed as it has. I know you don't have the time or the energy to sit down and read for half an hour, or even for fifteen minutes. So please browse through and pull out useful ideas when you don't have time to really read. Look at the pictures of happy, well-adjusted twins and triplets. Read the quotes from other mothers. You will discover that you're not alone in your difficulties or in your joys. You can also learn that just as others have found workable options where it looked like none existed, so you can find a constructive way to manage this life that at times seems so difficult.

If the voices of parents in this book are helpful to you, so your voice will be helpful to future parents of multiples. Nothing could be more appropriate for future editions than for me to pass on what you have learned. So I invite you to complete and mail in the Reader Question-naire.

This book grew out of my belief that twinship is a gift: to parents who can learn they are far more capable than they ever dreamed and to twins, who can learn so much about themselves from each other. My hope is that *The Joy of Twins* will make these gifts a reality for you and your family, too.

The Joy of
TWINS

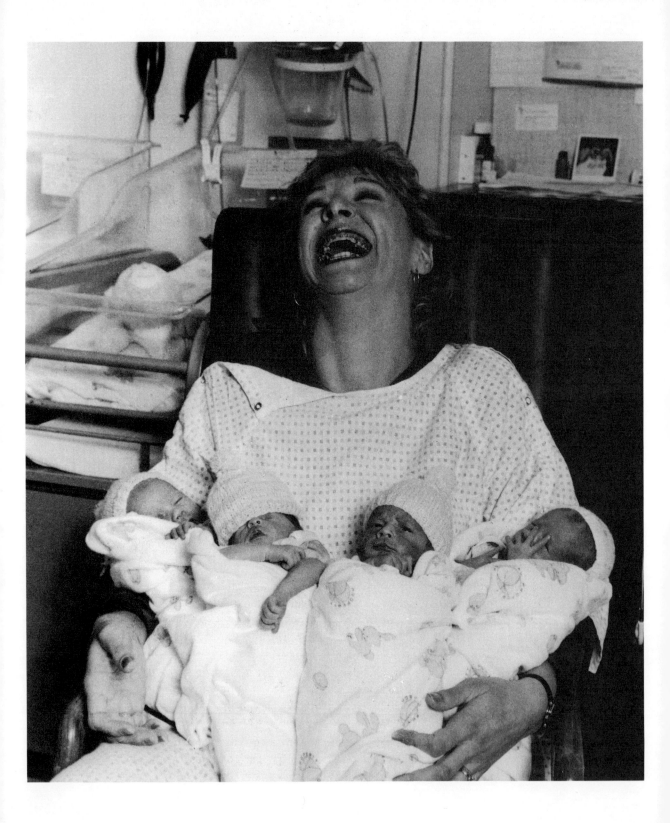

1 | Who Has a Multiple Birth and Why?

"We don't have twins anywhere in my family. I don't know how I ended up with them."

A miracle has happened. You conceived, and may have already given birth to, twins, triplets, or maybe more. Your most careful planning couldn't cover this option. But then, no one really plans to have a multiple birth, so saying you had an unexpected one is the kind of redundancy that only parents of twins or triplets would understand.

So now you have more than one baby, and more than a few questions about dealing with the situation.

Everyone has his or her idea of what it is parents of multiples want to know, ranging from news of the latest baby-care gimmicks to ideas on nurturing their children's individuality. But the first, and often the most urgently asked question has to be "Why me?"

There is no quick and easy answer to that question, but if you look in the right places, you'll find clues that can lead you to your own unique answer.

WHY ME?

If it seems that, lately, multiple births are more than infrequent accidents of nature; that everywhere one looks, there goes another twin stroller, it may be more than the old Volkswagen syndrome. (You know, you never notice Volkswagens—or pierced ears or leather jackets—until *you* get them; then you see them everywhere.) According to the National Center for Health Statistics, the number of multiple births in the United States is in fact on the rise. In 1985, there was a 6 percent increase in the number of multiple births, swelling the multiple-birth rate to its highest point since 1956. Nearly 80,000 live babies were born in multiple deliveries in 1985, compared to 74,600 born in 1984. Most of these multiple births were of twins, but even the rates of triplet and quadruplet births have continued to rise steadily, from 2.1 percent of all multiple births in 1983 to 2.4 percent in 1985.

What's making the difference? Changes in life-style seem to be the culprit. While the birthrate for identical multiples (babies that come from

one fertilized egg that splits and hence have the same genetic makeup) remains unaffected by any variables studied—they can appear like a bolt from the blue to anyone—it is commonly recognized that fraternal multiples (babies from two or more separately fertilized eggs who just happen to share womb space and are no more similar than other siblings) occur more frequently to certain people.

In fact, if American women really wanted to increase the multiple-birth rate, they couldn't be doing a better job. For example, more women are waiting until they are in their thirties to start a family, many are taking birth-control pills to curtail their fertility until they are ready for children, and increasing numbers are taking fertility drugs to get the ball rolling.

Mothers who have acquired a few gray hairs *before* having children are one of the signposts of the eighties. The norm used to be that a women had most, if not all, of her children before she hit the ripe old age of thirty. Perhaps because of the emphasis on career that came out of the women's movement, or perhaps because of economically rocky times, many women are now waiting until their thirties to even start having a family. In addition, Baby Boomers have swollen the ranks of women in their thirties. (There were 43 percent more white women aged 30–34 in 1979 than in 1970, while the number of white women aged 20–24 increased by only 18 percent during the same time period. Multiple-birth rates differ significantly by race. See how later in this chapter.) It's that huge group of Baby Boomers that has chosen en masse to wait until after their twenties to start a family.

The increase in over-thirty white mothers has been startling. For example, in 1985 one in four babies (single- and multiple-born) were born to mothers over thirty. That's a 5 percent increase since 1980, when one in five babies were born to mothers in their thirties.

Put those thousands of over-thirty mothers together with the fact that a woman's chances for a multiple birth increase when she's 35–39 years old, for reasons not completely understood by medical researchers, and you begin to get a clue as to why the multiple-birth rate is increasing now.

Those women who are 35–39 are three to five times as likely as younger women to release more than one egg when they ovulate, which can produce a multiple birth. That, of course, is only for fraternal multiples—children from separate eggs. The mother's age doesn't seem to have any effect on the rate for identicals—children from a single egg.

The increased number of women in their thirties and the larger number of them waiting to have their first births are probably the most significant factors affecting the number of multiple births in the U.S., but other forces are at work, too.

Are You an "Older Mother"?

There was no doubt that Sharon and her husband, Richard, both attorneys, wanted a baby. It was just a matter of when. At thirty-one, Sharon was advancing steadily in her law career, but she and Richard decided to wait just a few more years to have a baby until she was firmly ensconced as a junior partner in her law firm; until she could feel really confident about taking the six-month leave of absence she wanted when she had that first baby.

The leave turned out to be longer than anyone expected. Sharon, by now thirty-four, gave birth to fraternal twin boys, who at their appearance managed to give their parents, the doctor, and assorted medical personnel in the delivery room the surprise of their lives. The boys' birth was one of thousands of unannounced arrivals of twins that happen every year in the U.S. despite constantly changing technology for detecting multiple pregnancies.

There have been studies that show that a woman's fertility decreases as she reaches her thirties. Those women who are looking for help conceiving are finding it in an increased availability of technology for women who have trouble with ovulation—another reason for the increase in the number of multiple births.

There are two kinds of fertility drugs to help with ovulation. One is called clomiphene, commonly marketed under the brand name of Clomid. It works by stimulating the pituitary gland to tell the ovaries to do what they should be doing—producing and releasing mature eggs. Since it uses the body's own hormones to cue the overies, Clomid has not been associated with multiple births.

The other drug used to stimulate ovulation is called human menopausal gonadotropin, most commonly marketed under the brand name Pergonal. Pergonal bypasses the pituitary and introduces a hormone from the urine of postmenopausal women to make eggs in the ovaries come to maturity. A second drug, given several days after the Pergonal, is a releasing agent that prompts the ovaries to release the mature eggs to travel down the Fallopian tubes where they can become fertilized. That's where multiple births come from.

Although there are methods by which physicians can attempt to monitor how many eggs have matured and whether there are too many to release, still 20 percent of pregnancies resulting from Pergonal are multiple pregnancies. Of those, 95 percent are twin pregnancies. The higher-order multiple pregnancies get a lot of publicity, but as of 1984, there were only eleven sets of American quintuplets who have survived intact, and about another dozen sets of quints in which four or fewer have survived. In addition, there are about 150 families with quadruplets and one with a set of sextuplets.

Without drugs, twins in the U.S. occur about once in every 80 births. The incidence of triplets is once in every 80×80 births, or once in 6,400 biths. Quadruplets happen once in every $80 \times 80 \times 80$ births or once in 512,000 births.

While those higher-order multiples are not exactly appearing in droves because of fertility drugs, the chances of having such a birth do go up significantly with the use of drugs. For example, according to the formula used above, quintuplets would happen once in every 41 million births in the U.S. ($80 \times 80 \times 80 \times 80$), but when the mother has conceived as a result of using Pergonal, they show up once in just fewer than 5,000 births.

Millions of women take birth-control pills, and thousands discontinue their use each year in anticipation of getting pregnant. Obviously all of them do not end up with a multiple birth. But there is a select group of ex–pill users who do.

Did You Take Fertility Drugs?

Ann and Tom got married because they knew they wanted children. They'd been living together for three years and decided that since Ann was twenty-eight and they could plainly hear the tick of the biological clock, they'd make their union official and have a baby before Ann turned thirty.

They made the union official, but no babies appeared, and after over a year of trying to get pregnant, Ann finally consulted a fertility specialist. Following months of tests, the doctor told Ann she was ovulating irregularly, often not at all, and that a drug to stimulate ovulation might help her.

The drug worked. Within a year, Ann and Tom were the proud, if not slightly bewildered, parents of fraternal triplets.

Did You Use Birth-Control Pills?

Carol had always used the most efficient means of birth control she could find to ensure she adhered to the life plan she and John had devised. They had it all worked out in five-year segments: five years to get married, develop their careers, and travel for fun; five years to have a child and concentrate on parenting; five years to have a second child and buy a bigger house; and so on.

Carol used birth-control pills during the early years of their marriage. On their fifth wedding anniversary, John bought a bottle of champagne to celebrate the end of the first five-year plan. According to plan, Carol had discontinued her birth-control pills and bought a three-month supply of foam and condoms to be sure she didn't get pregnant too soon after she stopped taking oral contraceptives. Everyone said it was best to wait a few months to get pregnant after taking the pill.

But the romantic evening did its work all too well. Nine months after

Researchers have found in several studies conducted during the 1970s that women who use the pill for at least six months and who conceive in the first month or two after discontinuing its use at least double their chances of having twins, particularly twins of unlike sex. Conception by the third month after discontinuing the pill results in a normal frequency of twin births.

The studies, conducted independently by researchers at Harvard and Yale on a total of nearly twenty-five thousand women, showed that the doubled twin-birth rate was the same for both white and black women. Researchers theorized that the increase in twinning was caused by an increase in the hormone pituitary gonadotropin that normally follows discontinuance of the pill. That's the same hormone administered to women in the form of Pergonal to prompt their ovaries to mature and release eggs for fertilization. Former pill users who get pregnant in the first two months after stopping the pill seem to get the same surge of the hormone—in this case from their own bodies—that allows more than one egg to mature and release, which can result in a multiple birth.

Of course not everyone gets pregnant so soon after taking the pill, but the Harvard study showed that 28.4 percent of all oral-contraceptive users conceived within two months or less of cessation of the pill. That's a fairly large number of women who are doubling their chances of having a twin birth.

DO TWINS "RUN IN YOUR FAMILY"?

One of the most commonly misunderstood aspects of multiple births is the role of heredity in determining who does and who doesn't have them. The only hereditary factor recognized in multiple births is that if women on the *mother's* side have produced fraternal twins, that mother *may* also have a tendency to release more than one mature egg at a time. As far as medical researchers have been able to determine, there is not a consistent genetic trait passed from one generation of women to another that ensures either that more than one mature egg will be released from her ovaries at one time or, of course, that they will both be fertilized. In short, there are plenty of women who have all the "right" hereditary factors who never have anything but a single birth, and equally as many women who never even thought of having a multiple birth who are pushing twin strollers.

Also, the way most family stories are passed down, it is often unclear if twins in past generations were fraternal or identical, or if it was Great Aunt Rose's brother's wife or her sister who had the twins who died at birth. As we've noted before, only fraternal births are affected by things like heredity—identicals happen with the same frequency to anyone, cutting across lines drawn by race, number of previous births, age of the mother, and other factors.

In fact, variables like age, race, and number of previous births are much more important in determining who has a multiple birth than is a concept as vague in this case as heredity. As we've seen, older mothers have demonstrated a clear tendency to produce fraternal multiple births. The National Center for Health Statistics has also recorded an increase in multiple births for women who have had more previous births, up to four, and for black women. A higher fraternal twinning rate among black women around the world is so consistent, despite the mother's age or number of previous births, that researchers suggest that black women simply have a greater tendency to release two mature eggs than do white women. In the U.S., a white woman's chances of having twins are 1 in 105, whereas a black woman's chances are 1 in

their fifth anniversary, Carol and John welcomed a tiny boy and tiny girl into the world. They spent some of Carol's time in the hospital after the birth rewriting their second five-year plan.

73. That varies somewhat with geographical location; the highest twinning rates for whites are in the northeastern U.S., and the highest rates for blacks are in the north-central region.

Illustrating the statistics is one black woman in New Jersey who in 1983 gave birth to her third set of fraternal twins in ten years. At that rate, she could just about top mothers from the world's most twin-prone culture—the Yorubas of Nigeria, in whom twins occur in 1 of every 22 pregnancies. Researchers have theorized that the high twinning rate among Nigerians may be due to the high level of a substance like the female hormone estrogen in the yams that are a staple in their diets—but that doesn't quite explain the twins in New Jersey!

By contrast, twinning in Japan, and among people of Oriental descent, is among the lowest in the world. In Japan, twins occur only once in 254 births.

WHAT IF YOU ARE "NONE OF THE ABOVE"?

There are some other causes of multiples that researchers have come up with, although for the most part they are rare, virtually one-of-a-kind occurrences. But they can be nonetheless interesting to look at. For example, some researchers have theorized that twinning rates may involve psychological factors as well as biological ones. Two researchers at the Gregor Mendel Institute of Medical Genetics and Twin Studies in Rome found that fraternal twinning increased not only with the mother's age and number of previous births, but also with illegitimate and premarital pregnancies. Some American studies have shown higher fraternal twinning rates among children conceived within the first three months of marriage, which may explain a peak in twinning rates that occurred in the U.S. in 1946 after World War II. The average time to conception then, following military discharges, was 2.2 months shorter for mothers of twins than for mothers of singletons.

To explain this "eagerness factor" some researchers suggest that at the time of marriage, or upon return of husbands from war, or in an out-of-wedlock relationship, there can be a psychological state that stimulates the pituitary gland to produce more gonadotrophic hormones. Those are the same homones administered to nonovulating women in the form of the drug Pergonal to stimulate ovulation. They are also the same hormones that, in excess, can cause more than one egg at a time to mature and travel down the Fallopian tubes to become fertilized—producing a multiple birth.

Another unusual occurrence is when twins actually have two different fathers. One or two cases have been substantiated—one of them through paternity tests conducted by researchers at U.C.L.A.'s School of Medicine as reported in the *New England Journal of Medicine* in 1978. Double paternity can be explained by the fact that some women ovulate twice a month.

The last factor influencing multiple births has nothing to do with researchers, medical facts, or studies. It's just plain luck. Medical evidence can go a long way toward explaining who has multiple births and how often they happen, but it is not uncommon to be left with unanswered questions, even after the most diligent sleuthing to find out why a particular multiple birth occurred. As we've seen, the identical twinning rate is unaffected by any of the variables we've discussed here. Anyone can have them and no one really knows why. All they know now is that having identical twins has nothing to do with anything the mother or father did or didn't do. And even fraternal multiples, while their occurrence does seem to be influenced by various factors, can turn up in the most unexpected places—like in families with no perceived tendencies toward multiples.

So if you find yourself in the "none of the above" category, you can consider yourself lucky that Fate chose you to be privy to one of nature's miracles.

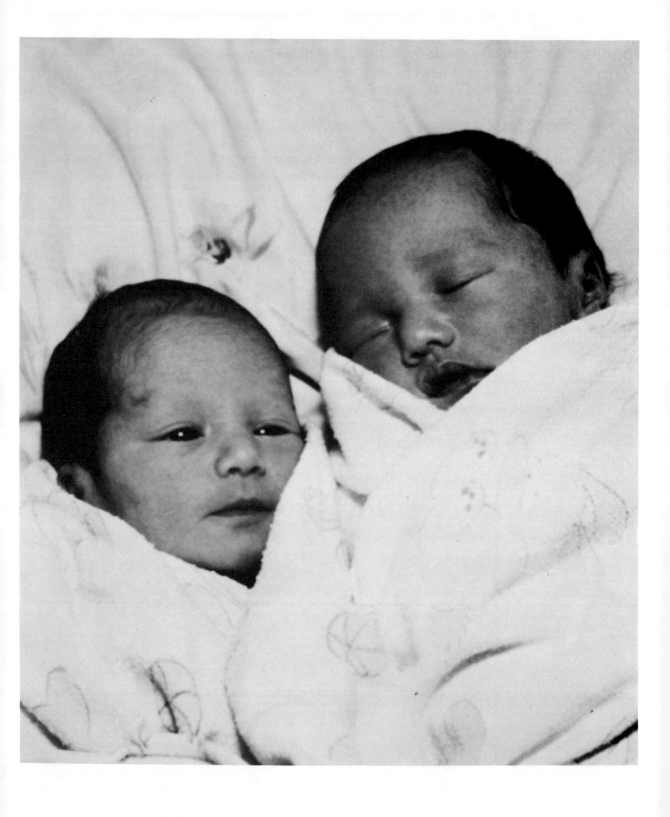

2 | Transitions

"We had a good birth, and the babies and I were fine. But as the day to leave the hospital neared, I panicked. No way did I want to go home alone with those babies. I wanted to take one of the hospital nurses with me!"

After weeks—and for some women, months—of swollen ankles, outgrown maternity clothes, itchy abdomens, and curious stares, the birth of your multiples may look like the blessed light at the end of a long, long tunnel. While some women find the birth of their babies a physical and psychological relief, others find that the transition from being pregnant with multiples to being a mother of multiples feels like an emotional roller coaster. And most mothers probably find themselves somewhere in between those extremes—bouncing around in the back seat of the emotional roller coaster part of the time, and seated confidently in the driver's seat as the competent mom the rest of the time.

Underlying this transition is the kind of help you can get for those first weeks at home, and the way you can arrange your home to make caring for infant multiples as convenient and safe as possible.

THE PREGNANCY-AND-CHILDBIRTH CIRCUS

With a multiple pregnancy, even more energy than usual may go into learning about the pregnancy and birth. You might feel like you are in the center ring of a three-ring circus. Many mothers who know ahead of time they are carrying twins count grams of protein religiously and pack in the calories to ensure adequate nutrition for their babies. They may limit their activities if they can, try to put their feet up at least once a day, and some even stay in bed for weeks or months to help the pregnancy get to term or near-term. Mothers carrying multiples put up with the extra water retention common to multiple pregnancy, the itching abdomen stretched beyond belief, the difficulty in breathing, sleeping, and moving with those growing babies still inside.

If nothing else, their rapidly expanding girth alone places many of these gestating mothers of multiples squarely in the center ring of the pregnancy-and-birth circus, with the limelight trained always on them.

The birth of multiples is in the second ring of the three-ring circus. Often, there is at least one doctor for each baby and one for the mom; plus the dad, the friend who's there to take pictures, and all the nurses. Mom isn't quite the star she was during her pregnancy, but for most moms that's okay, because the babies are her primary focus now, too.

During the hospital stay, mom and babies still get a lot of attention, but this is when the reality begins to set in that it may not be a snap to juggle breastfeeding or bottlefeeding two at a time, comforting two at a time, and caring for herself, her husband, and other family members.

Homecoming is the final act in the circus. Babies, flowers, plants, gifts, and mom are loaded into the car at the hospital and loaded out of the car again at home. And there you are. In the quiet of your own home, just where you longed to be. But wait, both babies begin to cry before you can even show them the cute rainbow-patterned nursery you spent so much time planning during your pregnancy. Your mother doesn't arrive until tomorrow afternoon. You feel silly calling a friend to come help the moment you step in the door. What exactly would you tell her to do, anyway? And you know your husband has to go back to the office tomorrow because he took all that time off to be with you and the babies while you were in the hospital.

The pregancy-and-birth circus is over. It's no wonder new moms cry a lot. Coming home can be worse than the day after Christmas.

WHAT HAPPENS WHEN THE PARTY'S OVER?

If you've had a single-born baby before, or if you know friends who have recently had a baby, you may have noticed that the transition from pregnancy to motherhood can be a rocky one even with only one baby to care for. Many people, inside the medical community and out, have blithely dismissed those up-and-down postpartum days, which sometimes include depression and even feelings of despair, as the unavoidable products of hormones run amok. While different hormone output following birth probably does play a part in how you feel, hormones have yet to be *proved* as the primary cause of depression and emotionality after childbirth. Medical literature, midwives, and most likely your neighbor can all offer examples of new fathers, grandmothers, and adoptive mothers who also have become depressed after the arrival of a baby.

Rather than simply hanging the blame on hormones—something over which we have little or no control—it seems far more useful to focus on what we *can* do, what we *can* change, and how we *can* adapt.

Not everyone gets depressed or has a rocky time emotionally after the birth of her multiples, but some studies show that 50–85 percent of all new mothers report feeling blue or down sometime during the first six months after their births, and another 10 percent report being more seriously depressed at some point during that time. Who are these women? They are likely to be new mothers who had high expectations before the birth, and they are likely to be mothers who are left alone after the birth. Some people believe that the high incidence of postpartum blues and depression in our culture occurs because, more than in most nonindustrial cultures, for example, we leave new mothers all alone at a time when they most need to be mothered themselves.

Students of anthropology know that while mothers in many nonindustrial societies often seem to have a shorter physical recovery from birth, they also usually have a period of being coddled as if they themselves were the fragile newborns, which in a sense they are, in their new roles. It is not uncommon in those cultures for a new mother to be housed in a separate dwelling in which the fire is never allowed to go out. She is the center of attention: warmed by the constant fire, fed, bathed, massaged, and cared for by other women. She is not expected to do anything but take care of her new baby for as much as six weeks in some cultures, and for as little as two weeks in others. In this cozy environment, the new mother doesn't worry about bonding, cleaning house, taking care of other children, cooking dinner, driving in the car pool, or returning to the office. And most anthropologists believe she isn't depressed.

During the last twenty years or so, there has been a cultural movement in this country to return to our birthing roots, and many women have sought to have as "natural" a birth as possible. We often seek the simple births and quick recoveries of the women who live in these nonindustrial societies. But we leave out the special care and support

"I think I cried at least once a day for about six months after my twins were born. Other times I'd be high as a kite at the thought of having these two wonderful babies. I've never been so emotional. I couldn't figure out what was happening to me. Sometimes I thought I might be going crazy."

that helps smooth the entry of those women into motherhood. Even childbirth education classes—now the major source of pregnancy-and-birth information in our culture—place enormous emphasis on every detail of pregnancy, labor, and birth, then skim over or leave out entirely what happens afterward, leaving isolated parents holding the babies and wondering what to do.

YOUR BODY IS YOUR FRIEND

For many mothers there are days when it seems you can't get off the emotional roller coaster. On those days it might help to know that there are good reasons for the way your body and mind behave after something as momentous as gestating and birthing more than one baby at a time. Just as being in tune with your body's birthing ways can help during labor, so being in tune with your body's healing ways can help your transition to motherhood with multiples.

In order to understand what it is your body is healing, it might be helpful to look at how your multiple pregnancy and birth have been different from a single pregnancy and birth. People who work with birthing women know that "surprises" during labor and birth can be extremely unsettling to the mother, to say the least. As a mother of multiples, you may have had more surprises than most.

1. *Did you have surprise multiples?* Reports vary, but it seems that in spite of the technological changes in the last decade, it is not a foregone conclusion that every woman knows she is going to have twins or triplets ahead of time. Some medical journals report that most multiple pregnancies are diagnosed ahead of time using ultrasound, but others say that 57–65 percent of mothers of multiples don't know they will have a multiple birth until one to two weeks before delivery, or until they are giving birth.

2. *Did you have a surprise cesarean section?* If you knew you were having multiples, you may have wanted to have a vaginal birth. Many women do, but you should know that close to half of all mothers of multiples have cesareans. According to the National Center for Health Statistics, in 1986, 64 percent of multiple births were by cesarean, and there is no reason to believe that number is any less today, since the cesarean rate for single births has steadily increased in the last decade. Of course some of those were planned cesareans, but nonetheless, many of you ended up with a birth that was not the one you planned.

3. *Did you have surprise interventions?* Even though you may have had a vaginal birth with your multiples, you still may have been surprised by the interventions you hadn't planned on. Whether you're pregnant or you've already had your babies, you know that twin or triplet pregnancies, healthy or not, are automatically labeled high risk. And high-risk moms are much more likely to have interventions during birth like: the use of one or two fetal monitors, the use of a variety of painkillers, oxytocin to start or speed up labor, amniotomy, imposed fasting, repeated vaginal exams, shaving, enema, episiotomy, and forceps.

4. *Did you have a surprise premature birth?* Between 50–60 percent of multiple births are considered premature—meaning the babies arrived before thirty-seven weeks gestation and/or they weighed less than five and a half pounds each. If you are a mother of premature multiples, you may have used one or more of the methods most often used by physicians to forestall an early birth: labor-stopping drugs, partial or full bedrest, and cerclage or surgically closing the cervix. But despite everyone's best efforts, the babies often come early anyway. For example, one study, reported in 1986 in the British medical journal *The Lancet,* focused on 212 women with twin pregnancies. It showed that when 105 of the women were assigned hospital bedrest, and the other 107 were sent home, the average length of pregnancy was almost *five weeks longer* among the women not confined to bed. So you may have done every little thing your doctor told you to do, and still been surprised by a premature birth.

5. *Did you have surprise complications?* After a healthy, happy pregnancy, you might have had serious complications during your multiple birth. Babies who begin labor in a perfect-for-vaginal-birth, head-down position have been known to move into all sorts of untenable angles during labor, resulting in complications ranging from an emergency cesarean for you, to resuscitation or other medical action for your babies. You and your babies may have had complications after the birth, like an infection they picked up in the hospital, or an infected cesarean scar you noticed later. Or you may have had toxemia, a complication seen in 20–30 percent of multiple pregnancies and characterized by high blood pressure, water retention, and protein in the urine. Although it is not a major contributor to fetal mortality for multiples, as it is for singletons, it can be dangerous to the mother, in a few cases resulting in convulsions and even death. Research shows that no single course of treatment for toxemia works consistently—including diet modifications and bedrest.

You may have had only one or two of these surprises or you may have had nearly all of them, but if you had a multiple pregnancy and birth, this list should look very familiar to you. What do the experts say are the results of these kinds of surprises?

"HOW CAN I FEEL SUCH LOSS WHEN I HAVE JUST BEEN GIVEN SO MUCH?"

It may seem hard to think about or acknowledge feelings of loss when you've just given birth to two, three, or more healthy babies, but there are a lot of reasons why some new mothers and fathers may feel that way after the birth of their multiples. One of those reasons is the element of surprise. As the list of surprises shows, many parents of multiples find that the end of the pregnancy and the birth just didn't turn out the way they expected it to, and behavioral scientists say that these kind of surprises often lead to those feelings of loss. Here are some examples:

1. *Did you get the kind of multiples you thought you would?* A new mother may grieve for the "death" of the fantasy she may have nurtured of a certain kind of birth and of a certain kind of baby. For example, one brown-eyed brunette mother of fraternal girls felt right at home from the start with her brown-eyed brunette girl, but couldn't imagine how she got a blue-eyed blond twin too. It wasn't part of her fantasy to have two so different twins, or to have one so different from herself. Another mother, this one of identical girls, was so caught up in her fantasy of having boy-girl twins that when the first girl was born, she started calling the second, yet-unborn, twin by the boy's name she had chosen. And a mother of premature boys found herself wondering what her two tiny babies might have been like if they'd had those last important weeks to finish their development inside her body. She felt nostalgic for the fantasy babies she'd dreamed of before the premature birth.

We all have expectations about how any important event in our lives will be, or about what a new and important person we are to meet will be like. Reality seldom is the same as our expectations for it, and some period of adjustment—which may be long for some and short for others —must follow.

2. *Did you have surprise multiples?* If you were surprised by the birth of two babies instead of one, please allow yourself a little extra time to adjust. Even if your multiples weren't a delivery-table surprise, accepting *reality* sometimes takes longer than accepting the *prediction.*

The birth of your twins might also have meant that you didn't have the kind of birth you had hoped for, or you may feel that you didn't handle the labor and birth the way you wanted to. (These feelings may also be a product of "birth in the eighties" when, for the first time in history, you can "flunk" childbirth.) All of these things are part of whatever "fantasy" or expectation you might have had of the labor and birth. Whatever disappointment you may feel in reality is worth grieving.

3. *Did you have a surprise cesarean section?* Many mothers, though certainly not all mothers, who have cesarean sections are most struck by the feeling of loss of control over their bodies, their babies, and their own lives. Many feel they were made a victim ("Why me?") or that their bodies were violated, and they often find it difficult to regain trust and confidence in the ability of their bodies to function correctly. ("My body didn't work right.") Often, their self-esteem also suffers. ("If I could have done it 'right' this wouldn't have happened . . .")

4. *Did you have surprise interventions?* Loss of control is one of the issues here too. Unless you were part of the decision-making process about which interventions would be used and which wouldn't, you may feel you lost control of an experience that you believe should have been most intimately yours. In addition, some medications used in conjunction with childbirth interventions can have an effect on how you feel, both mentally and physically. For example, some women report depression, anxiety, temporary paralysis, and headaches after being given some childbirth-related drugs. And some interventions result in unanticipated separations for the mother from the babies, her husband, her family, and her friends. For example, if you looked forward to holding each of your babies immediately after their birth and you ended up not seeing them for twenty-four hours, you may feel the loss of that special time.

5. *Do you mourn the loss of your prepregnant body?* You looked forward to the birth of these babies at least partly because you were tired of being so huge. For some mothers who feel "suddenly slim" by comparison, all it takes is one insensitive remark ("Now you look like a normal nine-month-pregnant lady.") to plunge them into despair. There is real fear that the incredible number of stretch marks and the unbelievable number of pounds left to lose after the birth won't ever go away. And even if they do, there is the belief that your body won't really ever be the same. It won't, but that isn't all bad. See more on body image in chapter 5, Mothercare.

6. *Do you mourn the loss of your prepregnant life-style?* If the idea of caring for one baby is formidable to most parents, the idea of caring for

Expressing instead of *repressing* your feelings at this tender and vulnerable time is the best way to resolve the ways you may feel after birth.

two or more infants at a time is overwhelming to some. The loss of spontaneity in your life, the changes in your relationship with your husband, and the demands on your time and energy as a mother can be surprisingly intense.

7. *What else do you mourn?* For some mothers, the birth of their children brings up old memories and feelings about their own childhoods and about their own mothers that they may have thought were long forgotten. It has been said that during childbirth a woman is opening not just physically, but psychologically as well. She opens her whole being, which is one reason some psychologists believe birthing women, or women who have recently birthed, are so vulnerable. It's not surprising that you find it unsettling to feel this vulnerable just when you are also faced with a challenging new life.

THE ONLY THING THAT'S NOT SURPRISING IS HOW YOU FEEL NOW

It is normal that there is an enormous range of feelings that wash over new mothers in the first days and weeks after giving birth. Most mothers would tell you these feelings usually have nothing directly to do with their babies. A new mother might not recognize exactly where the feelings come from, and she might not have a convenient label like *postpartum depression* for them—but she knows the feelings neither come from, nor are they directed at, her babies.

Many women find that in the first weeks and even months after the birth of their multiples they cry a lot, at both happy *and* sad events; or they cry about things that usually don't affect them. Some see in themselves chronic exhaustion or its opposite, chronic action ("If I stop working, I'll start crying."). They may find themselves more irritable than usual and they may over- or under-eat. Some say they have difficulty functioning on a day-to-day basis and have a hard time relating to their babies. Others find that they have more arguments with their spouse or uncharacteristic recurring colds, backaches, and headaches.

What a familiar list to every new mother!

There are probably thousands of *well-adjusted* mothers of multiples who could look at this list and find many, if not all, of those items in their own lives on certain days. All of these feelings, at one time or another, are within the normal range for women who have recently given birth. And if giving birth for you means that you had two, three, or four babies instead of one, how much more reasonable it is to expect that you will feel this range of emotions—and maybe an even wider range—that much more intensely.

If what you are feeling in the months after your birth is what *you* would call depression, it might be helpful to gain some perspective on the use of this feeling. Some psychologists see depression as a signal to the body to rest and recuperate after physical or psychological trauma. Even though some people may think that depression or grieving is inappropriate when you have so much to be happy about—*don't let them guilt-trip you into thinking you "shouldn't be feeling this way."*

COMING TO TERMS AND MOVING ON

As a mother of multiples, you may have had a much more eventful pregnancy and birth than a mother of a single-born baby and, as a result, you may feel you have more to settle, emotionally and physically, after the birth of your babies. Here are some things you can do to help come to terms with whatever your experience has been:

1. *Accept yourself and your decisions.* No matter what the outcome of your pregnancy and birth, second guessing after the fact ("I should have eaten better, rested more . . .") decisions you made in good faith does no good. As a mother, you need to believe that you did your best for yourself and for your babies. Because you did.

2. *Find support you need among those you love.* Surround yourself with people who share your beliefs and love for your babies. Particularly at this open, vulnerable time soon after their birth, neither you nor your babies need a negative word.

3. *Use your body.* Begin to reinvent your prepregnant body by getting whatever kind of exercise is appropriate for you. Even fifteen minutes of walking outdoors—preferably alone—will not only get your body used to moving in its old ways again, but it will allow you a few minutes of quiet reflection as well, to recharge your spiritual and emotional batteries.

4. *Pamper yourself.* Most of us don't ask for special favors unless we're sick. You may not be sick after the birth of your multiples, but this is the perfect time to think of whatever it is that makes you feel loved and protected—and ask for it. Some people have "cozy" foods that are especially soothing to them, like the macaroni and cheese their mother made when they were home sick from school, or the chicken soup their grandma brought over when flu season hit. To others a favorite novel, fresh sheets on the bed, and classical music on the radio make the perfect solitary break between feeding and diapering babies. And some find that being really pampered means simply having someone willing to listen attentively to whatever needs to be said. Try to

arrange the time and help to make as many as you can of these pampered moments happen. Or ask your husband or a friend to arrange them. For more ideas on taking care of yourself, see chapter 5, Mothercare.

5. *Be touched.* Touch is one of the most powerful of healers. Massage has for many cultures been an important part of birth and the period immediately following. It seems our culture is only just beginning to rediscover the value of touch as a healing force. For example, we know the importance of things like skin-to-skin contact between baby and mother, and mothers of multiples get plenty of that. But mothers seldom gets their share of healing touch. For many couples, touching means sex, and the woman who has just given birth may find that since she is told to wait six weeks until she has sex, she also waits six weeks for a loving touch. (And you may wait much longer than that if you're like many other normal mothers of multiples, for whom a return to a prepregnant sex life simply takes longer than it does for mothers of single-born babies.) Try substituting back rubs or general massage for sex during this time. And if a friend can't figure out what to give you when the babies are born, consider suggesting some baby-sitting time and an appointment with a good masseuse.

6. *Find new ways to express yourself.* It has been said that depression is creativity turned in on itself—creative energy that, with no outlet, rattles around inside and finally goes sour. During the first weeks after the birth, old ways you expressed yourself, through your career or your hobbies, will most likely not fit into your new life with multiples. For now, try to see the things that dominate your new life as creative acts. For example, by simply feeding your babies, whether you breastfeed or bottlefeed, you are molding, shaping—and creating—them. The byword for finding new ways of expressing yourself now is *simplify.* In those early weeks, you can also talk, write notes to yourself or others in a journal, sing, laugh, and cry—all are creative and expressive acts.

Later, you can try fitting in pieces of activities that were important to you before the birth. For example, you can arrange some time to do small, simple sewing projects perhaps, or you can subscribe to a professional journal you might not have taken at home before, to keep yourself conversant with others in your field.

7. *Look ahead.* Sometimes, in the midst of what seems like endless feedings, diaperings, and housework, it feels like time stands still. You are sure you will never again get a good night's sleep. You will never again have time alone or with your husband. And your babies will always demand about twenty-three hours of your attention out of any given day.

In rational moments, we all know those things aren't true, but in the heat of "battle," we often can't see past the diaper pail. For some mothers, it helps to look ahead sometimes. If your babies aren't sleeping well now, you might be able to lighten the situation by realizing that in two or three weeks they might be—babies' schedules *always* change. If you can see time as a continuum and this difficult day as just a tiny part of all the time in your life, you might not feel so stalled. Keeping a calendar close to the area where you change and dress your babies might help maintain a grip on time and the fact that it does pass—and that with each passing day your babies are taking steps, however tiny, toward independence.

HOW CAN WE BE EXPECTED TO BOND WITH TWO BABIES IN THE MIDST OF THIS?

When Marshall Klaus and John Kennell published the results of their research in the early 1970s on the bonding that takes place between parents and babies soon after birth, they probably didn't forsee how popularized and oversimplified it would become. On the plus side, because of their bonding research, many hospitals have recognized the importance of making it possible for parents and babies to be together in those tender, receptive moments after birth.

But on the minus side, many people have an oversimplified picture of bonding that could be called the "epoxy" theory of relationships. There is often a feeling among parents that if you don't get properly "glued" to your babies at exactly the right time, which only occurs very soon after birth, then you will have missed your chance. Bonding has come to seem for many like a one-time offer: miss it now and you'll forever regret it. Who knows *how* your kids will turn out if you don't bond right!

What did the human race do before babies were born in hospitals and hospitals had "bonding rooms"?

If we take a closer look at bonding and what the experts are saying about it now, and use a little common sense, maybe we can all take the pressure off "performing" correctly so soon after something as momentous as the birth of multiples.

Common sense and experience show that most (but not all) mother's can't wait to see and hold those babies they have carried for so many months and have worked so hard to birth. Studies show that holding, comforting, and breastfeeding babies soon after birth calms babies *and* mothers, and can certainly get many women off to a good start as they learn to be mothers. That contact can also help many

"I remember my friend trying to reassure me during the birth of my twins by telling me that the babies were fine. To tell you the truth, I couldn't care less about the babies at that point. I was exhausted from the birth, and the idea of the babies was still so unreal to me, I hadn't really thought of *them*. I was just thinking of the task at hand—pushing them out!"

fathers of multiples, because there's always another baby to hold, and he can be a needed and an integral part of the family picture from the first moment after birth.

For other parents, the reality and intensity of the moment may mean that they need a little more time to develop their attachment to their babies.

What about all those mothers and fathers who take some time to feel close to their babies? Some parents fall in love with their babies at first sight. Others take days, weeks, and sometimes longer to feel that way. Does that mean they are bad parents?

Once again, common sense tells us that we just can't make that kind of assumption. Generations of American babies born in hospitals spent the first days of their lives in nurseries, and only visited their mothers every four hours to be fed. That's the way it still is in many hospitals. This scenario may not be what we would call the ideal situation, but does it mean that *none* of those parents and children *ever* bond? And what about adoptive parents? Is it impossible for them to bond with their babies because they've missed the magic moment after birth? It's hard to believe that is so.

And it *isn't* so if you believe a new theory by Daniel Stern, a psychiatrist at Cornell Medical School. He sees personality development as a result of a long continuum of small events rather than the result of a single dramatic event during a certain developmental stage.

In other words, Stern says that your children are shaped by everyday acts throughout their lives. "An imbalance at one point can be corrected later; there is no crucial period early in life—it's an ongoing lifelong process," Stern said in a 1986 *New York Times* article.

With all due respect to Stern and psychological research, your grandmother could probably have told you that. For decades since your grandmother raised children, psychologists have believed that childhood was a kind of "parade of epochs" during which parents had to be sure to accomplish the correct emotional tasks at the correct time with their children. Stern's ideas fly in the face of those beliefs. Of course there isn't agreement in the behavioral-science community about all this, but as a parent, you might rest easier knowing:

1. There is a wide range of beliefs about your role and your timing in the formation of your children's personalities, and

2. No one *really* knows exactly how humans become who they are. Psychology is a relatively new and a very theoretical science. The theories may throw some light on child-rearing for you, but remember that they are *theories*.

3. Life is different for everyone. What constitutes nurturing for

children in one family may seem like smothering for children in another family. We each must find our own way, in our own context.

Parents of multiples are often concerned about bonding with two babies at a time. There have been studies that show that this is difficult, and some psycholgists even believe that humans are incapable of bonding with two babies at a time, thus the tendency of some parents to treat their twins as a unit—or one child in two bodies instead of two separate people. But when nurses in one hospital asked mothers of twins how they felt about bonding with two babies, not a single mother reported it to be a problem. The vast majority of parents of twins have no trouble developing a close bond in their own time to each of their babies. Ask parents who have large families how they can possibly bond to three, four, or more children at a time, and you might be greeted with a hearty laugh.

The bottom line on bonding with multiples seems to be that if you see bonding as a static event—a moment in time at which you must have eye contact and skin contact simultaneously with two or more infants—you may indeed be in trouble.

But if you see bonding as an ongoing process with all kinds of interesting curves and twists—a process that begins at the moment of birth and continues throughout your lives—then maybe you can give yourself and your twins or triplets some time and space to develop your own special bond.

"Holding my babies soon after their birth was great, but I was so tired, I didn't mind that the nurses took them away for a while. It really was about three days before I felt that I loved them."

GETTING HELP

One of the things that will help you have that needed time and space early on is having help with your multiples. From the day you find out you are having (or have just had) multiples, the first piece of advice you hear from every side is *"Get help!"*

That sounds good, but what pops into your mind when someone advises you to get help? For many people, it's some variation on these themes:

- "I can't afford to hire help."
- "My mother can't get much time off from work."
- "Even if I had help, I wouldn't really know what to ask them to do."
- "I'll be all right. I have to learn how to deal with the babies by myself sometime anyway."

All of these can be valid statements. But you might be glad to know that while hiring someone or corralling your mom as a helper are two options, they aren't your only options. Figuring out exactly the kind, the amount, and the cost of help you need is only a matter of looking carefully at the kind of life you lead. And looking at your new life realistically may be just what you need to see that a little help in the right places can improve the quality of your life tremendously.

DECIDING WHAT YOU NEED

This checklist might help you see more clearly just where and when you need help. The help you choose for the transition between hospital and home might be the help you use later, too. For example, an au pair (a young person from another country who comes to the U.S. to do child care in exchange for room and board) who arrives just before your babies are born can double as postpartum and long-term help. Or the high-school girl next door might be the one you hire to help after school in the early weeks after the babies come, and she might be the one to work more hours for you during the summer.

Once you know what kind of help you need, you can review your options and begin to develop a plan that will suit your needs.

• Do you have other children? If you do, will you need to have them cared for so you can use your time in other ways (with the babies, by yourself, with your spouse or friends)? If you don't know how you will want to use your time, can you arrange child-care with a person who is willing to care for the older children alone, the babies alone, or a combination of the two so that child-care time is flexible?

• Do you prefer to have someone come to your home for child care, or will some or all of your children be going out to daycare, preschool, etc.? You might consider in-home care, both for convenience and to protect the babies from illnesses that can be carried home from child-care centers by older siblings.

• Will you be, or are you now, recovering from medical complications of the pregnancy and birth, a cesarean section, for example? If you and/or your babies are in need of home medical care, you may be eligible for reimbursement for the cost of that help from your insurance company or for help from Medicaid. To find out, check your insurance policy, contact your insurance agent, and call the Medicaid office in your state. (It's usually listed under Medicaid Information in the white business pages.) Federal and state governments share the cost of Medicaid programs, but they are administered by individual states, each of which makes its own rules. In many states, you do not have to qualify for welfare to receive Medicaid. Many middle-income families with large medical bills are eligible for help. You may also be eligible even though you are covered by other insurance.

• Will you be relying on your health insurance or a government agency for whatever help you receive with the babies? If you know about your multiples ahead of time, make a point of it to see if you are entitled to help in the form of a home visitor or visiting homemaker. Call your county or state social services department, health department, or public health department to see if you qualify. In some states, a few insurance companies and health-maintenance organizations have recently expanded their coverage of things like doula—or homecare— services, which are explained later in this chapter. Check your insurance policy, or talk to your agent to find out if yours is one.

• If you won't have any aid in paying for help after the birth, can you open a separate savings account during your pregnancy to start saving for those costs? Even a little bit shaved off the family budget over a period of time can add up. Friends and relatives wanting gift suggestions can also donate to the cause.

• If you know you won't have any money to pay for help after the babies arrrive, consider some of the trade or barter options listed below.

• Which of these is most important to you: a clean house, a picked-up house, a hot meal, clean clothes, time for yourself, time for you and your spouse, more sleep, time with friends, time with other children? Look carefully at your priorities, particularly if you can only choose one kind of help. Try not to jump to conclusions about what's really important and what makes you feel less harried. For example, it's easy to assume that you'll need help with housecleaning, but many women have found that during their postpartum days it is no big deal to get family members to pick up and do light housework. But it is a big deal to get dinner on the table every night. For these women, the job they most need help with could be cooking instead of cleaning.

WHO CAN HELP?

The options for help are wider ranging than you may think. Here is a list of some of them. The last part of the list might spark your own thinking about creative ways to get what you need without spending a fortune.

Au pair

These are young people, usually females, who want to come to the United States from a variety of countries, usually European, to combine a work situation with a cultural experience. If this option looks good to you, you might want to arrange for an au pair as your postpartum helper, who could then become a long-term helper.

Historically, it's been catch-as-catch-can in finding and recruiting an au pair. If you knew someone who had an au pair, and the au pair had a friend at home who also wanted to come to the United States, you were in luck. The hitch with au pairs has been that they can only get a tourist visa which allows them to be in the United States for six months at a time (renewable for another six months), and which means that if they are employed, they are working illegally. It also means that if they are caught, they are deported. And under a new immigration law that went into effect June 1, 1987, employers of illegal au pairs can also be slapped with fines ranging from two hundred and fifty dollars for a first offense, up to ten thousand for more than one offense.

Despite their illegal status, many girls are willing to set up a reasonably believable, but bogus, scenario to get past immigration authorities. For example, they must provide proof that they are only visiting this country as a tourist and have some means of support, other than working for a living, while they are here. That proof is usually provided by phony letters from parents or friends at home and in this country.

Most au pairs receive a small salary and room and board in exchange for child care and some household chores. It can be a good deal for a year's worth of child care if you get an au pair who fits in with your family and your needs. For some people, though, it has been a disaster, mostly because families usually take the girl (and she takes the family) sight unseen.

One solution to the hit-and-miss nature of getting an au pair comes in the form of a pilot program called Au Pair in America. Started by the American Institute for Foreign Study Scholarship Foundation in Greenwich, Connecticut, the program offers a more controlled approach to recruiting young European visitors as au pairs. It matches applications from potential employers with au pairs, and sets standards for pay offered and work expected. Visas for young girls in this program are obtained through the U.S. Department of Information Services. Since they get a cultural exchange visa instead of a tourist visa, they don't have problems with immigration authorities that girls working on a tourist visa (and their employers) can. The pilot program will be re-evaluated in 1988 by the federal government, which is then to decide if it will continue. To get in touch with Au Pair in America, see the Resources list in the appendix.

Whether you find her through an organization or by yourself, an au pair probably won't come cheap. Through Au Pair in America, you can expect to pay about one hundred and fifty dollars a week for a maximum five-and-a-half-day week of no more than nine-hour days over a twelve-month period, plus travel expenses to your home. As the host family, you will also be asked to pay tuition fees of up to three hundred dollars a year for the au pair to attend personal or cultural enrichment courses in a local adult-education program. That's more than you would pay if you found the au pair yourself, but through the organization you have a better chance of getting a good match, and they guarantee a replacement if you don't. They also provide counselors to deal with problems that may arise between the family and the au pair, and assure that there will be no immigration problems.

If you do find an au pair yourself, you work out your own combination of salary and travel expenses. In either case, you also must have an extra bedroom in your home for her.

Doula

One of the newer options for help after the birth of multiples is one of the doula services that are springing up around the country. *Doula* is an ancient Greek word meaning helping woman or servant. Doula services concentrate on helping the mother in any way she needs help. They will usually do things like cooking, light housekeeping, keeping up with the laundry, taking care of children, and running errands. Many of these services employ women who are knowledgeable about breast-feeding, who can offer support and answer nursing questions. They are also qualified to answer questions about bottlefeeding, infant care, and personal postpartum care.

Some doula services are run by registered nurses or midwives, some by professional counselors, others by mothers who wish they'd had a caring woman to help when they needed it. In most states, doula services are not paid for by insurance, but that may be changing in some eastern states.

Doula services commonly charge between ten and fifteen dollars an hour. Most require a minimum of four hours a day and may work for a family for an average of ten days, but that figure can vary to fit your needs. And since a doula isn't exclusively providing child care for the babies, doula services don't usually charge extra for more than one baby. That may vary, so ask the service you contact.

For names and addresses of some doula services, see the Resources list in the appendix.

Visiting Nurse, Home Health Aide

You might want to consider these options if you and/or your babies will need medical help at home, because of birth or prematurity complications, for example, but you don't have to require medical care to hire a visiting nurse. Home health-care services usually provide registered nurses or health aides acting under the supervision of a registered nurse. Their rates vary, but expect to pay roughly ten dollars an hour for a health aide, and more for an R.N. (a higher rate is often charged on holidays). Hourly charges usually decrease with more hours worked each day, and there are sometimes special rates for a live-in or sleep-over arrangement. Some services may charge extra for more than one baby, so be sure to ask.

Some home health-care services have special postpartum nurses, and their care often, but not always, focuses on the infants and you, not on your household and family.

Insurance coverage of home health care varies, so you should check carefully to see if your insurance will cover all or part of the cost. It may be cheaper for you and your babies to complete your recovery at home than it would be in the hospital, and that fact may be attractive to your insurance company. Some aspects of home health care are also tax deductible, so if you require medical help of this kind at home, be sure to check with the IRS or an accountant to see which deductions may apply to you.

See the Resources list in the appendix for national associations to contact to locate a reputable home health-care agency near you.

Other Hired Help

You can work out a variety of arrangements with a variety of people to help take up the slack in those first weeks after the birth of your babies. Here are some ideas:

• Hire a high-school girl to come over for a couple of hours after school every day or a few days each week. She can give you time to take a nap or go for a walk, or she could pick up other children from school, help get dinner started, and generally take the edge off what is for many mothers the hardest time of the day.

• Hire a young adult or college student who wants a part-time job to come in for a few hours each morning to help get the family out the door to school and/or work, then catch up on chores like laundry or cooking extra meals for the freezer.

• Make a standing appointment for the first few months after the babies are born for a baby-sitter to come one evening a week. Use this time to be with your husband. You don't even have to go out, and you probably shouldn't in the early weeks. Tell the baby-sitter you'll be staying in, then lock yourselves in your bedroom (or the den, or wherever you can feel reasonably private) with a bottle of wine, some munchies, and some taped music, or maybe a VCR and a rented movie. For not much money and even less energy on your part, you can have some private time. For most parents it may take some concentration at first to ignore the fact that your children are still in the house, but it could be worth the effort. Or you could schedule a Saturday afternoon date and have the baby-sitter take the babies out for a walk.

• If your husband travels a lot, or has fairly regularly scheduled business appointments in the evening, hire a high-school girl to come help with dinner and getting other children to bed. Or just have her hold the other fussy baby. Not all babies are fussy in the evening, but studies have shown that more than half are—between about 5 P.M. and 11 P.M.

—just when you are ready for some peace and quiet. For this reason, you might consider this kind of help even when your husband is home.

The cost for any of these options varies from about a dollar-fifty an hour to about five dollars an hour, depending on your area and the age and experience of the sitter.

Nonpaid Options

A real advantage to having multiples is that most parents find that family and friends are eager to help. When helpers don't come through, it is often because the parents haven't told potential helpers *exactly* what they need. You can find out how to do that better at the end of this section.

Here are some ideas for nonpaid help. They aren't the only ways to get help you don't have to pay for, and you can tailor these ideas to fit the resources of your community and the needs of your life-style. Use these ideas as a springboard for more creative thinking about how to get help that won't break your budget.

• Check for *support groups*. Call your local hospital to see if they have classes for parents expecting multiples or if they have postpartum groups for parents. Look in your telephone book for listings of clubs for parents of multiples or, if you are nursing, for La Leche League groups. Meeting other parents of multiples before yours are born or when they are still infants can help you establish a network of friends who will be your support group. You can help each other just by being willing, available, and understanding company when your babies are small, and by trading baby-sitting when your children are a little older. If you get a good support group of only a few other mothers going, you can decide as you go along what your needs are and how you, as a group, can meet those needs.

• Whether you are pregnant with multiples or have young babies, you can *appeal for help to your church or another charitable or service organization* (YWCA, Girl Scouts, etc.). Often church youth groups are happy to take on a community project—and you and your family could be that project. If you give them a proposal—a more specific request than just asking for general help—they might be willing to supply that help as a group or individually. For example, if you can list specific times you need help, or specific chores you need completed, they can plan how much they can do to help.

• You can suggest to those relatives and friends who don't know what to give as a *shower gift* that they give frozen home-cooked dinners.

Since meal preparation is a big stumbling block for many mothers of infants, the more planning you can do ahead of time for easy or gift meals, the better.

• Contact the *home-economics teacher* of your local high school and see if your needs can fill *her* needs for some real-life experience for students in child development or cooking classes. Some home-ec classes sponsor small child-care centers for toddlers while the students are learning about child development. Others might be willing to send a student or two at a time to your home at specific hours to put some of the skills they are learning about to use, by helping you with cooking or child care.

• *Grandmas and grandpas* whose own grandchildren live far away might be willing to take on yours as local substitutes. Some senior citizens' centers even have programs to match families with their clients to benefit both. It can be a help to you to have your older children establish a special friendship with another adult they can spend some time with. And a caring older person might be a good source of support for you—a willing ear and a helping hand that can make you feel loved and them feel useful.

• *Your own parents* can be a great source of help and comfort if they live nearby. Even if relations with them have been strained in the past, some mothers find that their own graduation to motherhood produces a new rapport with their parents. Don't expect your parents to walk in and take over, but do ask them to help with specific tasks or child care, just as you would with any close friend. And remember that, just as with any close friend, you don't have to agree with every opinion about mothering your own parents may have. In the end, you will spend far more time with your children and have a far greater influence on them than your parents will. So in a sense, it doesn't matter if your mother-in-law insists on using cloth diapers when she visits instead of your disposables, or if your own mother insists that the babies wear their snowsuits outdoors in fifty-degree weather.

But for some people, having their parents help is too emotionally charged. If that is the case for you, make other arrangements and invite your parents to visit to enjoy the babies without working.

• Check the telephone book under city services to see if your town has a city-sponsored *parenting center*. These are excellent sources for help, advice, contact with other parents, and sometimes for short-term, drop-in baby-sitting. You might also check for similar services with your pediatrician, family practitioner, childbirth educator, library, Chamber of Commerce, or the hospital nurses on the maternity floor.

"The hardest thing for me after my twins were born was that I had to ask for help all the time. At times I felt like I couldn't go to the bathroom without making sure someone was there to pick up a baby if he needed it. I had been a responsible working woman for ten years before they were born, and suddenly I was like a little girl again who had to ask permission to go out."

• One of the best ways to avoid handing over your hard-earned cash for services is to *trade something* else for the service. For example, if you have an extra bedroom, you could trade room, or room and board, for a certain number of hours of child care and light housework a week. Or if your husband or your children have a particular skill that a family you know could use, you might work out an arrangement to trade jobs with them. For example, one father of multiples who is an engineer did a home energy audit for another family, who traded that for an agreed-upon amount of child care.

• Another good way to trade for help you need is to *form a cooking co-op* with a few other friends. If each of five people cooks one big, freezable dinner a week to distribute to the other families in the co-op, you each have several noncooking days. It would even be helpful for many people to not have to cook just one or two days a week. In that case, you could trade meals with just one other family. When it's your turn to cook, you simply double the batch you make for your family and give the extra batch to the other family. They do the same for you, and you each get some days off from cooking. This might be a good thing for you to do before your babies are born, and then after you are through the postpartum period. In between, you stand a good chance of getting some extra meals as a gift just after the babies are born.

• Don't overlook your *family* as a resource. Chores they all get used to doing during your pregnancy and soon after the birth can become part of their regular repertoire. Studies have shown that families of multiples in which everyone pitches in to help feel they come out stronger and happier for their efforts. You can make all your family members, even siblings as young as four, feel needed by assigning specific tasks they are able to do. It takes some planning, particularly with young children, but it can work. Choose a task you know your child can accomplish, and teach him how to do it before you expect him to do it on his own. Break the job down into component parts—like just sorting the laundry—to make it easier. Your child will eventually learn how to do the whole job when he learns it step by step. Be ready with praise and try hard not to redo work you've assigned him to do. The quality will improve as he gets older and more adept, but the important thing is that you have begun to set a precedent—that his help is needed and appreciated. Jobs to consider relegating to children as young as four: setting the table (use unbreakable everything); sorting, folding, and putting away laundry; picking up toys; dusting; vacuuming; feeding pets. Be sure to rotate jobs, and keep it fun if you can, so what starts as a positive, helping time doesn't turn into a drag for all concerned.

The same applies to your spouse and any extended family you have around. Most of them are happy to help, but need to be asked.

IF YOU WANT HELP YOU HAVE TO ASK

Our culture doesn't supply a built-in support group of extended family or village women to help new mothers. If you want help—and you may find you need it more than you thought you would—you are going to have to build it in yourself. As a culture, we value independence, and many women in recent decades have been concentrating on developing that independence. But the first weeks after having multiples is not the time to be alone and independent. Studies have shown that new mothers who have some kind of support—either hired help or friends and relatives willing to pitch in—are less likely to be depressed later, are less likely to have serious problems with mothering their children, and are more likely to be successful with breastfeeding. It could yield long-term benefits to you and your family if you construct this foundation of support to smooth your way into a new life as a parent of multiples. Here is a summary of some of the ideas in this chapter, along with a few new ideas, that may help you plan your support for this transition:

1. *Know your needs.* Use the checklist earlier in this chapter as a guide to decide what is most important for you: cooking, cleaning, child care, etc.

2. *Know who can help you fill your needs.* Use the list of options to spark your thinking about who can help supply the time or help you need.

3. *Know how to find the people who can help.* Once you've decided what kind of help you need, decide if you can find that person through word-of-mouth, newspaper ads, local agencies, or a few phone calls you or a friend can make.

4. *Know how to pay the person.* Decide before making an offer to a potential helper either how much your budget can stand, or exactly what you can trade for his or her services.

5. *Know what to ask for.* If you've done your homework about your needs, this part should be easy. Be as specific as possible. Asking for ten hours of child care and four hours of housework a week from a church youth group is a lot easier for them to deal with than is a plea from you for "any kind of help." Be specific with friends and relatives,

too. Many will ask how to help. If you say, "Oh, you don't have to," or, "I don't know," they will either not help or do something that you don't really need. Give them a break and say, "Thanks for offering. I'd love it if you'd do my grocery shopping sometime this week. Here's my list."

6. *Know how to ask once.* One way to avoid feeling at the mercy of everyone else's willingness to offer help is to set up as much help as you can ahead of time so you only have to ask once. For example, one mother of twins reported that her favorite baby gift came from her best friend who did all her family's laundry for two months after the babies came. She would come over to the new mother's house once or twice a week, make coffee, and spend the afternoon chatting, holding babies, and washing and folding laundry. The mother didn't have to ask for help over and over, she had some welcome time chatting with a friend, and the laundry never got out of hand.

Another mother, this one of triplets, set up a standing date with a woman friend for the evening her husband always went bowling with his buddies. Her friend would come over with her five-year-old, who played with the babies part of the time. The moms each got to catch up on the other's lives, the husband kept his contact with his friends, the babies loved seeing the older child (who felt important being the helper, and was duly rewarded for her help), and the mother of triplets wasn't trying to deal with babies alone in the evening.

PLANNING AHEAD IS THE KEY

The one thing most parents will agree on is that they have to give up spontaneity when their children are born. It may seem hard to give up that aspect of your life, but as you wave good-bye to acting on whims, you may learn to welcome planning ahead. The value of seeing what you need and planning for it may never be so apparent as when you are the parent of two, three, or four babies at once. Loose ends can mean chaos when you have multiples. Spontaneity isn't fun when you realize you haven't planned for someone you can call on for help when your husband suddenly has to be out of town. Or when you discover that your expensive new twin stroller won't fit through most store doorways. Or when you see just as the cribs are delivered that they are too big for the only bedroom left in your home for the new babies.

As you plan for changes in your life-style to make the transition to parenthood smoother, so you must plan for changes to your home that can make it easier to accommodate more than one new baby at a time. Here are some things to consider as you plan for your multiples.

As You Plan the Nursery

Plan for Safety

• Check for appliance cords, drapery cords, draperies, hanging covers of any kind, trunks with lids that open and close.

• Check to see that cribs are not close to furniture babies could climb onto or pull over, or too close to operational windows. Remove heavy plants or other objects that could be pulled over.

• Check to see that rugs are nonskid and that bare floors are not slippery. Carpeting or cushioning around or under crib and changing table is a good idea.

• Be sure the light level is appropriate for the tasks you plan in the nursery. A nightlight bright enough for you to see by is a must.

Plan for Comfort

• Consider buying or borrowing a changing table to avoid bending or stooping to change diapers.

• Consider using a radiant panel heater over changing and/or crib area if the room feels drafty. These can be wall- or ceiling-mounted and usually come in plain (to blend with the wall color) or decorator (to look like a picture on the wall) styles, and simply plug into an outlet. Prices range from about $120 for an on-off model, to about $150 for one that comes with a thermostat, and they are available from electrical supply houses or hardware stores. If your babies were premature and you can get a doctor to prescribe the extra heat for their room, you might be able to have your insurance pay for at least part of the cost.

• Use open shelves mounted over or next to the changing table so you can reach needed supplies without leaving the babies.

• Include a rocking chair in the nursery if possible.

• If there is room, consider adding a small bed or couch to the nursery for lying down to nurse.

• Choose a bedroom close to your room and/or a bathroom or other water source.

• Use low-maintenance, easy-to-clean everything.

• Be sure to set up a branch diaper-changing station—either something portable that you can easily take with you, or a permanent changing spot near where you spend the most time, so you don't have to keep running back and forth to the babies' room. For more on choosing the type of diaper you'll use, see chapter 4, That First Year.

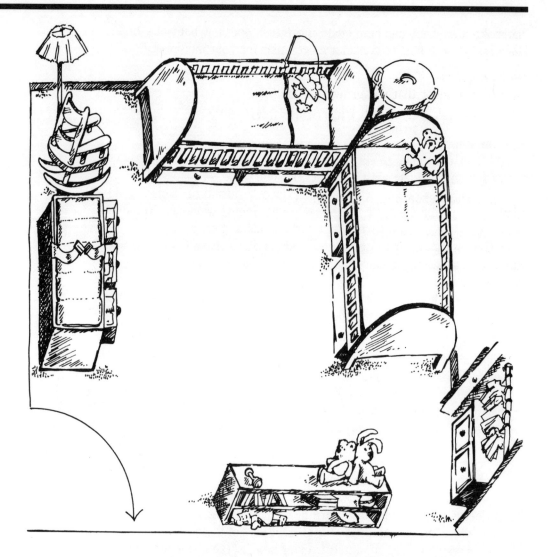

• Decide how many cribs you want. Many parents of multiples use just one crib to start with, or a combination of a bassinet and a crib until the babies get bigger. If space is a concern, consider putting the dresser in the closet—baby clothes that hang aren't long enough to require much space. Double up on uses: try one of the changing tables that combines a dresser with changing space; use space under the crib(s) for storage. Consider building in storage and/or dresser space around and under windows, but be cautious about making permanent changes until you have lived with your multiples for a while and can be more realistic about needs.

• If you don't have a washing machine and/or a dryer, decide before the birth of your multiples what can be done about that. Laundry for more than one baby can be significant, even if you don't wash your own diapers.

Plan for Looks

• Use a décor that will grow with the babies, so you won't feel the need to redo it for years. If you haven't painted, papered, etc., before the birth of your twins or triplets, get friends to do it for you while you're in the hospital.

• Use bright, simple colors for stimulation, and natural light when possible. Consider changeable décor over the crib at babies' eye level —like a bulletin board with different pictures, designs, and colors (until babies can get up and reach the board). Include music in your plan— quiet tapes can be soothing for babies and parents. Think of textures you can include: hard, smooth floors for rolling balls and trucks; soft, padded areas for cuddly reading or quiet times.

• If the nursery is too small, consider setting up a play area in another part of the house. Even a corner in the living room with a basket for toys and some floor pillows for reading would help.

• Simple is better than elaborate, fussy, or fancy—for you and for your babies.

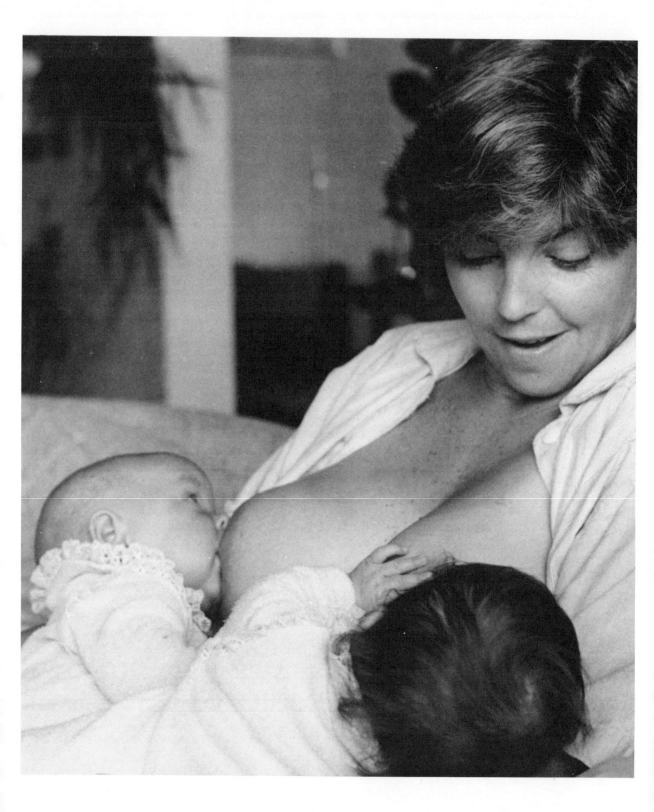

3 | Feeding the Masses

"Breastfeeding saved the day for me. I don't know how I could have cuddled both of them and still rested as much as I did if I hadn't breastfed my twins."

"I didn't want to breastfeed my twins; it seemed like too much trouble. My twins did fine on bottles, and my husband got to help with a few feedings too."

Perhaps the most creative thing you can do as a mother, besides gestating and giving birth to your babies, is to feed them well. The way you feed them and what you feed them continues to create your children, day by day. You have the power to point your multiples in the direction of good health, for as infants they are totally dependent on you to nourish them.

Making decisions about feeding affects your children so directly (and you indirectly—constantly crying babies are a strain no mother needs) that the decision deserves careful consideration. As a mother of multiples, it might be helpful for you to know, and believe, that you do have a choice about how and what you feed your babies. You can choose to

"I know people who can't breastfeed one baby. How am I supposed to believe I can breastfeed two or three babies?"

bottlefeed (and you can choose among a number of kinds of formulas), or you can choose to breastfeed. That may seem a simple statement of two obvious choices to some, and it may seem an outrageous idea to others. But it is a fact that with the proper support and information, you can choose how you'll feed your babies from a position of strength, knowing that there is a choice. Conversely, if you don't know how to handle both of these feeding methods, you don't really have a choice.

In this chapter, we'll look at these two ways of feeding your babies and a third you might consider. Before you decide on how to feed your babies, you'll want to know how your body makes milk, how your milk is different from various formulas, and how each may effect your babies, whether they were born at term or were premature. There are some specific how-tos for mothers who breastfeed multiples and others for mothers who bottlefeed multiples. And the bottom line in this chapter, as well as in your life with multiples, is how you measure how well your children are doing with whatever feeding choices you have made—and the measure may *not* include studying those infamous growth charts at the pediatrician's office.

CAN IT REALLY BE DONE?

Here's what happened to one mother who believed she had a choice about how and what to feed her twins. It may sound familiar to a lot of mothers. It began with her fervent desire to breastfeed her twins. Her obstetrician cautioned against it, for her sake as well as her babies'. "You'll be too tired," he explained. Her pediatrician said, "Well, you can try it if you want to, but we'll watch the babies' weights carefully." And her husband, a first-time parent too, was unsure she could produce enough milk for two babies, but he was willing to go along with what she wanted.

So she tried it. At first everything was fine, and the special time nursing each twin separately made her feel she was gettng to know them each better. But then her nipples became sore. Nursing became more and more painful and difficult. She dreaded putting her babies to her sore breasts and then wondered if the babies were getting enough milk. Finally, her pediatrician suggested she quit nursing. She did. As far as he was concerned, the problem was solved—the babies were simply being fed another way, it was easy to tell how much milk the babies were getting, the mother's nipples were healing, and everyone was fine.

Well, not quite. The mother felt terrible. She had tried nursing, and she had *failed*. The doctor was right and she was wrong. And she found herself wishing all those women who boast of breasts filled to overflowing, and of how easy and "natural" breastfeeding is, would just shut up.

What may seem on the surface to be a simple decision about feeding has become an emotionally charged, guilt-laden topic for many women. How did we get to this point over a bodily process that has sustained the human race for millennia?

First, it's important to remember that the human race is indeed here because of breastfeeding. Bottlefeeding as a norm didn't begin until the turn of the century. In the U.S., bottlefeeding arrived on the heels of the industrial revolution, just in time to provide the missing link for the suffrage movement. Women's roles were changing, and for the first time, women were often expected—and just as often they elected—to work outside the home. Who would feed the baby? Well, there was Bossy. And industrial cleverness eventually produced a rubber nipple facsimile acceptable to infants.

Bottlefeeding was a great invention that met a serious need. But it brought about another effect—the baby got thrown out with the mother's milk, so to speak. With the introduction of the bottle, thousands of years of mother-to-daughter and grandmother-to-granddaughter information about breastfeeding (and childbirth, for that matter) vanished. At the same time in the late nineteenth century that women were leaving home to be part of the industrial revolution, doctors were setting up shop in hospitals, where women would now give birth. For the first time in history, the management of childbearing and child-feeding became the domain of men instead of women. The facts, folk medicine, and healing lore of women were lost.

And breastfeeding was obscured in a fog of medical misinformation. Between the turn of the century and the early 1960s, it was assumed that many mothers couldn't, and probably didn't want to, breastfeed one baby, much less twins or triplets. But then, just as bottlefeeding followed on the heels of one cultural movement, the resurgence of breastfeeding came in on the coattails of another. In the 1960s, there was renewed interest in our cultural and biological roots. Natural childbirth and breastfeeding became the choice of the avant garde. At the same time, medical researchers began to discover that human milk possessed nothing less than amazing nutritional and immunological qualities. As women passed their newly rediscovered knowledge of breastfeeding from one to another, and as some doctors began to read and believe the latest research, it became apparent that indeed, the vast majority of women can breastfeed. The next step may be to recognize that because of how the breast works, we each can choose to feed just about as many babies as time and energy allow.

But before we get to that point, we have to figure out why, during this resurgence of breastfeeding as a choice, so many of us try (with great conviction and enthusiasm) to breastfeed, and then give up (with equally great disappointment and sometimes anger and resentment too). Why do we have so much trouble performing a simple bodily function that nearly any female of childbearing age in the 1860s could do?

IF WE KNEW NOW WHAT THEY KNEW THEN

Part of the answer is that although breastfeeding has enjoyed a comeback, it has come back with bottlefeeding rules; which, not surprisingly, don't work at all for breastfeeding. For example, a new mother may be told that:

1. She should only breastfeed her babies every three or four hours.
2. She should only nurse ten (seven? twelve?) minutes on each side.
3. And she should be sure to clean her nipples before nursing.

These instructions sound suspiciously similar to those another new mother might hear:

1. Be sure to adhere to a four-hour schedule with bottlefeeding.
2. Your babies should each take three ounces of formula at each feeding.
3. Be sure to sterilize the bottles and nipples before feeding your babies.

Both sets of instructions are attempts to standardize feeding practices by setting feeding times, amounts, and techniques. Treating all babies the same doesn't often work well with bottlefeeding, and it's downright disastrous for mothers who want to breastfeed.

The rest of the answer to why many of us have so much trouble with breastfeeding is that most of even the best-informed new mothers (by 1980s standards) don't have what the young uneducated mother in the 1860s had. Most of us don't have a granny to say, "It'll be okay, honey. Lots of people get sore nipples. It feels like they're going to fall right off if you let that little baby suck one more time, doesn't it? Well, you just rub some of this salve on your nipples from time to time. And that baby's eight days old now, right? Sore nipples usually don't get any worse after ten days. They're probably about as bad as they'll get now, and they'll be getting better day by day now. You'll see. Why, I remember when I was nursing your mama . . . ."

How many breastfeeding mothers in the last twenty years could have benefited from a kind word and a helpful hint spoken by someone who had breastfed her babies?

Breastfeeding Without the Kindly Granny

The reality is that most of us don't have a kindly granny who breastfed our mothers, most of our mothers didn't breastfeed us, and most of our pediatricians know little more than our mothers do about breastfeeding. Does that mean breastfeeding isn't really an option? Not necessarily. It just means you may have to work a little harder at finding what you need to make it an option.

Mothers were breastfeeding their babies long before anyone knew about those amazing nutritional and immunological qualities of human milk. So simple knowledge of what's in your milk or how it's formed isn't crucial to making breastfeeding an option. But loving, helpful support is.

As you will see in the explanations that follow, you don't have to worry about producing enough milk if you let your babies suck when they want to. But if you feel embarrassed, inhibited, uncertain, criticized, and scrutinized (in other words, you don't have loving support), you might have difficulty with your let-down reflex, and then all those gallons of milk you produce have no way of getting to your babies. At the same time, it's important to know that *all* of these difficulties can be dealt with using some of the ideas that follow.

Our culture doesn't provide a convenient structure of support for breastfeeding mothers any more than it does for mothers who have just given birth. If you want breastfeeding to be an option for you, you must construct your own structure of support. Here are some ways to do that:

1. Talk to a representative of La Leche League International. *La leche* means "the milk" in Spanish, and the milk they talk about here is mother's milk. The group was organized in 1956 as a mother-to-mother network providing breastfeeding information and support. They offer mother-led meetings at members' homes, and local groups provide telephone counseling for nursing moms. Being able to call someone who is knowledgeable and supportive at any time has been a godsend to many nursing mothers. Some La Leche League chapters have special groups for nursing mothers of multiples. The La Leche League number is usually listed in the white business pages of the telephone book. Childbirth educators, obstetricians, pediatricians, family practice physicians, and maternity nurses may also have names of La Leche League counselors or groups in your area. You should know, though, that some people, both mothers and health-care providers, are uncomfortable with

the level of dedication to breastfeeding among members of La Leche League. But if you want the best-informed answers to breastfeeding questions, this group is the one with the most up-to-date information and the best breastfeeding success rate.

2. Check with local Mothers of Twins or parents of multiples groups for other mothers nursing multiples. National surveys done in 1985 show that 50 percent of mothers of multiples breastfeed their babies while still in the hospital. A little more than 15 percent of them are breastfeeding at five to six months, and 9.6 percent are still breast-feeding at twelve months. (Compare those numbers to 57 percent of mothers of single-born babies who breastfeed while still in the hospital, 21 percent breastfeeding at five to six months, and 9.3 percent still breastfeeding single-born babies at twelve months.)

3. Find a relative or friend through the grapevine who has recently breastfed a baby or two. An experienced nurser is the ideal helper for a new mom. Choose someone whose mothering style you like and call her before your babies are born. She'll probably be willing to come to the hospital to help you get used to nursing more than one baby and to help you figure out the nursing positions that work best for you and your babies. Starting right with breastfeeding can head off problems that can come later when you are home alone juggling two babies.

4. If you can't find an experienced nursing mother, then hook up with someone from your childbirth preparation class or a nursing mother you met in the hospital. You can be a great support to each other just by being company. But to avoid falling into the blind-leading-the-blind syndrome (in which your combined lack of knowledge and experience undermines both your efforts), decide early on to help each other find accurate answers from reliable sources to your nursing questions.

In order to ensure an ongoing relationship with this nursing mother (or any other person you know you will look to for support), consider making a standing appointment with her to meet once or twice a week at least for the first couple of months. You can meet at each other's house or in a nearby park if weather allows, so you'll each get practice going out with your babies.

5. Another option for help may be a human lactation center. Many have sprung up around the country, and often they exist in conjunction with a medical school, but not always. When they do, they may function as a teaching center for medical students to learn about lactation (something that has been missing from medical school curricula), and offer classes and counseling for nursing mothers. In other situations, they are a teaching and counseling center just for mothers, and they employ

medical or childbirth education specialists trained in lactation and breast-feeding. Many offer telephone hotlines to answer questions. See the appendix for a list of lactation centers, or check with your health-care provider or a university medical school, if there is one near you.

Finding loving support is the most important preparation for breast-feeding you can do. Finding a source of accurate, reliable information is the next most important preparation for breastfeeding.

IF I HAVE TO DO ALL THIS PREPARATION, WHY BOTHER WITH BREASTFEEDING?

No matter where you look for information these days, you just can't get away from the fact that breast milk offers your babies the best possible nutrition. Commercial formulas approximate the composition of human milk, and they do it better now than their evaporated-milk and whole-cow's-milk predecessors did. Formula companies do continue to update the composition of their products as discoveries are made about properties of human milk. And despite all the research that has been done on human milk in the last twenty years, discoveries continue to be made about its properties.

If you are deciding how to feed your multiples, here are a dozen reasons why you might consider breastfeeding.

1. Breast milk offers the best *nutrition.* According to the American Academy of Pediatrics, one of the most remarkable characteristics of human milk is that its composition changes to adapt to the specific nutritional needs of the infants being fed. So if you were to analyze breast-milk samples from a dozen women, you would find that while the same nutrients were present in all their milk, they existed in a different balance for each mother. And if you followed any one of those women during the course of breastfeeding her babies from birth on, you would find that the composition of her milk changed over time to meet the needs of her babies as they grew. The composition of breast milk even changes during a single feeding.

Perhaps the best way to understand the properties of human milk is to look at them in comparison to some properties of cow's milk and formula.

> • *Protein* in human milk is easier to digest than that in cow's milk and some formulas because it forms a small, soft curd in the babies' stomach. Cow's milk and some formulas form a larger, harder curd that doesn't break down as easily in human stomachs. (Since cow's milk is made for calves, it no doubt

One more note on pre-paring for breastfeeding: "Toughening" your nip-ples during your preg-nancy has never been proved to make a bit of difference in how sore you do or don't get when you first breastfeed your babies. Some degree of nipple soreness happens to just about everyone. It's a normal part of ad-justing to this new task and seems to have more to do with your skin and hair color (those with fair coloring seem to have more sensitive skin) than with how often you scrubbed your nipples with a rough washcloth during your pregnancy.

breaks down just fine for them.) The smaller, more digestible curd of human milk is one reason breastfed babies may eat more often than bottlefed babies. Human milk is used in the babies' body more fully and is digested quickly. Cow's milk takes longer to digest and its nutrients are not as available to the baby.

• *Fatty acids* in human milk play a key role in brain development during the first months after birth. According to nutritionists, 60 percent of the solid matter found in the brain is composed of transformed fatty acids. Human milk has seven to eight times more essential fatty acids than whole cow's milk. And unlike either cow's milk or formula, the fat content in human milk is not constant. The largest concentration of fat occurs at the end of the feeding. Researchers believe that the changing composi-tion of human milk during each feeding may help develop an appetite-control mechanism in breastfed babies. Protein concen-trations also increase significantly at the end of the feeding, leading researchers to believe that the richer milk signals to babies the end of the feeding. They believe that it isn't lessening availability of milk that signals the end of the feeding, since they can usually get more milk from the breast by pumping after the baby is finished. They also believe that it isn't because the baby is full. Babies who seem to be finished nursing on one breast eagerly continue to nurse when offered the other. Conse-quently, results of this study, in which the milk of two hundred women was tested throughout individual feedings, also ques-tioned the practice of having mothers limit nursing to ten min-utes on each side (or to any prescribed amount of time), since they found that the higher concentrations of fatty acids and pro-teins occurred in less than ten minutes for some women, and after sixteen minutes or more for others. The common denomi-nator for all the mothers was that the baby, not the clock, could always tell when to stop.

• *Lactose,* a sugar that, when digested, helps in the development of the nervous system and brain, and in the absorption of cal-cium, is more abundant in human milk than in the milk of any other mammal.

• *Iron* in human milk, contrary to earlier beliefs, is sufficient for normal-birth-weight, full-term babies until they are six months old or until solids are introduced. The lower concentrations of protein and phosphorus, and higher concentrations of lactose and vitamin C, make the iron in human milk more available to babies than was previously thought. The American Academy of

Pediatrics confirmed the effectiveness of iron in human milk in 1978.

• *Less is more* for many minerals and vitamins in human milk. Breast milk has less sodium, potassium, calcium, phosphorus, and vitamin D than cow's milk, but all of these are found in a more usable state for humans in breast milk and in the quantities that human babies need, not in quantities that calves need. Vitamin C in breast milk is more reliant on the mother's diet than are some other nutrients, and vitamin A and the B-complex vitamins are also found in just the right concentrations for human babies in breast milk.

It is easy to see from this quick nutritional rundown that breast milk has everything your babies need. Breastfed babies who are not on solids yet do not need vitamin, mineral, or iron supplements, nor do they need bottles of water or juice or anything else. All your breastfed babies need is a mother willing to sit down often and nurse. Which leads to the next reason to consider breastfeeding.

2. *You must rest* in order to do it right. A well-rested, healthy body has a much easier time making milk than an overworked, underslept one does. That may be easier said than done for a mother of infant multiples, but breastfeeding can gently force her to get the rest she needs. Considering how often breastfed babies usually want to nurse, a new mother of multiples has to spend a considerable amount of time sitting around, preferably with her feet up and her head lolling comfortably on a pillow. It may seem frustrating at times to have to take time out to nurse your babies, but it is always a good reminder to "stop and smell the roses" as your little ones grow so quickly out of your arms. It's also a good time to enlist the help of older siblings. They can feel needed by doing small chores or fetching a drink of water for you while you nurse. Younger siblings can sit with you and share some quiet moments. You might keep a special basket of "quiet" toys near where you usually nurse that your toddler can pull out at these special times.

3. For many mothers, breastfeeding is *less of a hassle* than bottle-feeding. The fact that more mothers of twins than mothers of single-born babies are still breastfeeding when their babies are twelve months old means that there must be some kind of payback for those breastfeeding moms. That fact makes it hard to believe that breastfeeding could be more difficult for them than it is for mothers of single-born babies. If you gather the information and the loving support you need, breastfeeding may be a way that you give yourself a break after your babies are born.

4. The *immunological* properties of breast milk are well documented. This could be another way you give yourself a break after your babies are born. While breastfeeding your babies doesn't mean that they will never get the sniffles, it does mean that they have antibody protection against serious illness. Some of these immunoglobulins line the intestines with an antiseptic material that helps fight pathogens, from bacteria to the polio virus. Others specifically protect the mucus membranes throughout the body. As a result, breastfed babies have a lower incidence of severe ear infections, respiratory viral infections, severe bacterial infections (like meningitis), diarrhea, vomiting, and even of sudden infant death. When breastfed babies do get sick, the illnesses seem to be less serious and shorter-lived than those for bottlefed babies.

Breastfed babies get an especially high dose of these protective factors from colostrum, the first fluid secreted by the breast after birth. Colostrum permits the formation of an intestinal flora (the good guys) that resists infection, while limiting the multiplication of undesirable bacteria (the bad guys). That, combined with the greater digestability of breast milk, means fewer babies with tummy aches.

As if all of this weren't enough, breast milk also helps prevent allergies. Eczema and other allergies have been documented as occurring seven times more frequently in bottlefed babies than in breastfed babies. Colostrum plays a big part in preventing allergies by helping the walls of the intestine become impermeable to large molecules like those of whole, nonhuman proteins found in whole cow's milk. Absorption of these foreign proteins can produce an allergic reaction in some babies, but even one feeding of colostrum can help "seal" the intestinal walls to prevent allergy.

If there is a history of allergies in your family, you might want to be especially conscious of the value of breastfeeding to help prevent allergies in your babies. You might also want to know that especially sensitive babies might react to foods eaten by their mothers. For example, some breastfed babies who are particularly intolerant of cow's milk and cow's-milk products (butter, cheese, etc.) also cannot tolerate their mothers' drinking milk or eating cheese. You'll know that your babies are having problems with this if they have a lot of intestinal gas, cry a lot, and/or seem generally miserable. If the problem is with your diet, you can pinpoint the offending food or foods by eliminating them one at a time from your diet until you see a corresponding change in your babies. If you do find you need to eliminate dairy products, be sure to supplement your diet with other forms of calcium.

5. Breastfeeding is a built-in way to establish a close *physical relationship* with your babies, which, for many mothers, strengthens the

bond they feel with their children. If you are concerned about being equally close to each of the babies, this is one way to put your mind at ease. Whether nursing their babies separately or together, mothers of multiples report that the time spent holding and nursing their babies contributes significantly to feeling confident that they are getting to know each child well. Does that mean you can't have that close, physical relationship if you bottlefeed your twins? No. It just means that it comes with the territory if you breastfeed, and that you have to arrange for it if you bottlefeed.

6. If your concern is not that *you* need to be careful about bonding with your babies, but that *they* may need help in sorting out which of the people who help care for them is their mom, breastfeeding again offers some built-in answers. Recent studies at Vanderbilt University have shown that within twenty-four hours of their birth, breastfed babies can distinguish the smell of their own mother's milk from that of other mothers. And by the time they are only a few days old, they distinguish the smell of their own mother's skin from that of other mothers. Breastfed babies consistently score higher on these tests than do bottlefed babies. Of course scent is just one indicator of identity, but the fact remains that breastfed babies, because of the physical relationship with their mothers, get tuned in to those cues sooner than bottlefed babies.

7. If *development* is your prime concern, you might like to know that visual stimulation, one of the important ways newborns receive information that motivates certain kinds of development, is most effective when the thing your newborns are looking at is nine to twelve inches from their faces. It just so happens that the average distance from the face of a nursing baby to his or her mother's face is nine to ten inches—the perfect distance for your newborns to learn to focus their eyes and pick up signals from human expressions.

Some dentists believe that muscle action and the combination of pressure and suction required of babies in order to nurse effectively contributes to the normal development of the palate and jaw, and later to the ability to form sounds for speech. While orthodontically correct nipples and pacifiers are common now, some dentists still feel that some difficulties with the position of teeth that require braces in later years are the direct result of bottlefeeding.

8. Some health-care professionals believe that *postpartum depression is less common* among women who breastfeed their babies. While causes of postpartum depression are far from clear, a case can be made for the positive effects of the slower pace and the "mothering the

mother" that breastfeeding requires. The lack of these often accompanies depression when it hits.

Another consideration, when you think about handling your feelings after the birth, is that breastfeeding stimulates the pituitary gland to produce prolactin. In breastfeeding circles, prolactin is known as the calming hormone, and nursing mothers report that they feel a soothing, even tranquilizing effect from nursing—the product of this hormone. Mothers breastfeeding twins have been known to produce as much as three times the prolactin as do mothers nursing one baby.

Prolactin and oxcytocin are both associated with mothering feelings or the "mothering instinct," and breastfeeding stimulates their production.

9. You stand a good chance of *regaining your prepregnant body* quicker if you breastfeed. It begins with the surges of the hormone oxytocin your body produces when you breastfeed soon after birth. Oxytocin makes your uterus contract (which some mothers feel as clearly as they felt contractions during labor), which in turns helps to stop bleeding and shrink this organ that has been stretched far beyond its prepregnant size (about the size of your clenched fist). Breastfeeding mothers often find that their uterus returns to this prepregnant size quicker than those of bottlefeeding mothers.

Mothers nursing one baby need about five hundred extra calories a day to produce enough milk. Mothers nursing two babies need twice that amount, and mothers nursing three babies need three times that. For many mothers of multiples, those early breastfeeding days are like none other. For once in their lives they can eat as much as, and for many women even more than, they want and probably lose weight. For the breastfeeding mother of twins, three thousand calories a day is a requirement for at least the first couple of months while she is establishing her milk supply. Once it is established, she may want to eat a little less, maintaining nutritional quality, to begin to return to her prepregnant weight. For many, but not all, women, healthy weight loss is not difficult after giving birth to twins.

10. Your *premature* multiples can reap special benefits from your milk. Researchers from Georgetown University working with others from the U.S. Department of Agriculture found recently that milk from mothers delivering babies one to three months early has nearly twice as many long-chain fatty acids, the kind that are vital to the growth of brain cells and the formation of the lining around nerve centers.

Milk from mothers with premature babies was also found to be easier to digest, and it has nearly 70 percent more of the easily assimilated medium-size fatty acids, which provide energy for growth, than milk from full-term mothers has.

The catch here, researchers found, is that only the mother of the premature baby can offer her baby these extras. Pooled milk, even if it was collected from other mothers of premature babies, doesn't offer the same benefits because the fatty acids break down even when stored in what has been considered the best conditions. They found that human milk must be stored at minus 94 degrees Fahrenheit to preserve the fatty acids so needed by premature babies. But while that temperature may preserve the fatty acids, it may also break down many of the immunological properties of breastmilk. For more on breastfeeding premature babies, see the section in this chapter on how breastfeeding works.

11. While it does not provide foolproof birth control, breastfeeding your multiples can help with *child spacing*. Babies sucking at the breast stimulate the mother's pituitary gland to produce the hormone prolactin. Prolactin triggers the production of progesterone by her ovaries. In turn the high level of progesterone during breastfeeding (which also occurs at the end of a woman's menstrual cycle and during pregnancy) signals her ovaries not to ovulate. You have the best chance of keeping your prolactin and progesterone production up and ovulation down if you are nursing exclusively. Introduction of bottlefeeding or solids, an interruption in nursing (where you don't nurse for several days), or even some extreme emotional upsets can change your hormone production enough to allow ovulation to resume.

You probably won't know that your progesterone level has fallen enough to allow ovulation until you have your first period, and just when that happens varies considerably from mother to mother, and from pregnancy to pregnancy. Anyone who knows mothers of multiples can come up with examples of breastfeedjing mothers whose periods—and thus ovulation—started six weeks after the birth of their twins, as well as those whose periods did not resume for up to two years after the birth.

Since you cannot know exactly when ovulation will resume for you, if you're serious about not having another child at all or about waiting a considerable amount of time until you do, you will need to use another form of birth control. But as a general rule, breastfeeding stimulates prolactin, which triggers progesterone, which suppresses ovulation.

12. Last, and certainly not least in the list of reasons to consider breastfeeding, is that if you do breastfeed first, long enough to establish your milk supply, you can then truly have a *choice* in how you feed your babies, and offer bottles of either your milk or formula later. But if you never establish your milk supply, that choice won't be as available to you. Certainly mothers can relactate—or rebuild their milk supply after stopping breastfeeding—and adoptive mothers who have never given

To summarize those dozen reasons to consider breastfeeding, they are:

1. better nutrition for babies
2. "enforced" rest for mom
3. less of a hassle for mom
4. more immunities for babies
5. physical bonding for all
6. mother identification for babies
7. development benefits for babies
8. soothing hormones for mom
9. body benefits for mom
10. special nutrition for premies
11. child spacing helps for mom and dad
12. a true choice in feeding methods.

birth are also able to breastfeed their babies. But learning to nurse and training your body to produce milk in those situations are much more difficult and take much more tenacity than they do right after the birth of your babies.

HOW YOU FEED DOESN'T HAVE TO BE AN EITHER/OR CHOICE

So far, we've mentioned two ways to feed your babies. The first option is breastfeeding; the second option (which will be discussed in greater detail later in this chapter) is bottlefeeding. But you don't have to make a black or white decision between these two. Why not a third option: begin with breastfeeding and take advantage of the need to rest while you nurse through your own recovery. Offer an occasional bottle, or have your partner, a friend, or an older child do that so the babies are familiar with bottles. Then, if you go back to work, or when your milk supply is well established and you want to supplement with bottles of formula (or later on, bottles of juice), add the bottlefeeding option.

Three good reasons to try this combination are:

1. Your babies will get the strongest dose of all the good things offered by human milk if they have colostrum and early milk.

2. You will learn how to breastfeed and will have milk, so you will be able to choose between bottles and breast.

3. You will reap the benefits of breastfeeding—among them are hormones to help stop bleeding after birth, to contract your uterus to its original size, and to keep you calm and motherly.

You are more likely to feel right about the decision you make if:

1. You have done your homework about the feeding method or methods you choose, so you know what you're doing and why.

2. You understand what's important for you in the way you live and choose a feeding method or combination of methods that fit your structure.

3. You make a decision and are consistent. Confusion and ambivalence rub off on babies and can show in fussy behavior. You don't have to be swayed by other opinions if you have done your homework and are clear about what you are feeding your babies and why you are feeding them the way you are.

IF YOU CHOOSE TO BREASTFEED

When you choose how you'll feed your babies, it might help to remember that if you choose to breastfeed, you can also choose for how long or short a time you will nurse your babies. While nursing takes a commitment to learn how to do it well, just as learning any new skill does, you needn't feel that you have made an irreversible decision. And you needn't shy away from making the decision to nurse because you believe there's no turning back if you find you don't want to nurse after you've tried it.

By the same token, you don't have to stop nursing after a few weeks or months if you don't want to. As we've seen, slightly more mothers of twins than mothers of single-born babies are still nursing at twelve months. How easy it will be, in terms of social pressure, for you to continue nursing if you want to nurse longer than the norm, or even to nurse your babies at all, may have something to do with where you live. According to surveys done by the National Center for Health Statistics, as many as 77 percent of all new mothers living in the western part of the U.S. (from the Rockies to the coast) breastfeed. By contrast, as few as 45 percent of all new mothers living in the southeastern part of the U.S. breastfeed. Of course the varying popularity of breastfeeding in different parts of the country doesn't mean you can't do what you want wherever you live, but if you live in an area where the incidence of breastfeeding is low, you might want to know that you may find more criticism if you breastfeed. And you may want to be extra careful about lining up loving support to cushion yourself.

No matter where you live, lining up loving support is the first step to successful nursing. The next, if you choose to nurse your babies, is to get as much good information on breastfeeding as you can. Use the information earlier in this chapter as a guide and consult the organizations and books listed in the appendix as guides. The third thing you can do to help ensure success is to understand basically how breastfeeding works. Knowing the basics might help you to find your own answers to questions that can arise while you are breastfeeding.

Colostrum is the first fluid to appear when you begin lactating. It has the strongest dose of some nutrients and immunological factors your babies will get. It aids in gut closure, or sealing the lining of the intestine, and it helps clear out the meconium (the dark green or black first stool common to newborns) in the babies' intestines.

First milk may appear as early as the end of the first day or on the second day after the birth of your multiples. The third- or fourth-day appearance of milk you may have heard about is often the result of newborns being on four-hour schedules and is probably based on the amount of sucking done by one baby. If you are letting your babies suck at will, whenever your milk does come in is exactly the right time for you and your babies.

Production of milk is based on a simple principle of supply and demand. More sucking = more milk. That's why mothers can nurse more than one baby. Your body produces the milk it is asked to produce. If you let the babies nurse whenever they want to (and breastfed babies usually want to feed more often than bottlefed babies, because their bodies use breast milk more efficiently and their little bellies empty sooner), you will have the amount of milk they need. If you don't let them suck when they want to, your body will respond by cutting down on production. When you introduce bottles or solids, your body will accommodate that change by producing a correspondingly smaller amount of milk. That's why, if you want to nurse and use bottles, you need to wait at least six weeks and ideally three months (until you have a stable, plentiful supply of milk) to introduce the bottles.

Let-down is the way your body gets the milk to the babies. When your milk supply is well established, you will probably be producing at least a half-gallon of milk a day (which one mother of twins discovered she was producing when she was away from her nine-month-old twins for twenty-four hours and so had to pump and discard all her milk). But if it doesn't get to the babies it's all for naught. The let-down is a physical response to the physical stimulus of the babies nursing, or to an emotional stimulus like hearing your babies cry. The catch for some women is that the physical response can be colored by emotions. This is where loving support comes in. If you feel yourself to be judged, watched, and criticized; or angry, embarrassed, and irritated, your let-down reflex can be affected.

Some helps for a good let-down reflex:

Relax. Visualize waterfalls, milk flowing, etc. Arrange yourself and your babies comfortably (see illustrations). Choose a position you all find cozy; use pillows to prop your arms, head, feet, or all three so you feel absolutely no tension anywhere. Listen to soothing music.

Traditional beliefs contend that having a glass of wine or a beer will relax you and increase the flow of milk. But researchers have reported recently that alcohol may cause exactly the opposite effect. Alcohol that reaches the infant through breast milk can make some babies too lethargic to continue nursing and may inhibit the milk-ejection or let-down reflex in some women. Non-caffeinated herbal tea or some other drink you find soothing might be a better relaxer.

Time is not only the great healer; it's also the great teacher. Give yourself and your babies about six weeks to get good at nursing. You are all learning a new skill, and your body is learning to adjust to the babies' needs. It's best, during these early weeks, if you keep supplemental bottles to a minimum so you establish a plentiful supply of milk.

Eat well while you learn to nurse. You need about five hundred calories a day for each baby over what you normally eat to maintain your weight. A new mother of twins who breastfeeds may find herself eating about three thousand calories a day and still slowly losing some of the fifty to sixty pounds she was likely to have gained during her pregnancy.

Studies of undernourished women in some Third World countries show that their breast milk is not significantly different from that of well-nourished women. Their babies receive the nutrients they need, and the mothers' bodies pay the price. You'll want to eat as well or better than you did when you were pregnant for your own good, and you can be confident that your breastfed babies will be well nourished. There are mixed reviews on the value for babies of vitamin supplements taken by nursing mothers. But while the milk of mothers on vitamin supplements might not be significantly different, the well-being of the mothers might be. You'll be able to keep your health and energy up if you eat well and continue to take your prenatal vitamins, along with extra calcium (you need more when you are nursing than when you were pregnant) and an iron supplement, especially if you needed an iron supplement during your pregnancy.

Drink as much water as you can hold, and then drink a little more. Maternal nutrition is an obvious requirement for healthy mothers and babies. But what's often overlooked is how much you drink. No matter how you eat, if you're not drinking enough, your milk production can fall. Usually nursing mothers—and especially nursing mothers of twins —are so thirsty that drinking enough is not a problem; it's a compulsion. But to keep from forgetting, it might be a good idea to keep a half-gallon jar of water in the refrigerator and drink all of it each day. That, combined with whatever juice, milk, or other beverages you have, should be enough. (You might want to try not to include soft drinks, especially diet soft drinks, as part of your beverage requirement. Cyclamates may cause diarrhea in babies.) You'll know you aren't getting enough water if your urine is scanty and/or a concentrated yellow. Your urine may also look a dark yellow if you are taking vitamin C supplements. If you're not sure whether you're getting too little water or just taking a lot of vitamin C, it never hurts to drink a little *more* water, just to be sure.

THE JUGGLING ACT

One of the most frequently asked questions of a mother of twins who breastfeeds is whether she feeds them simultaneously and how in the world she gets them to be on the same schedule if she does.

Many mothers prefer to feed their babies at the same time whether they are nursing or bottlefeeding. Some only do it when both babies happen to be awake at the same time, and some prefer to wake the sleeping baby when the other wants to be fed. It certainly makes life a little easier for mom when she can feed both babies and be done with it.

Whether or not you are able to get your babies to conform to the same schedule may have to do with whether they are fraternal or identical twins. Identical twins tend to have similar biological rhythms. Most (but not all) identical twins will get hungry at about the same time and will eat about the same amount. And it will be somewhat easier to breastfeed most (but not all) identical twins at the same time because they often have the same sucking abilities and take roughly as long to empty the breast. For that reason, you needn't be too concerned about switching indentical twins from one side to the other each time you nurse to keep your milk supply even.

Identical twins who differ greatly in size at birth probably won't get hungry at the same time or eat similar amounts. Neither will fraternal twins, who are genetically no more alike than any single-born siblings. Mothers of fraternal twins often report that their babies' eating schedules have virtually nothing to do with each other, and these mothers aren't often able to get their babies on the same schedule. In addition, fraternal twins—particularly boy-girl twins—may have widely different abilities and styles of sucking, and you may want to be sure to have them switch sides each time you nurse to avoid one breast becoming noticeably larger than the other. In terms of nutrition, there's probably nothing wrong with each baby developing a favorite side on which to nurse, but the stronger nurser will elicit more milk production, and some mothers might not appreciate the aesthetics of the lopsided look.

As a breastfeeding mother of multiples, you may not have to keep track of which breast was nursed last, as a mother of a single baby might. You also may not have to burp each baby each time you nurse. Breastfed babies typically take in less air when they nurse than do bottlefed babies, and some really don't need help burping after nursing. Since you might be holding two babies at a time when you nurse, you might try skipping the burping routine and see if your babies miss it.

If you want to breastfeed both babies together, you will need to learn how to juggle them and yourself into position. Early on, you can enlist the help of whoever is with you. But later, there are bound to be many times when you are alone with the babies and need to nurse them together. Necessity will be the mother of invention, but it might eliminate some trauma for you and your babies if you practice getting into position with them before you're alone with two screaming, hungry babies.

First, while you still have someone with you, decide what is your most comfortable, practical nursing spot and claim it as your own. It may be a favorite easy chair, it may be the corner of the living-room couch, or it may be your big bed. Ideally, the perfect nursing spot has:

- enough room for all of you
- a table or nearby surface for food, drink, and reading material
- a light within reach that you can easily switch on or off
- a radio within reach, or a television with remote control
- a telephone close by that you can switch off
- a window to gaze out of
- a comfortable place to prop your feet

Use pillows to prop your arms and your babies so everyone is comfortable and relaxed, then memorize which pillow works best where, so you have a simple set of steps that you can easily follow to get into your best nursing position. The goal is to be propped so that one or both of your arms are free for eating, drinking, or waving to siblings.

Once you have figured all this out, practice doing it yourself with

someone there. So far, you can see that the two keys to being comfortable while nursing are learning how to arrange pillows effectively and remembering to have goodies and entertainment available. The third key is figuring out how to get the babies there. Mothers of multiples are often warned never to walk while holding both babies because of the danger of tripping. While that's a reasonable thing to say for someone who's never had twins, many mothers do it anyway. But if you've got an armful of babies, and you walk to your nursing area and sit down, how do you get your nursing flaps down and the babies up to the breasts to nurse? Here are some suggestions:

• One idea is to have a nursing spot that's wide enough so that a baby can lie down on either side of you. Then you take one baby at a time to the nursing spot, being sure she is protected from rolling off, and sit down between them. Look around before you start—do you have something to drink, eat, read, etc.? Then get yourself and/or your pillows ready, and pick up one baby with one hand. Yes, you can pick up young babies with one hand, particularly when you are surrounded with pillows. You can do it by sliding your hand and forearm under the baby's back, supporting the neck and head. It might be easier to lift the baby in this position to the opposite breast, but you can figure out what's most comfortable for you and your babies. Get that baby settled,

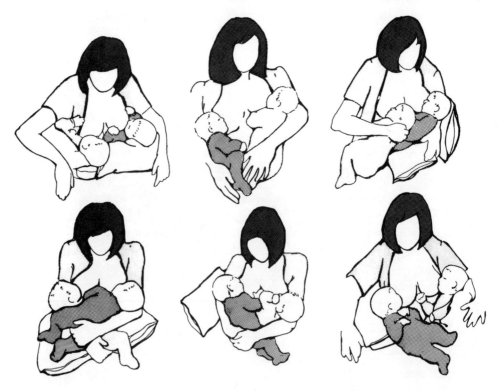

then pick up the other one with one hand, and get her settled. Lean back, relax, and close your eyes.

• Another way to do it is to use infant seats as a transfer point. Have the babies in infant seats in front of your nursing spot. Sit down and get yourself arranged. You might want to have one baby lying next to you. That's baby number one. Lean over to pick up baby number two. Get baby number two settled, and pick up number one next to you with one hand. If you have baby number one next to you, you avoid having to lean over while nursing to get her from the infant seat.

• A third method is to lie down while you nurse. This one may take some practice, but some mothers find they can sleep well in this position, and use it when they get up for those middle-of-the-night feedings in the first weeks. This works best on a couch, but you might try it in bed too. Sit on the couch holding one baby vertically in your left arm, as you would to burp him. Have the other baby lying perpendicular to you with his feet pointing to your right thigh. Be sure to have him protected from rolling off the bed or couch. Lie down on your side next to the baby, still holding the other one. Now you have one baby on top of you and one next to you, and your back should be supported by the couch back or by pillows arranged on your bed. Your hands are free enough to get everyone nursing, and once that is done, you can doze off.

The next step in the juggling act is what to do when your babies have nice full tummies and they've gone to sleep. There you are, trapped beneath two sleeping babies. What do you do? If you're lying down, and if you're in bed, you might gently lower the baby on top to the bed, and go to sleep yourself. No, you won't smother or squash your babies. Mothers have been sleeping with their babies (and the rest of the family too) for hundreds of years. (See chapter four, That First Year, for more on sleeping arrangements.) If you're sitting up in your nursing spot it helps if you have enough room next to you to lay one baby down. Lower that baby by leaning over. Then either lower the other baby to the couch or gently place her in the infant seat. If you have used enough pillows to keep your arms free while nursing, you don't have to lower the babies at all. Just be sure they are stable on the pillows, and get up and walk away. You can either leave the babies on the couch protected from rolling off, or gently lift them into their infant seats.

If this all sounds like a three-ring circus, it is, at least for a few weeks. But you might like to know that much of the pillows and propping aren't neccesary once your babies develop enough head and neck control to get to and stay at the nipple themselves. You might want to use some for your own comfort, but you won't have to go through the kind of major setup you do when the babies are very young. Babies also learn how to nurse more efficiently as they get stronger. They probably won't take as long to eat, and most likely won't eat as often as newborns do, when they are even a few months older.

TROUBLESHOOTING

No matter how much preparation and help you have with breast-feeding, you may find that you have difficulties as you learn this new skill. For detailed information on dealing with these, you can refer to one of the books in the Resources list in the appendix. To handle more routine questions, check the following list of problems and solutions.

1. *Sore nipples.* Virtually everyone feels some degree of soreness when she begins nursing, and mothers nursing two babies may feel a bit more, simply because there is unavoidably more sucking time. But just as most people feel some muscle soreness at the beginning of a new exercise program, it's normal for most mothers to feel some nipple soreness when they first begin to nurse. As with muscle soreness, nipple soreness does go away as your body adjusts to this new acitivity. For many mothers, nipple soreness peaks at around ten days, and diminishes after that. That doesn't mean you have to be sore for ten days—some mothers never feel particularly sore; others do, and may take a little longer than ten days to feel comfortable. As with most aspects of childbearing and child-caring, it is very individual.

While no single remedy has proven perfect for all mothers with sore nipples, there are a variety of things you can do:

- Perhaps the best thing you can do is try to keep from getting sore in the first place. Many childbirth educators and other health-care providers recommend washing your nipples with a washcloth or exposing them to sunlight and fresh air while you are pregnant. Some lactation experts say that these prctices probably don't condition your nipples for sucking. But they can condition you to handling your nipples and breasts and seeing how it feels to have your nipples touched all the time.

- Once your babies start nursing, it is a good idea to use *pure* hydrous lanolin (available at pharmacies—it's not a cosmetic preparation) on your nipples between feedings. It might help prevent extreme soreness, and you might find it soothing if you do become sore. You needn't wash it off before nursing.

• Another way to avoid soreness is to be sure the babies are holding the nipple correctly. They should each have all of the nipple and most of the areola (the dark area around the nipple) in their mouths. If they have less than this, they may be nibbling on the nipple itself, which would make anyone sore.

• You may avoid soreness or help deal with soreness by changing nursing positions frequently to see which suits you and your babies best.

• If you do become sore, try nursing one baby at a time and begin the feeding on the least sore breast. That will get the let-down going, and once the milk is flowing, the baby doesn't have to suck so hard.

• Try introducing the nipple to the baby by holding it between your thumb and forefinger and getting it well into his mouth to avoid the initial "ouch" of the baby adjusting his grip.

• A nonaspirin painkiller before you nurse can help ease the soreness.

• Exposing sore nipples to air also helps. If you don't have enough privacy to walk around with the flaps of your nursing bra down, you can use breast shields (not nipple shields), which are sold in some pharmacies where nursing supplies are sold. You could contact a local La Leche League representative for the one nearest you. Or, one nursing expert recommends getting a couple of those little tea strainers and wearing them inside your bra over your nipples for a few days. Tea strainers or breast shields will allow your nipples to air dry and keep irritating cloth off of them, without your having to walk around half dressed.

• With all their built-in immunities, colostrum and breast milk are also great healers. Let either of these dry on your nipples to help heal sore or cracked nipples.

• Perhaps the best things to remember are: 1. Sore nipples— even very sore nipples for some people—are a normal phase of adjustment to this new activity, and 2. They do heal. The rule of thumb is to keep nursing—all will be healed and forgotten in a couple of days. Don't take the baby on and off the sore breast during the feeding—that's the action that produces the soreness. And if you cut down on the number of nursings, you will either become overfull (and most mothers nursing twins don't have trouble with engorgement if they're nursing regularly), which can be painful in itself, or you will eventually diminish your milk supply because your body will adjust to the lowered demand.

• *Do not* use soap, alcohol, petroleum jelly, or other drying or greasy preparations on sore nipples. Nature and time will heal them.

2. *Plugged ducts and breast infections.* It's not how many babies you're nursing, it's how you're caring for the mother who is doing the nursing that can have an effect on whether you get plugged ducts or breast infections. Each of these is usually the sign of a mother who is not getting enough rest, not getting the best nutrition, or who is missing feedings. It's probably impossible to feel well rested with infant twins. You can't control their behavior when they are infants but you can control your own behavior. Some mothers who counsel breastfeeding moms even see a pattern to breast infections—they often occur at about six weeks, three months, and six months after the birth. Somehow those are times when many new mothers feel ready to jump into their old routines again, without considering that their new routine may be demanding more energy than they realize. Try to resist the temptation to do too much after your babies are born, even if you do feel great. If you will be going back to a job outside the home, try to limit what you do in your off hours. See chapter 5, Mothercare, for more on taking care of yourself.

A red, sore spot on your breast may signal either a plugged duct or an infection. Apply warm, wet compresses to the area, and nurse frequently on that side to keep the breast as empty as possible. Neither of these conditions affect the quality of your milk. If you develop a high fever and flulike achiness, you might need an antibiotic to combat the breast infection. Check with your doctor. There are antibiotics that can be safe to take while you're nursing. Be sure not to stop nursing on the sore side—a buildup of milk will only make matters worse.

3. *Jaundice.* A third difficulty concerns not you, but your babies. Estimates are that as many as 70 percent of all newborns show some degree of jaundice—a slight yellowing of the skin and eyes. Jaundice is not a disease, it is a sign that the baby's body is breaking down excess fetal blood cells produced during the last weeks of your pregnancy to ensure the growing babies had enough oxygen. Bilirubin is a by-product of that action, and it is processed by the liver as waste. When the baby is processing a lot of bilirubin, it sometimes takes the newborn's liver a

while to catch up, and the excess bilirubin gives the skin and eyes of the newborn a yellowish cast. Bilirubin amounts are determined by blood tests.

Your babies are more likely to appear jaundiced if they are premature, if you have a stressful delivery, or if you are diabetic or seriously ill at the time of their birth. Normal physiologic jaundice usually shows up between the second and fourth day after birth and disappears within a week or so by itself. It is harmless, and exposure to sunlight (indirect if it's very hot) usually helps speed the bilirubin disposal process.

What all this has to do with nursing twins is that there are many myths surrounding breastfeeding and jaundice. Normal physiologic jaundice is not a reason to stop breastfeeding. In fact, research has shown that jaundice is more common in hospital-born babies than home-born babies because of the infrequent (every four hours) nursing often encouraged in hospitals. Breast milk apparently helps speed the processing of bilirubin in the newborn. Your babies won't need extra water to help with jaundice either. Breast milk is 80–90 percent water, and additional feedings of water only interfere with the establishment of your milk supply. It has also been shown that the use of bottles for newborns weakens their sucking reflex within just four days.

A second kind of jaundice, pathologic or "abnormal" jaundice, usually occurs within twenty-four hours of the birth, and may be caused by blood incompatibility between infants and mother. This rare form of jaundice may be treated with transfusions for the infants, and it is not a reason to discontinue breastfeeding or to add water or anything else to your babies' diets.

A third form of jaundice, called "breast-milk jaundice," occurs in about 1 percent of babies. Some believe it is caused by the way the mother metabolizes fat, and some believe it is caused by a hormone in the mother's milk, but there is no consensus on either cause. It usually begins after the fourth day of life (typically during the second week) and may last longer than other forms of jaundice, up to a couple of months. Many doctors will recommend that the mother stop nursing for forty-eight hours (although they don't know why that seems to work), during which time she can pump her milk. There is no reason to stop nursing altogether. Studies have shown *no* ill effects on babies with breast-milk jaundice, even when they are jaundiced for a long time.

The trend in the 1980s has been to use phototherapy to treat jaundice in which bilirubin levels reach 20 milligrams per decaliter of the baby's blood. (The normal level is around 6 mg/dl.) While that figure is based only on studies done years ago on sick, not healthy, infants, it remains the number most commonly in use. It is also generally accepted that bilirubin levels for premature and sick infants aren't allowed to go as high before phototherapy or exchange transfusions are used.

Babies in phototherapy are placed naked in an enclosed bassinet, similar to an isolette, with fluorescent lights. Their eyes are protected. Exposure to fluorescent lights—or sunlight—does speed the breakdown of bilirubin. Some health care providers caution that no long-term studies on the side effects of phototherapy have been done, and the procedure does produce a number of side effects in some babies that should be considered. Some of them are:

- hyperthermia
- riboflavin deficiency
- rash
- short-term growth impairment
- mutations on the DNA molecule
- apnea (interrupted, stop/start, or abnormal breathing patterns)
- lactase deficiency and increased excretions of some vitamins
- dehydration
- diarrhea

And of course, hours spent under the phototherapy lamps separate newborns from their mothers. In many cases, exposure to sunlight accomplishes the same as phototherapy, without the side effects.

If your babies are placed in phototherapy, some physicians urge that mothers nurse their babies briefly every hour (not every four hours) to avoid dehydration and to supply the breast milk that will aid in breaking down the bilirubin. In many hospitals, you can request the phototherapy setup be placed in your room instead of down the hall in the nursery, so you can continue to nurse frequently.

And if you are trying to nurse babies in phototherapy frequently, you will probably notice that they are very lethargic. That is partly from the warmth of the lights, and partly from their elevated bilirubin levels. You may have to cool the babies with cool washcloths, tap their feet, move their arms, and generally work at rousing them in order to nurse them. Continued nursing is what will break the cycle of jaundice/lethargy/infrequent feeding/jaundice.

In rare instances, particularly in the case of pathologic jaundice, bilirubin can pass into the brain, causing permanent brain and nervous-system damage. But there has never been a single case reported of brain damage resulting from breast-milk jaundice. Studies have also shown that there is no neurological difference between jaundiced and not jaundiced infants at seven years of age, there is no correlation between neonatal bilirubin levels and IQ at five years of age, and no relationship between bilirubin levels up to 23 mg per 100 ml and IQ scores at five years of age.

WHAT ABOUT BOTTLEFEEDING?

Surveys done by the National Center for Health Statistics and Ross Laboratories in 1985 show that 54.4 percent of mothers who chose to bottlefeed their babies did so because they thought it was more convenient. In the same survey, 62.5 percent of the mothers who chose to breastfeed their babies did so because they thought *that* was more convenient.

There's the bottom line about infant feeding. Heaven to one mother may be sitting down and nursing several times a day; and to another it may be handing the bottles to her husband or her helper at feeding time. The value of any form of feeding ultimately lies in the eye of the beholder, but there are factors that can help you decide which feeding method—or combination of feeding methods—is best for you and for your babies.

Two factors to consider when you decide how to feed your babies are:

1. Nutrition—How can you give your babies the best possible nutrition?

2. Life-style—Which feeding method or methods fit best with the way you and your family live?

No matter how you choose to feed your babies, it will only work for you (and them) if *you* like it and feel confident with it.

HOW DO YOU CHOOSE A FORMULA?

Surveys show that most new mothers leave the choice of the type of formula they will use to their pediatrician or to the hospital where their babies were born. If you do that, the formula you are getting may be a free sample supplied to your doctor or the hospital by a formula manufacturer. But just because a sales representative for a formula company succeeded in placing a lot of samples with your doctor or your hospital doesn't mean that particular brand of formula is best for your babies. There are other ways to decide on a formula.

For example:

• You can find out what is best for your babies by trial and error. But with two or more babies to care for, you and your infants may be paying a steep price in frayed nerves and aching tummies before you find the right formula.

• Or you could find out about formulas by reading up on them and by reading the labels. By matching what's in the formulas with what's important nutritionally, and with what's important to your babies individually, you may sidestep any serious problems. For example, if allergies, particularly to dairy products, are common in your family, you might want to look into formulas that do not have cow's milk as a base.

Measure the Formula Against a Standard

According to formula manufacturers, health-care providers, nutritionists, and babies, the standard for judging the merits of any infant formula is how closely it resembles human milk. Many formulas do a pretty good job, but formula manufacturers will be the first to admit that no formula does it perfectly.

Current technology doesn't allow the replication of the kinds of immune qualities found in human milk. And as they continue to discover nutrients in breast milk they didn't know existed, formula companies continue to adjust their formulas accordingly.

For example, Ross Laboratories, makers of Similac, and Mead Johnson, makers of Enfamil, the two biggest-selling formulas in the U.S., both recently added the amino acid taurine to their formulas. Taurine, among other things, plays a role in cardiovascular regulation and nervous-system excitability. Cow's milk contains only negligible amounts of taurine, and the human body can't make it from other amino acids. Until a child is ready to eat meat and fish, the only other source is human milk.

While no formula exactly duplicates human milk, a good formula must closely resemble human milk. It should be:

• relatively low in protein (11 grams per liter of human milk compared to 42 grams per liter of 2 percent cow's milk)
• relatively high in fat (45 grams per liter of human milk compared to 20 grams per liter of 2 percent milk, or 36 grams per liter of whole milk)
• and lower in levels of ash, calcium, phophorus, sodium, and potassium than cow's milk. (See the chart on page 67 for more complete comparisons between the compostion of human milk and substitutes.)

A careful reading of labels of commercial formulas will show which types come closest to being like human milk. Most of them are available in three forms: liquid concentrate, liquid ready-to-use, and powdered. Generally speaking, the liquid ready-to-use is the most expensive and the powdered form is the least expensive. Surveys show that the liquid concentrate (to which you add water before feeding) is by far the most-used form.

Depending on how you count, there are about six types of commer-

Composition of Milk or Infant Formulas per Liter

Milk or Formula	Calories	Protein (gms)	Fat (gms)	Carbohydrate (gms)	Ash (gms)	Calcium (mgs)	Phosphorus (mgs)	Sodium (mgs)	Potassium (mgs)	Iron (mgs)	Protein Source	Fat Source	Carbohydrate Source
Human milk	750	11	45	68	2.0	340	140	161	507	0.2	Casein, lactalbumin	Human	Lactose
Whole cow's milk	670	36	36	49	7.0	1,220	960	498	1,440	trace	Casein	Butterfat	Lactose
Evap. cow's milk	660	28	32	69	7.0	1,027	827	498	1,212	2.0	Casein	Butterfat	Lactose
Similac PM 60/40	676	15	37.8	69	2.2	400	200	160	580	15.0	Casein, demin. whey	Coconut & corn oils	Lactose
Enfamil Premature	810	18	45	83	4.5	660	560	340	830	15.0	Casein	Soy & coconut oils	Lactose, sucrose
Similac	676	15	36.3	72.3	3.0	510	390	230	800	trace	Casein	Soy, coconut, & corn oils	Lactose
Enfamil	670	15	37	69	3.4	550	460	280	700	1.4	Casein	Soy, coconut, & corn oils	Lactose
Isomil	676	20	36	68	3.8	700	500	320	770	12.0	Soy	Soy & coconut oils	Sucrose, corn syrup
Meat-based formula	650	28	33	62	4.0	980	650	180	380	13.7	Beef hearts	Sesame oil	Modified tapioca, cane sugar, sucrose
Nutramigen	670	22	26	88	5.6	630	470	315	680	12.6	Casein hydrolysate	Corn oil	Modified tapioca, sucrose
Pregestimil	670	22	28	88	6.0	630	470	315	680	12.6	Casein hydrolysate	Corn & MCT* oils	Dextrose, modified tapioca

* medium-chain triglycerides

cial formula: cow's-milk-based, cow's-milk-based "humanized," soy-based, meat-based, predigested, and a small group of special formulas for special problems.

1. *Cow's-milk-based.* These formulas use nonfat cow's milk as the source of protein, vegetable oils as the source of fat, and lactose or corn syrup solids as the added carbohydrate. Vitamins and minerals are added to approximate the levels found in human milk.

To make a formula like this, the cow's milk is first skimmed, then diluted to decrease the amount of protein and minerals to more closely resemble the amounts found in breast milk. Vegetable oils (coconut oil, corn oil, soy oil) are added to the milk to replace the fat found in cow's milk, which babies have more trouble digesting. Lactose (milk sugar) is added to equal the levels of lactose in breast milk. Lactose is the sugar that is transformed in the body to galactose, which is the only sugar capable of being used to build the babies' brain cells.

There are iron-fortified versions of these formulas, usually recommended for babies over six months of age unless they were premature. (Iron stores in the newborn term baby's liver usually last about six months; in the preterm baby iron stores usually last about two months. Some pediatricians prescribe iron supplements or an iron-fortified formula anyway, which works for some babies, but produces gastrointestinal problems for others, like diarrhea, excessive spitting up, and excessive and often painful gas.)

2. *Cow's-milk-based-"humanized" formulas.* Since the term "humanized" was first used in the 1970s, its meaning has changed considerably. Originally it just meant that the formula had a lower protein content, closer to that found in human milk. Now it more often refers to the whey content of the formula. If you were to make cheese from cow's milk, the by-product—the liquid left after the solids had formed a curd—would be whey. Cow's milk typically breaks down to 80 percent casein (curd) and 20 percent whey. Human milk breaks down to 60 percent casein (the softer, more digestible curd), and 40 percent whey.

Makers of humanized formulas use nonfat cow's milk and basically make cheese from it to extract the whey. The whey is then added to other nonfat milk in proportions similar to human milk. Some formula makers also demineralize the whey and then replace the minerals with the lower level of minerals found in human milk. Cow's milk has high concentrations of calcium, phosphorus, and potassium that are difficult for the young infants' kidneys to process.

Humanized formulas also have the vegetable oils, lactose, and vitamins added that basic formulas have.

Some believe that humanized milk, particularly the types using de-mineralized whey, are more digestible than other formulas because they more closely resemble human milk. For that reason, they are often used for low-birth-weight or premature babies. Others believe that adding whey that has not been demineralized to formulas for normal term babies is using a lot of processing for a product that doesn't make a lot of difference in a baby's tolerance of the formula.

3. *Soy-based formulas.* These formulas have been used in the U.S. since the 1950s for babies who were either allergic to cow's-milk protein or unable to digest milk sugar (and had proved it by excessive spitting up, diarrhea, and intestinal gas), or who, because of family history, were likely to be allergic to these.

Originally, formula makers used the protein from soy flour as the base, which produced a tan-colored milk, loose, smelly stools, and a lot of diaper rash. Today, formulas based on soy flour are rarely used in the U.S. By the 1970s, soy formulas based on protein from water-soluble soy isolates (soy protein extracted directly from the soybean) have almost completely replaced soy flour formulas. These are white in color, nearly odorless, and are rarely reported to have the objectionable side effects of their predecessors.

Soy formulas usually use soy oil or coconut oil as the fat, and of course soy protein, in amounts comparable to (and usually somewhat higher than) protein found in human milk. If you want to find a formula for babies who have difficulty digesting lactose, or milk sugar, some soy formulas use corn syrup solids as the main carbohydrate.

One national survey found that soy-based formulas were used by about one-fourth of new mothers. More of them used the ready-to-use and the liquid concentrate forms than the powdered form.

4. *Meat-based formula.* These are formulas made for babies with allergies or difficulties in digesting substances like cow's milk, soy, and lactose. They are generally made from beef heart or lamb, with added fat (sesame oil) and carbohydrate supplied by modified tapioca starch and sucrose. Meat-based formulas are usually not available over the counter. If you think your babies cannot tolerate either cow's milk or soy formulas, you might discuss this option with your pediatrician.

6. *Predigested formulas.* Babies who have major and prolonged diffi-culties digesting other types of formula sometimes do better with a predigested formula. These are very specialized and two to three times as expensive as other formulas, but if you and your babies are at the end of your collective ropes, you might look into these.

These formulas are called predigested because the protein, fat, or carbohydrate, or all three, are modified to make them easily digestible.

Homemade Formula

Mix well: One 13-ounce can WHOLE evaporated milk fortified with vitamins A and D, 19 ounces tap water, and 1 ounce (2 tablespoons) sugar (table sugar or corn syrup. Do not use honey. It has been known to cause botulism in infants under six months). Pour into sterilized individual bottles, cover, and refrigerate. It may also be refrigerated in a covered, clean bulk container.

Be sure to use whole evaporated milk, not skimmed. And be sure to use evaporated milk, not condensed. Evaporated milk is milk that has been concentrated (and sterilized in the process) by removing half the water. The extended boiling process also makes the milk somewhat more digestible. Condensed milk has sugar added and is used for baking.

You will need to supplement the formula with vitamin C drops, and you might want to use a multivitamin too, since the processing of evaporated milk can destroy nutrients. If there is no fluoride in your water supply, you might want to add that, too, in amounts prescribed by your pediatrician.

In some, the fats used are called medium-chain triglycerides, which need no digestion and are well absorbed by the infant. In others, there is no lactose. Corn syrup solids and modified tapioca starch are used instead.

Predigested formulas are used for babies who are allergic to both soy and cow's-milk formulas, as supplements for breastfed babies who are likely to be highly allergic, or for babies who are very allergic to cow's milk. These babies are likely to be allergic to soy also.

7. *Special formulas.* There are a number of formulas specially made for babies with special problems. For example, there is one for babies who cannot tolerate carbohydrates, another for babies who cannot properly absorb nutrients from other formulas, one for babies with PKU (phenylketonuria—no tolerance for phenylalanine), and another with no sodium at all for infants with severe congestive cardiac failure. These are generally only available through a physician, who would be treating your babies anyway if they had problems of this nature.

Are There Any Other Alternatives?

Two other choices remain—homemade formula and goat's milk.

When many of today's mothers were babies, they were fed evaporated milk mixed with water and Karo syrup. According to the National Center for Health Statistics, in 1984, only 0.1 percent of newborns in the U.S. received this kind of formula, and fewer than 10 percent of babies received homemade formula when they were five to six months old.

The switch from homemade to commercial formulas probably is the result of better research on infant nutrition needs, better advertising by formula companies, and more awareness of allergy and digestive problems associated with cow's milk. But for some mothers, properly prepared and properly supplemented homemade formula may be the least expensive alternative. Needless to say, whipping up batches of formula from scratch is not how most new mothers of multiples would choose to spend their "free" time. But it you want to do it, follow the recipe in the margin.

Before there was commercial formula, and before there was evaporated milk, many mothers used goat's milk if they weren't breastfeeding their babies. They probably used milk from other animals too, but goat's milk is the only one that has carried over to our culture and our time. In fact, infants and children in many parts of the world still commonly use goat's milk as a substitute for human milk.

Goat's milk is somewhat more digestible than cow's milk because it has more medium- and short-chain fatty acids than does human milk. It is comparable to cow's milk in all other minerals and vitamins except vitamin D and folic acid. Goat's milk is commercially available in some areas. If you use it, be sure it is fortified with vitamin D, and that you add folic acid to your babies' diets too, since goat's milk is deficient in both of these.

WHAT IF NONE OF THESE WORK?

For some babies, there just is no comfortable substitute for human milk. For some mothers, there may be a substitute, but it is so expensive that it is prohibitive.

If for any reason none of the formulas that "should" work for your babies did work, do you have any choices left? The answer is yes. For the really tough cases of formula intolerance (also known as miserable-babies/miserable-mother syndrome) there are local human milk banks. They don't exist in every city, but milk can sometimes be transported for special cases. Contact your local La Leche League representative to find out if this could work for you.

Purchasing milk from banks can be extremely expensive, although fund-raising and other creative approaches have helped many mothers.

That brings us to the last (and a less expensive) alternative: relactation. Relactation is reestablishing your own milk supply, which is sort of a misnomer, since it can be done whether or not you have nursed before. Successful relactation takes know-how and dedication. You are most likely to find the help you would need to do this from a lactation counselor at a lactation center or at a La Leche League meeting.

BOTTLEFEEDING GEAR

A standard amount of equipment is usually recommended for mothers planning to bottlefeed. After some experience, you may find you need a little more or a little less, but to get started, you will need about a dozen bottles for each baby, with nipples, caps, and neck rings.

Although some nipples and neck rings are interchangeable from one brand to another, it would be a good idea to buy all the same brand to be sure of a fit. You can choose from plastic bottles, bottles with plastic liners, or glass bottles. According to national surveys, for safety reasons, most new mothers use plastic bottles or the plastic bottles with liners. If you choose those, you will need an average of five to eight liners a day, per baby. Glass bottles with rubber, instead of plastic, nipples might be a good choice for babies who seem to be allergic to plastic. If your babies get contact dermatitis—a rash—where they are touched by plastic pants, disposable diaper edges, or plastic teethers and pacifiers, they may be sensitive to the tiny amounts of plastic that get into the milk from plastic bottles and liners.

Most new mothers opt for one of the orthodontically shaped nipples that are now on the market. These attempt to mimic the shape of a mother's nipple when a baby breastfeeds, since the part that goes into the baby's mouth is relatively long and narrow, with a little bulb at the end. But some people say that the shape of the nipple doesn't make much difference, since it can't really copy the shape of a human nipple anyway. The human nipple becomes long and *flat* when a baby is nursing, and a plastic or rubber nibble would collapse and stick together if it did that.

Most likely the more important issue about nipples is that they are easily cleanable and that the babies can get milk out of them at a comfortable rate. A too-small or clogged hole frustrates the baby and may make her suck too hard, collapsing the nipple. A too-large hole

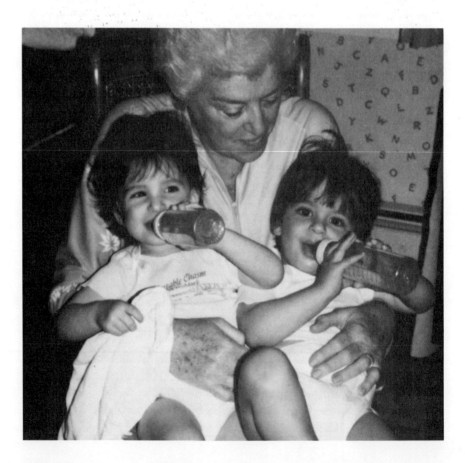

may choke the baby and make her develop an abnormal tongue thrust to keep all the milk from gagging her. You will be able to tell if your babies are comfortable by the way they drink. A hot needle can enlarge a tiny hole, but a nipple with a too-large hole must be discarded. Also discard any nipples that feel sticky to your touch. Saliva and milk or formula eventually deteriorate the surface of the nipple, and as it becomes stickier, it will stick to itself and not allow the milk through.

KEEPING IT CLEAN

Most health-care providers no longer routinely recommend that you sterilize all your feeding equipment if you have modern refrigeration, a clean water supply, use commercial formula, and carefully clean the bottles and nipples. In most cases, dishwasher clean is fine. Washing with hot, soapy water, and a good bottle brush is also fine. If that is how you are cleaning your bottles, all you have to do is mix the formula (according to makers' directions for powdered or liquid concentrate), pour it into the bottles, and refrigerate.

You may want to sterilize the bottles, if, for example, your babies are very young and were premature, or if you are unsure of the cleanliness of your water supply. If you do want to sterilize, there are two methods to choose from.

1. *Terminal method:* Use clean bottles as described above. Mix formula using tap water (or boil water for two minutes if you are unsure of its cleanliness), and fill bottles. Put a nipple upside down on each bottle and put the collars and caps on loosely so the steam can get to all the parts.

Stand the bottles (close together so they won't fall over) in a large pot or sterilizer. Fill with water to about ⅓ the way up the bottles. Cover and bring the water to a boil and boil for twenty minutes. Leave the cover on and let the water cool gradually. Quick cooling can form a skin on the milk. Remove the bottles when cool and refrigerate. Use within forty-eight hours.

2. *Aseptic method:* If you are using water to prepare the formula, boil it for two minutes. Boil everything you will use (bottles, nipples, caps, tongs, measuring tools, can opener, etc.) in a covered pot for twenty mintues. Mix formula in a sterile container and fill bottles. Put on nipples, collars, and caps, and store in refrigerator. You must use the bottles within forty-eight hours.

Some mothers, who don't use either of these methods but who want to be a little more sure about cleanliness than "dishwasher clean," boil all the bottles, nipples, collars, and caps once a week for twenty minutes in addition to their regular cleaning.

KEEPING TRACK

With two or more babies to feed, you might want to label bottles. Generally speaking, it is really not a problem if one baby drinks from the other's bottle (and it isn't a problem later to feed two babies from a single spoon). Rather, your labeling would help you keep track of how much each baby has consumed. If either or both babies do not finish their bottles at a single feeding, you can refrigerate them and allow them to finish within an hour of the feeding, but don't keep the half-used formula any longer. Formula with a little saliva in it is an excellent breeding ground for unfriendly bacteria.

If you find your babies are consistently not finishing their bottles at a feeding, just put a little less formula in each bottle to begin with to avoid throwing away so much.

Another way some mothers of multiples keep track of how much each baby is eating is by keeping a simple chart of feeding times and amounts. This is probably more common for mothers bottlefeeding than for mothers breastfeeding. And it's probably more common among mothers who have very small or premature babies. You needn't become a babyfood bookkeeper to do this. Just have pencil and pad handy where you usually feed the babies, and jot down who took how much at what time. After the first few weeks, when you and the babies have established eating and growth routines, you probably won't need to do this.

HOW TO DO IT

Just as you tried to find the formula that most closely resembled human milk, when you feed your babies, the best way to bottlefeed is to find the position that most closely resembles the one you would use to breastfeed them.

Some mothers of multiples hold and feed one baby while the other bounces, rocks, or swings in the appropriate baby equipment. If you have a helper around, this is a great time to use him or her to feed the other baby or babies. But one way or another, you should plan to distract the other baby while one is feeding. In the early days, one baby may be sleeping while you feed the other. But later, as babies become more aware of routines and of each other, one hungry baby may not be willing to sit placidly by and watch you feed the other. If early on, you can establish a routine of something reasonably enjoyable for one to do while the other is being fed, you may avoid problems later.

But inevitably, the day will come (and probably sooner than later) when you have two crying, hungry babies, and only two hands to feed them with. You can't simultaneously cuddle two babies and hold two bottles. What you can do is hold one baby and lay the other on the couch or bed next to you. Hold the bottle for the baby in your lap, and prop the bottle for the other baby. Roll a cloth diaper into a cylindrical shape, and prop the bottle with it so the nipple is easily accessible to the baby and the milk fills the nipple. Then roll another diaper to prop the baby. A very young baby may need this second diaper placed snugly against her back to help keep her on her side and in a good feeding position.

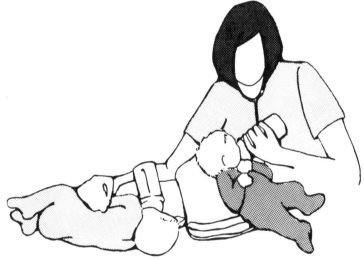

Once you are all settled, you can talk to each baby, and (if you can hold bottle and baby in one hand for a few seconds at a time) you have a free hand for caressing or patting. You may find that one baby is often more accepting of being the one who gets the propped bottle, or is more willing to wait to be fed. You may feel comfortable letting your babies establish this order. But some mothers report that the baby with the propped bottle takes less formula compared to feeding times when that baby is held. Since there is solid evidence that all babies benefit from being held, and since most mothers of multiples are very aware of treating their babies equally, you might feel more comfortable alternating who gets the propped bottle.

However you decide to manage propping bottles for your multiples, you can know that your sensitivity to your babies' needs will override any ill effects you may fear from bottle propping. Twenty or thirty years ago, bottle propping was not only done, but recommended. Today, the value of touch has been well recognized, and every child-care book admonishes mothers against bottle propping. But those books weren't written for mothers of twins or triplets. You know that reality for you is very different from reality for mothers who have one baby at a time. It follows that what will be acceptable—and necessary—for you will also be very different.

As your babies get teeth, you will need to be careful about allowing them to fall asleep with a bottle of juice or milk. Babies and toddlers who habitually do this can suffer from severely decayed teeth because of the small amounts of the liquid that can remain pooled in their mouths all night.

Feeding each baby will take about twenty minutes. All babies are different, but if you notice it taking inordinately long for one baby to feed, check the nipple to be sure the hole isn't too small or clogged.

Here are a few tips to get you started right with bottle feeding:

• You don't really have to warm the bottle before you feed your babies. Try different temperatures and see what your babies like. Cool formula in summer and warm in winter might make sense. Extremes will probably be unacceptable to most babies.

• Cuddle your babies, one at a time, in the crook of your arm as if you were breastfeeding. Remember, that nine-to-ten-inch distance from your face is the optimum for newborns who are learning to react to facial expresions.

• Control the flow of milk to the baby by loosening or tightening the collar on the bottle.

• Tilt the bottle so the milk completely fills the nipple. The baby will swallow less air if you do.

• Try burping the baby after every ounce or so at first. Bottlefed babies unavoidably swallow more air than do breastfed babies. You may help the baby avoid a painful bellyfull of air after the feeding if you burp as you go along.

• Tiny bubbles moving from the nipple back along the bottle will show you the baby is getting milk.

• If your babies are on different formulas, or if they have different feeding times, try color-colding their bottles—Julie always gets the yellow bottle and Erica always gets the pink bottle, for example.

• If your babies seem happy and do well on the formula you are feeding them, then leave well enough alone. Don't switch formulas just to see what will happen.

• Most babies spit up some—maybe even a couple of times a day, or even a little bit after each feeding. Many babies have a mild bout of diarrhea from time to time. Neither are reasons to start jumping from formula to formula. Prolonged, serious difficulties are. Your babies may have a cow's milk or lactose intolerance if they:

> —have severe diarrhea, wheezing (purring in the chest), persistent colic, excessive gas, asthma, vomiting, bronchitis, frequent inner-ear infections, or runny nose.

> —have anemia despite drinking huge amounts of milk daily. Usually this happens to babies over six months old who are allergic to cow's milk. The allergy can produce mild bleeding in the intestines, which results in anemia—a lack of sufficient iron in the blood. Babies who have this kind of anemia typically appear pale and thin-skinned, have dark circles under their eyes, may be sluggish and extremely irritable, and may have a runny discharge from the nose.

> —break out in hives if cow's milk touches their skin. This is quite rare, but definitely indicates a serious allergy that can send a baby into a coma if he drinks cow's milk.

If you think your babies have a cow's-milk or lactose intolerance, you should be in touch with a physician. The first step should be away from cow's milk—or humanized-cow's-milk-based formulas, not just to another brand with the same base. Often the switch is made to a soy formula, but many children who are allergic to cow's milk are also allergic to soy. That doesn't mean you shouldn't try it; it just means soy isn't a cure-all for sensitive babies.

The next step after soy should be to the predigested formulas described earlier in this chapter, unless it is found that your babies have a specific problem requiring a specific formula. The other alternative is to feed the babies human milk.

HOW CAN I TELL IF MY BABIES ARE DOING WELL?

Whether you are breastfeeding, bottlefeeding, or using a combination of methods, the goal is the same: You want healthy, happy babies who are growing well.

But what happens when you go to the pediatrician's office, and he puts the babies on the scale, measures their lengths, and proclaims that they are "pretty low on the chart." Is that reason to run out and start pumping formula into breastfed babies? Do babies on formula have to add cereal and two fruits? Does it mean their growth is retarded and you are a bad mother?

The answer to all of those questions is no. To understand that answer, it might help to understand the charts against which your babies may be measured. Those charts were formulated for the most part about twenty years ago from a small sample of bottlefed babies. Researchers recorded the average weight and length of those babies at different ages, and devised the chart to show where any other baby's growth stands in relation to them.

Perhaps the best use of the chart for your babies is to compare their growth *not* with those of bottlefed babies twenty years ago, but with themselves. For example, pay attention to the curve each child develops as he grows, not necessarily to where he falls on the chart. It's more important that babies maintain *their own* relatively steady growth rate than it is for them to compare well with the babies from an old study.

If you are breastfeeding your babies, they may not weigh as much during the first year of their lives as the bottlefed babies whose weights set the standard for the charts. And if you are five feet tall and your husband is five-foot-nine, your babies are probably going to be in the lower ranges of the chart for length. In neither of these cases should you worry or suddenly change your babies' diets because of their position on the chart. Normal for them may well be smaller than what is normal for some other babies.

What should concern you is if you see a drastic change in the growth rate for your babies. For example, if they have been consistently in the 10–15 percentile for height and weight and suddenly drop to the fifth percentile, you would want to examine why that happened. It may be they were sick and not eating for a while, and once normal eating patterns resumed, their weights both jumped back up. But a sustained and drastic change deserves closer examination.

Another thing to remember about growth is that twinship is not, in and of itself, a reason to be physically small. Many twins are quite small as infants because they were premature or because of other pregnancy- and birth-related problems. But small premature babies usually catch up with their age group in size by the time they're two or three, and possibly younger, depending on their birth weight.

If you have babies who are growing more slowly than you or your pediatrician thinks they should, before making sweeping changes in their diets, consider this standard from a medical text on breastfeeding for discerning the difference between healthy slow-growing infants and failure-to-thrive infants:

Slow Gainer	Failure to Thrive
alert healthy appearance	apathetic or crying
good muscle tone	poor tone
good skin turgor	poor turgor
at least 6 wet diapers/day	few wet diapers
pale dilute urine	strong, dark urine
stools frequent and seedy (or if infrequent, large and soft)	stools infrequent or scanty
8 or more nursings a day lasting 15–20 minutes each for breastfed (consumption of adequate-for-age amounts of formula if not)	fewer than 8 feedings often brief
well-established let-down reflex	no signs of functioning let-down reflex
weight gain consistent but slow	weight gain erratic—may lose

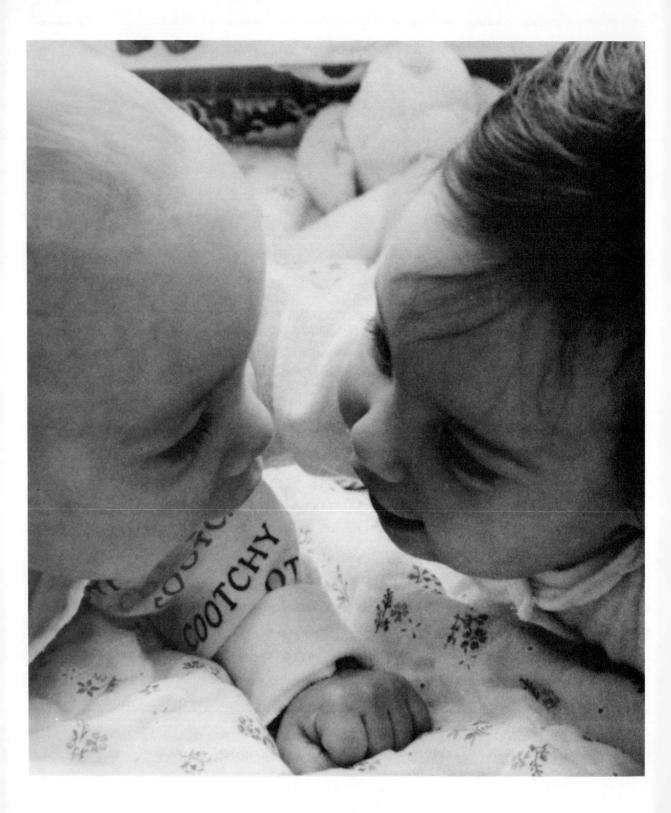

4 | **That First Year**

"My husband told me when the babies were born that he didn't expect me to do *anything* but take care of them and myself. That attitude took a lot of pressure off me."

You've gotten past the early recovery from the birth of the babies. The frozen dinners from friends have stopped coming. Your husband has gone back to work. And the novelty of your multiple birth has dimmed just a little. Now, the reality of months of caring for two or more totally dependent infants looks to some moms like a long, lonely road.

A partner with an attitude like the one in the quote above can help a lot, and is exactly what every mother of multiples needs. But it's not exactly what every mother of multiples gets. You may have a wonderful husband who is willing to help, but he travels a lot on business so he's not really available. You may have a loving family who wants to pitch in, but the other children are really too young to take care of themselves. What will you do with two or more new babies *and* everyone else to care for?

The key to doing more than just surviving during the early months with multiples is having a workable, satisfying routine.

In many ways, your life can be immeasurably enriched by the birth of your multiples. But there is one quality your life will most likely lose —that of spontaneity. Of course that happens with the birth of any single baby, but the loss of spontaneity is often more pervasive, and the feeling of that loss is often more intense, for parents of multiples.

That's why a reasonable routine is so important to you. With all the demands on your time and energy, absolutely nothing outside of feeding, diapering, and laundering will happen if it isn't planned for, and even then, there will be plenty of times when the best-laid plans will go awry.

Despite ups and downs, you *can* bring order from chaos. How well you do that will depend on three things:

1. *Attitude.* This includes your attitude and the attitudes of those around you. Once again, you need to be aware of surrounding yourself with people who support your decisions, your style of mothering, and most important, your ability to find creative and healthy ways of handling your new life with multiples. Those who see your situation as a disaster, a tragedy, or an insurmountable burden, and those who see you as a beleaguered victim, cannot add to your sense of competence.

The same is true if you see yourself as a victim. You can put yourself on a positive track by choosing to see yourself and your multiples as capable beings. All those old sayings about self-fulfilling prophecies ring especially true when you look at how confidence can beget confidence, and how criticism and self-doubt can beget a sense of failure.

2. *Expectations.* We all have expectations for ourselves, for our babies, and for the people around us. And we all know that the source of disappointment and even depression often lies in unrealistic or mismatched expectations. One way to avoid those is to be crystal clear about our own expectations and to share those with people who matter.

For example, just before or soon after the birth of your multiples may be the best time to clarify your priorities. You can be especially clear if you actually write them down and put them in order. When you do this, it is important that you ask your partner to do the same. Then you need to compare lists. If having time alone is number one on your list, and having time to work out gets top billing on his list, then you need to figure out exactly how you can realize even a part of what's most important to each of you—and still take care of two or more infants.

The reality may be, for the first few months or for the first year, that neither of you gets all of what's most important to you. It is more often the norm that everyone's schedule revolves around the babies' schedule. But if you each understand what is crucial to the other, and if you each can allow even a bit of time for that crucial item, you might end that first year feeling at least a little balanced about your lives and not completely martyred.

In the same way, if you each understand clearly what you expect from each other, you may avoid other difficulties. For example, it may become apparent after you have been home with your babies for several weeks that the hours between 5 and 7 P.M. are the babies' fussiest, and therefore the hardest of the day for you. Your husband won't know unless you tell him that those two hours consistently put you over the edge. If he knows that, he may be able to arrange his schedule so he is home as close to 5 P.M. as possible. If he doesn't know how he can help you, he probably won't read your mind to find out.

3. *Planning.* The more you can understand the needs that have to be met (yours, your babies', your spouse's, your family's), the better you will be able to plan for them. That doesn't mean that *everyone* gets *every* need met, but with clear priorities, most of you can get the most important ones taken care of.

Perhaps the most important part of this kind of planning is flexibility. Your workable routine may fall apart when one of the babies is sick, or when you finally catch the terrible cold that's been shared by the entire family. It happens to everyone. But if you're used to working from a plan that takes everyone into consideration, you know you will be able to pull it all back together again and find some order in the chaos.

Another way you must be flexible in planning your routine is that you must be willing from time to time to throw the whole thing out. Babies change all the time. Their needs change, their feeding schedules change, their happy times and their fussy times, all change. You can take comfort from that when the pattern is an unpleasant one, and you may find a bit of extra joy in that as you strive to really appreciate the pleasant patterns. But you can always know that neither pattern will last forever.

Nor will your plan, your routine, last forever. You may find that when your babies are newborns, your routine is pretty simple and tightly scheduled. But as they get older and require a little less from you and will accept more from others, you may find that you will have a little more freedom to add activities to your personal routine.

WHAT DO YOU DO ALL DAY?

If you asked a mother of very young infants what she did all day, she would probably say she fed and diapered babies. And she'd be just about right. There's no question that those two activities usually dominate the new mother of multiples' life for several months at least. If you looked at a day centered on a family with younger or older multiples, it would look different because the routine would be set up to satisfy different needs. For example, the mother of three-month-old twins might not be meeting with a playgroup yet, and the babies might not be satisfied amusing themselves with toys while she did something else. If you looked at a family with older twins, you might see the mother more involved with outside activities, perhaps hiring a baby-sitter more often to accommodate them, or being more easily able to take her toddlers with her for some activities. Families with other children in addition to multiples, and families in which both parents are employed outside the home have still other workable routines. See chapter 7, Going Back to Work, for ideas on setting up those.

If you look closely at the life of a mother of even fairly young twins, you'll see there are other things going on in a workable routine beside feeding and diapering. Those things can be the parts of a routine that make the day work instead of making everyone miserable. Here's one routine that works for a mother of nine-month-old breastfed twins.

5:30–6:30 A.M. The girls wake up at 5:30. I am convinced they have an alarm clock hidden in their room. It seems that magically, on the dot of 5:30, two little pairs of eyes pop open simultaneously, and they are ready to go. I, however, am not. I arrange myself on the couch in the living room with them, and with a little nursing, all of us doze off again for forty-five minutes. Then it's up and at 'em. I change their diapers and leave them in pajamas until later.

At this age, they like to crawl and roll around on their blankets on the floor and play with one another until breakfast. They also spend some time now with their dad, who gets up around 6 A.M. so he can play with them a little before he goes off to work.

7 A.M. Ready for rice cereal and fruit. No eggs yet because of allergies. A quick nursing before breakfast takes the edge off, so they are reasonably happy waiting in their high chairs while I warm up their cereal. A toy, a book, or a cracker usually distracts them enough for me to get ready.

Months ago I abandoned my horror at using one dish and one spoon to feed them. Switching from spoon to spoon and dish to dish seemed ridiculous after I inadvertently gave each the wrong spoon a few times, with no apparent ill effects. So I decided to loosen up and leave behind the every-baby-has-a-spoon idea. Much simpler!

7:30 A.M. Another diaper change, and back to the floor with toys to play while I eat and then clean up blobs of rice cereal from the floor and two high chairs.

I have become adept at taking the fastest shower of all time, usually with two little heads peaking at me around the shower curtain. The bathroom, as well as the rest of the house, is child-proofed so I just cart both girls around with me wherever I need to be. I seem to do everything with an audience these days, and the girls mimic my tooth-brushing (even though they don't have any teeth yet) with the little brushes we bought for them and admire each other's hair as they "brush" first their own, then their sister's.

8:15 A.M. They've wandered out to the living room without me, and I find them busily rearranging our books. My husband must have taken one out of the tightly-packed bookcase last night and forgotten to re-place it with another book. Our secret to childproofing bookcases is to jam the books in there so tightly most adults can't budge them.

9 A.M. I throw the first load of laundry into the washer, and return to find one girl has pinned the other, and is apparently delighted with the feeling of power. She calmly remains spread-eagled on top of her sister, watching the girl on the bottom scream and squirm to get away. I disengage them and wonder if the one on the bottom will always be the "victim."

9:30 A.M. Diaper-change time again. I'm so glad we broke down and bought a large changing table, even if it was more expensive than the smaller models. It folds out from the top of a sturdy dresser, has a four-inch rim on three sides, and safety belts. I don't have to bend over to change the girls, and the table is big enough so that both girls can be changed at the same time.

It's never hard to tell when it is morning nap time: The girls get fussy and I get tired of trying to pick up the debris we always seem to have scattered around the house. I arrange them and me on our king-size bed, and catch a thirty-minute snooze myself as they nurse to sleep. Then I ease my arms out from under them, and since they scoot in their sleep now, I put each into her own bed. Then I toss the laundry from the washer into the dryer and dump a second load into the washer. A few minutes remain of the girls' nap, so I make a cup of tea and sit down to read the newspaper.

11 A.M. I can hear them giggling and calling to each other in their beds. I let them play for a few minutes, since they sound happy, then go in and change them and get them dressed. Today is playgroup day, and all the moms have agreed that for now, late morning seems to be the best time to meet, since the little ones have all had a nap by then and are happy. I nurse the girls sitting on the couch, then take a couple of minutes to get ready while they play on the living-room floor. I never used to go out of the house without makeup; now I'm lucky to remember to comb my hair! Fortunately, most of the mothers I hang around with these days are in the same boat, so it doesn't seem to matter as much as I thought it would.

I wrestle both girls into snowsuits, then strap one into an infant seat on the living-room floor for safekeeping while I take her sister out to the car and strap her into a car seat. I return for the second girl, lock the front door behind me, and strap her into the other car seat. Then I remember I left the diaper bag and snacks for the girls to eat in the car on the kitchen table. Feeling guilty about leaving the girls alone in the car even in my own driveway, I decide to "risk it," and run to the house, unlock the door, retrieve the bag, and run back to the car. Whew. The girls are still there.

Getting out of the house with the girls when I'm alone is still hard. I can't wait until I can say, "Get your coats on, girls, we're going to playgroup!" But even though it is a hassle to get two babies into and out of snow gear and into and out of the car, it's worth it for me to go to playgroup. Catching up on the adult world with the other mothers, even if the talk is sometimes baby-oriented and I'm the only one there with twins, makes me feel like part of the human race again. I get cabin fever when I don't get out. So no matter how hard it is to do it with two little ones, it's worth it.

1 P.M. Home again from playgroup. The mothers in the group take turns bringing snacks for mothers and for babies, and rotate whose house the group meets at. It's great to talk with the others while all the babies play on the floor. And it's interesting to compare notes on how each of the babies is developing. Just when one of us thinks our baby is the only savage child with the infuriating habit of throwing food at her mother, we find that four of six babies in the group are doing the same thing! And just when one of us thinks she must be the worst mother in history for getting genuinely angry with a nine-month-old baby who dumps his whole bowl of rice cereal on her head as she bends to pick up the toast he already tossed to the floor—she finds three others who have had the same feelings. We always end up laughing about it and usually find some better way to deal with our feelings and our babies. It really recharges me to talk to those other mothers.

1:30 P.M. Snowsuits off, diapers changed, and we're all cuddled up nursing on the bed. The other good thing about playgroup is that the babies love it, and they are usually so wiped out by the time we get home, they nap well in the afternoon. I'm usually pretty tired by now too, so I end up dozing off with them again for a half hour or so, and then I have to get back to the laundry and think about dinner. While the girls finish their nap, I do the washer-dryer shuffle again, and try to remember if I have a dinner I made earlier stashed in the freezer, or if I have to start from scratch. I decide it's half-and-half, defrost in the microwave what I find in the freezer, and rifle the refrigerator to see what I can add to it. By 3:15, I hear the girls again, and it's back to change them, nurse them, and let them play while I heat some puréed chicken and vegetables for them. They eat some, but not much, preferring instead to spit the food out and rub it into artistic swirls in their hair and on their highchair trays. We are approaching what I call the witching hours—the low point of the day for all of us. I'm tired of pulling them apart in the wrestling matches. (The girl who was on the bottom this morning is on top this afternoon. I decide not to worry about who is the "victim.") I'm tired of picking up after them. I'm tired of trying to do laundry that never gets done. I'm tired of changing diapers. And by the way they are acting, they're pretty tired of me, too.

4 P.M. Since I know the babies and I feel this way every afternoon, I have arranged with a friend down the street to meet for an afternoon stroll with all our babies (she has just one). We do this almost every day around 4 P.M. Sometimes I even cook dinner in the morning if I find time, so I will be able to "hit the streets" with my neighbor in the afternoon. After shoving strollers through three inches of snow one afternoon, the snowflakes falling in my girls' eyes as they lay in their stroller bundled up to their little red noses, we decided we should have T-shirts printed with DESPERATE MOTHERS CLUB on the back. We may look crazy out there with strollers in the snow, but we always return laughing, which we think is better than sitting home alone listening to fussy babies cry. We also often sit and nurse our babies and have a glass of wine until we see one or the other of our husbands drive up. Before we figured this schedule out, afternoons were pretty awful for both of us. Now, even crying babies aren't so bad when someone shares the time with you.

5:30 P.M. My husband has adjusted his work schedule since the babies were born, so that he leaves a little earlier in the morning, since we're all up anyway, and returns a little earlier in the evening. His earlier return also allows him time in the evening to do yoga exercises for a while and then go for a short run. I'm still too tired most of the time to run, so my form of exercise is mostly walking now.

While he exercises on the living-room floor, the babies delight in crawling over and around him—which also allows me to finish getting dinner ready. When he is done exercising, I put the babies in their highchairs and feed them while he is out running. Dinner is pretty basic for us. Absolutely nothing that takes more than 20–30 minutes preparation, which means a lot of take-out food, salads, and tuna.

What makes any routine work is knowing the needs to be met, and finding ways to at least partly satisfy them.

"Heaven to me, when my twins were two or three months old, was going to the grocery store all alone to read the magazines."

"I couldn't believe I'd feel like Queen for a Day by just going out for a cup of coffee with a friend in the evening when my babies were small. I can't tell you how self-satisfied I felt sitting at the diner counter with an adult and a whole hour of conversation stretching before me."

When my husband returns from his run and cools down a bit, we strap the babies into bouncy chairs, and they bounce away while he and I eat dinner. I have friends who do the same thing with swings, but our kitchen isn't big enough for two swings. So we each take a baby and bounce the springy chair with one foot. Motion is the best insurance we've found against crying babies during dinner. We joke that for years to come, eating will probably trigger a strange jerking of the foot for each of us. After dinner, my husband cleans up while I bounce both chairs and we get a few minutes to catch up on each other's day.

7 P.M. I'm fading fast, so bath time is shared time. I do one girl in the Tubby, the inflatable tub in the big bathtub, and my husband does the other. Fresh diapers, clean pajamas, and we all settle on the couch to nurse. In an hour, they're both asleep, and we tiptoe them into their beds. I'm pooped, but restless. My husband suggests I go out for a while. For my big night out, I decide to browse in a favorite old bookstore to see if I remember how to read. To my delight, I find I do, but I'm too tired to commit to reading an entire book, so I return home empty-handed, but somehow refreshed.

9 P.M. I know the girls will be up somewhere around 3 A.M. to nurse, but I really want to spend some time with my husband, so we chat over tea for half an hour, and when I can't keep my eyes open any longer, he trots me off to bed. This is when he stands in as a mother to tuck *me* in. I fall asleep trying to figure out how I can get a baby-sitter at the last minute so I won't have to take the girls to the supermarket with me tomorrow.

WHAT MAKES IT WORK?

This routine may look all wrong to some people. But it is just right for this mother. The reason is that she tailored it to be that way. That means she made sure that the most important needs for her, her husband, and her babies were met in the best way possible.

No routine is going to make anyone happy if it doesn't meet needs. If your need is to work out, to have some extra sleep, to have time alone, or to have time with other adults, you can find a way to at least partly meet that need. You might not be able to meet it in exactly the same ways you did before your multiples were born, but you will probably find that even partly fulfilling the need is better than trying to ignore it until your children grow up.

You can see how that can work by looking back at this mother's routine. Here are some things that made her routine work:

1. *Adjust.* Although the babies set the schedule by their waking, sleeping, and feeding times, the mother adjusted her schedule as much as she could to fit theirs. She may not have gotten a full night's sleep, but she napped briefly twice during the day.

2. *Rearrange.* This mother changed what she could to make life simpler for herself and for her babies. For example, she used one spoon and dish for two babies, generally fed and changed them at the same time, waited until half the day was gone to dress them to cut down on the number of soiled outfits, and arranged her house so she wasn't constantly chasing after them saying no or worrying about their safety.

3. *Schedule.* Time away from home was built in for babies and for the mother. Babies get bored and grouchy, just as adults do, when they do the same thing day after day. And sometimes the energy just isn't there for mothers to think up new and fun things to do with the babies each day. Standing appointments or meetings are usually a simple and effective addition to your routine.

4. *Gear up.* The equipment she used, like the bouncy chairs, changing table, and inflatable bathtub, genuinely helped the mother instead of getting in the way.

5. *Get/give support.* The playgroup mothers gave this mom the acceptance and understanding she needed as her life changed to accommodate multiples. Since they didn't judge her by her makeup or degree of organization, she could be a little easier on herself. And she could, in turn, offer the same kind of acceptance to the other mothers. Her husband offered support too, by being flexible with his schedule.

6. *Share.* Explaining to her husband that she wasn't really an out-of-patience witch all day, just for the last two hours of it, convinced him to change his schedule to make the hard hours a little shorter for her (and their evening a little pleasanter for both of them). She also told him how wonderful it made her feel to get out without the babies once in a while, so it wasn't difficult for him to take over in the evenings a few times a week to give her that break.

> **"I was in no shape to do as much working out after my babies were born as I did before, but I found that all I needed was a fifteen-minute jog around the neighborhood to feel renewed."**

> **"When the twins were tiny, I missed my sleeping-in time on Saturday mornings so much. But when they were a few months old, we figured that my husband could get them up, give them a bottle, and take them out for an early walk that one morning each week. I couldn't believe how pampered I felt having that extra hour of uninterrupted sleep."**

BASIC ISSUES

As you develop a routine that works for you, there are basic issues you will probably see, no matter what your specific situation is. Here are some ideas on how to handle those basics, which include crying (theirs and yours), sleeping, feeding, bathing, and housekeeping.

To tailor a routine to fit your life, first survey the needs to be met, then—

Adjust
Rearrange
Schedule
Gear Up
Get/Give Support
Share

CRYING (THEIRS):

Why *do* babies cry? Many mothers associate crying in very young babies with feeding—either from hunger to be fed or from gas that comes from being fed. But researchers and experienced mothers know there are many other reasons why babies cry. Understanding what they are might give you some ideas about how to deal with your crying babies.

• *Individual differences.* Although it may be hard to think of newborns as having personality differences, it is true that they each react differently to stimulation and to the lack of it. One study showed that in the first week of life, some newborns cried as little as ten minutes a day, and others cried as much as one hundred ninety minutes a day. Some cried consistently on awakening; others always cried just before falling asleep. The only pattern researchers discerned in this early crying was that most of these newborns cried more and longer in the late afternoon and evening, and less frequently in the morning hours.

If you have had children before your multiples, you know well how different each baby can be, despite your best efforts to treat them similarly. You will probably see these kinds of differences with your multiples too, particularly if they are fraternal. Their biological rhythms will be no more similar than those of any single-born siblings, and they will have their own way of reacting to life. Even though identical twins may be more physiologically similar, it is just as likely that each will have his or her own approach to the world.

What all this means is that some babies just cry more than others by their nature.

• *Labor and Drugs.* Research has clearly documented the effect on babies of drugs given the mother during labor and birth. Differences in infant behavior have been noted for babies whose mothers had general anesthesia, local-regional anesthesia, or epidural analgesia. These babies tended to cry more, were more generally irritable, more difficult to comfort, and more likely to sleep in short bouts. Some of the behavior differences were still apparent in the babies a month after the birth.

• *Gender Differences.* Many studies show that male babies are more vulnerable to all kinds of stresses almost from conception. Some also show that they tend to cry more and be fussier, especially during the newborn stage. But one behavioral scientist points out that newborn fussiness in boys may be more closely related to circumcision than to gender. Judy Dunn, a behavioral geneticist at Pennsylvania State University, notes that the behavior of three-week-old uncircumcised boys is not significantly different from that of girls of the same age, but the behavior of circumcised boys is.

• *Hunger.* Of course babies cry when they are hungry. For breastfed babies, that may seem like all the time, because their bodies digest breast milk more quickly than they can digest formula. For some babies, that may mean they want to be fed every thirty to forty-five minutes during growth spurts. For others it means crying to be fed every two or three hours. And for bottlefed babies, it may mean crying for a bottle every three or four hours.

Some studies show that sucking, an integral part of feeding for small babies, is also an important need. In one study, premature babies who had to be fed through a tube were allowed to suck on a pacifier while being fed. Researchers found that those babies grew and matured faster than premature babies who didn't get to suck. But other studies show that the most calming factor for babies is the feeling of a full stomach, not the comfort derived from sucking.

• *Temperature.* It won't be surprising to find that babies sleep better in a warmer environment. One study showed that babies kept at 88–90 degrees Fahrenheit cried less and slept more than babies who were kept at 78 degrees. Diapers play a part in this. It isn't necessarily a wet or dirty diaper itself that bothers babies, but the cooling (or the rash) that can result.

• *Contact.* Did you ever wonder why they wrap those newborns so tightly in the hospital nursery? Or why so many cultures swaddle their babies and even tie the closely wrapped bundle onto carrying boards or onto the mother's body? It's because, generally, very young babies seem to be happier that way. If you have newborns, you've heard the noisy effects of undressing them, even if you made sure the room was warm, the babies were fed, etc., etc. Most newborns don't like to have their clothes off. And just plain throwing a blanket over them doesn't usually make them any happier. What does work for most babies is swaddling with soft cloth, or skin-to-skin contact.

• *Evening.* Many, and some would say most, babies cry more and are harder to comfort in the evening. So far, no one has come up with a really good reason why this is. Some say breastfed babies cry more in the evenings because their mothers probably have less milk at that time of day. But even mothers who supplement their milk with a bottle of formula at that time report their babies are still fussy. The only facts revealed by studies on the topic are that evening crying peaks for some babies around two months of age and that evening crying occurs no matter what the mother or anyone else does.

> "Why are those babies crying again? This happens every evening. They *can't* be hungry, they just ate. It's driving me crazy."

• *Pain, Sudden Stimulation.* If you stick a baby to get a blood sample, she will cry. And most babies will also cry when they are startled, for example by a loud noise.

WHAT CAN YOU DO ABOUT CRYING BABIES?

Most experts agree now that what you shouldn't do is let very young babies cry to keep from "spoiling" them. You can't spoil young babies. Crying babies are not nearly sophisticated enough in their thinking to be manipulating you; they are only responding to needs they feel and letting you know about them the only way they can.

On the other hand, real life for parents of multiples means that you *will* have crying babies whose needs don't get met immediately. As a mother at home with your babies, you will be outnumbered, even if you don't have any other children. If your babies are already here you know that it is often impossible to take care of everyone simultaneously. Does that mean you are stunting the emotional development of your multiples because you have only two hands? No, it doesn't. Common sense will tell you that it is unlikely that every wonderful, accomplished, well-adjusted human being in the world today had a parent who was instantly available every moment of his or her life.

And a careful reading of the most recent research in the behavioral sciences shows a change in how we understand human behavior. The focus is changing from a belief in the overbearing influence of environment to an acknowledgment of the effect of inherited traits on human behavior. To a larger degree than was thought before, your children are who they are, and your every move is not necessarily irrevocably shaping their lives. Another trend is a move toward seeing the big picture in child-rearing and away from seeing psychological and emotional development as a "parade of epochs" during which you, as a parent, had better do the "right" thing at the "right" time or you will have forever lost your chance to positively influence your children.

So when you are sure you are damaging your multiples by not being able to satisfy their needs instantly, you can comfort yourself with these thoughts:

• It is the overall tenor of how you care for your twins or triplets that matters more than specific instances in which they have to wait for your attention.

• Your multiples will never have to unlearn the belief that they are the center of the universe, as do most single-born chidren. They will

learn by degrees from the beginning that we all have to make room for others in our lives. In a very elemental way, the necessity of sharing what matters to them will be a way of life for your multiples, not an ability that is often painfully learned much later in life.

• Responsiveness has more to do with your attitude toward meeting your multiples' needs than it has to do with beating a stopwatch. One baby may still cry while you're tending the other, but you can know that your loving care and responsiveness to your babies in quiet moments can go a long way toward making you, and eventually, them, feel more tolerant of those times when you just can't get to one or the other.

There are several time-honored ways to help calm a crying baby (or two). Here are some of them:

1. *Rocking.* Mothers all over the world almost instinctively will rock a fussy baby. And in many cases rocking works. The reason it works may be that it provides constant, rhythmic stimulation. You'll have to

experiment to see if your babies prefer to be held upright on your shoulder or shoulders, or if they prefer to be held horizontally. Both positions can accommodate two babies at a time when they are small. For the vertical position, simply sit in a rocking chair holding a baby to each shoulder, using a hand to support each head, and a forearm to support each back. To rock them horizontally, try sitting in a rocking chair with both babies on their tummies across your lap.

As they get older and bigger, you can still rock both vertically, but you might try some variations on the horizontal position. Some babies like to be rocked sideways instead of front-to-back. In that case, stand with one baby draped on her tummy over your forearm, her head nearest your elbow, and supported as needed by your other hand. You can then sway from side to side.

Of course you can also sit in a rocker with a baby in the crook of each arm, as you would if you were breastfeeding, but remember that for babies, lying back like that may make a tummy ache worse—if that's what you think is bothering them. And, if you are breastfeeding, they will probably automatically want to nurse if you hold them in this position, so keep that in mind if you don't want to nurse them right then.

However you choose to position yourself and your babies to rock, keep in mind that the purpose is to replace the erratic movements of crying with the smooth, regular, calming ones of rocking. Pay attention to what kind of rocking works best for your babies. Large, swooping motions work for some; small, gentle ones work for others, with plenty of variations in between. Keep trying until you find what works best for you and your babies.

2. *Swaddling.* Remember how much young babies seem to like contact. Try wrapping a fussy baby snugly in a receiving blanket, with her head toward one of the blanket corners. Fold the corner nearest her feet up toward her tummy. Tucking her arms at her sides, fold first one side around her, then the other, and tuck the tail into a fold if you can. Hold her securely.

Some studies have shown that swaddling in some form is the most effective method for calming babies. This is primarily true for young babies, and it may work for a reason similar to why rocking works: It cuts down on the amount of erratic stimulation the baby gets—in this case from its own thrashing and startling. Once babies are several months old, they may not like to be restrained that much, but they will probably like the kind of contact that comes from variations on swaddling.

One of those variations that can work for young babies as well as older ones is a baby carrier. There are several made for twins that allow you to carry a baby on the front and one on the back, and one that allows both babies to face you on the front. This can work for small babies, but once they get very big, they could be too heavy to carry around this way.

Another alternative is skin-to-skin contact. Keeping in mind that young babies like to be wrapped up, undress yourself, get in bed, and snug the diapered baby to you with a blanket or a shawl under the covers. Or keep both babies close to you, warm and secure underneath your nightgown. The babies can nurse and sleep at will—and so can you. Some fussy babies like to be in a warm bath with an adult, and some will actually fall asleep in the water on an indulgent father's chest or in his mother's arms. This of course would work best with one baby at a time.

3. *Sucking.* There is some evidence that sucking physically relaxes a baby, and pacifiers certainly work to stop many babies from crying.

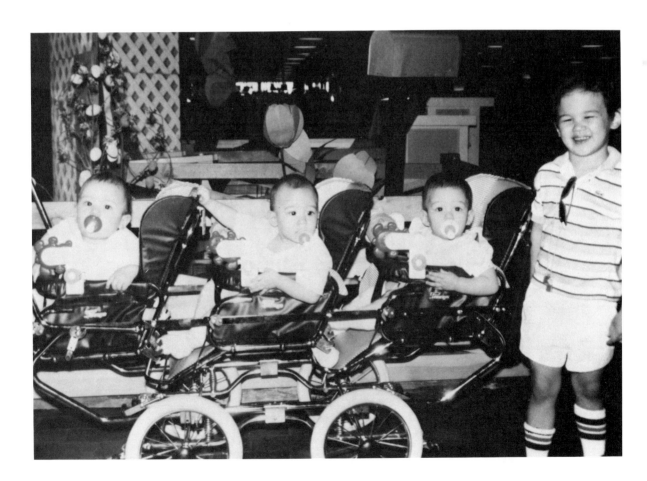

They may also work for reasons similar to those for rocking and swaddling—the regular, rhythmic motion of sucking reduces the amount of movement in the rest of the baby's body, including the number of eye movements the baby will make when given something to look at. Just be sure, if you use pacifiers, that you are not ignoring empty stomachs or stretching the time between feedings.

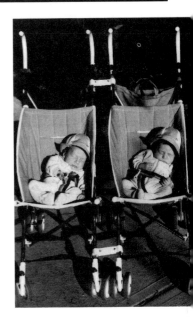

Within a few months, some babies will find their fingers and suck on them to calm themselves. Thumb or finger sucking used to be frowned on at any age, but some mothers and health-care providers now see it as the first step an infant makes in learning to calm herself. The majority of children give up the habit of their own accord when they are ready to —usually around the age of five or six—and often because of subtle and not-so-subtle peer pressure rather than because of anything a parent says or doesn't say. There is no agreement among dental professionals on whether sucking of this kind actually harms tooth formation or palate structure. The only consensus seems to be that it is completely individual, depending on where the child places the finger or thumb in her mouth, how often she does it, how hard she sucks, how long the practice goes on, and what her genetic history is concerning the arrangement of her teeth and the size of her mouth.

Many mothers of multiples remember clearly the day one of her twins sucked her thumb instead of screaming for attention. For those mothers, it was a turning point toward sanity.

4. *Sound.* For some babies, constant and rhythmic sound can be soothing. Some babies will be calmed by the "white noise" sound of a vacuum cleaner or a vaporizor, and some like to fall asleep to those. There are recordings available of sounds the baby has heard in the womb—the whooshing of blood in his mother's veins, the beating of her heart—and some parents report success in calming babies with these. The principle of *regular and rhythmic* can guide your choices here, too, in finding sounds that can calm your crying babies. Try rhythmic music, or your own singing or talking in a chanting or singsong voice.

5. *All of the above.* In one study, babies who were swaddled, *and* rocked, *and* sung to, *and* were allowed to suck were calmed faster than those on whom one method at a time was used.

These are not by any means all the ways to calm a crying baby. But they are a starting point. One of your jobs as a parent is to get to know your babies and what pleases each of them. You will discover those special soothers that work for your babies as you discover who they are.

"Before I had my twins, I was well established in my career and felt reasonably in control of my life. After they were born, I cried every day for about six months. It was so out of character for me I couldn't believe it. Strangely enough, I would not have described myself as being depressed."

NOW THE BABIES ARE CALM, BUT THE MOTHER IS CRYING

A much neglected fact is that new mothers—and that includes many mothers with months-old babies—often cry a lot. A lot means that most of them cry at least once a day, and many of them cry more often than that. And perhaps the strangest fact of all to the uninitiated is that they cry at the drop of a hat. Literally. Seeing certain television commercials, meeting old friends, being tired, meeting new friends, being alone, feeling overwhelmed, and loving her babies are all perfectly legitimate reasons for a new mother to cry.

While the teariness that comes with motherhood for many women may be disturbing or seem out of character, you should know that it nevertheless is a *normal* part of the transition to motherhood—of multiples or single-borns—for many women. (See chapter 2, Transitions, for more on this.)

Giving birth is a tremendously powerful and opening experience, no matter what the details of your birth were. As we've noted, a woman is extraordinarily open both physically and emotionally as she gives birth, and that openness remains, for many women, for weeks or even months after the birth.

It can be that emotional openness that brings you to tears at the sight of a toddler's happy face, or of your babies sleeping peacefully. And even though it may be out of character for you, that kind of tenderness is not a bad thing. It is natural that babies call forth love and open people's hearts. Allow yourself the luxury of being touched in a way you may not have been before.

Crying, for mothers of multiples particularly, may be a response to fatigue, or to the fear and frustration they may feel in their early days of learning to care for more than one baby at a time. That, too, is a normal response. Allow yourself time to learn this new skill and to bring a rhythm and order to the chaos you may feel. Your whole life is being reorganized by someone else, and it may be happening with more intensity and urgency than you have ever felt. It's not surprising that you feel overwhelmed at times.

What can you do about crying? First, accept that you are more tender and open than before, and give yourself the emotional room to express that. Explain that to your partner or to close friends, especially if your crying makes them uncomfortable. And second, mother yourself. Nourish yourself with good food. Take care of your body, which has just produced this miracle of two or three or more babies. And ask to be mothered by those close to you. Keep a list by the phone of things you need or favors you'd like, so when friends call, you'll remember to ask their help or support in specific ways. (See chapter 5, Mothercare, for more ideas.)

WILL THEY ALL EVER SLEEP ALL NIGHT? WILL I EVER SLEEP ALL NIGHT?

The answer to both those questions is yes, but probably not right now. There are whole books on getting your baby to sleep through the night—which for most people means to sleep uninterrupted from at least midnight (and preferably a little earlier), until 5 or 6 A.M. Some of the suggestions will work for your babies, and some of them won't. None of them is guaranteed. In no child-care practice besides feeding will you see as many differences from baby to baby as you will in sleep patterns. We all know adults who always have trouble falling asleep. And we all know others who can nap at a moment's notice. The same range of behavior is there for babies.

One of your most important—and sometimes most difficult—jobs as a parent is to bring a sense of rhythm to your newborns. They are born without that, as you can see even in the irregular way newborns breathe at first. Your routine, your consistent loving care, brings the first rhythms of this world to your babies. Helping them to learn to sleep when everyone else does, taking into account individual differences, is one part of that rhythm.

What most babies are born with is the rhythm they lived by in the womb. Remember those sleepless nights you had in the last weeks or months before their birth? You could feel two or three babies inside having wild wrestling matches every night. They would be still during the day while you were moving around and then bounce into action as soon as you settled down for the night. Knowing that, it's not surprising that your babies' waking and sleeping patterns soon after birth are the reverse of your own.

Most parents, in fact it's probably safe to say all parents, would love to help their babies establish a routine that would allow both the parents and their babies to sleep well and at the same time, if only they knew what to do. You can find hints galore that are meant to help little ones sleep, from friends, books, and relatives. Some of those hints may help, but there are two in particular that probably won't.

The first is solid foods. Of course your Aunt Tillie insists that the only way she got little Bernie to sleep through the night was to stuff him full of cereal at 6 P.M. It's impossible to tell, though, if little Bernie would have slept through the night anyway by the time she resorted to cereal. And for many babies, the introduction of solid foods, especially if it's done before three to six months, may mean a big tummy ache or an allergic reaction. (See the section on feeding solids later in this chapter for more on this.) Neither of those are conducive to a good night's rest.

Studies on newborns have shown no correlation between sleeping through the night and the age at which the babies were fed solids. The same study showed some correlation (but not a statistically significant one) between being able to predict when a baby would sleep through the night and his weight. But alas, there was no magic weight at which all babies could be expected to sleep for five to eight uninterrupted hours.

The second approach you may hear of is to let the babies "cry it out." When you think about it, how much sense does it make to think that a two- or three-month-old baby will calm herself by being left alone in a dark room? For babies, crying is their only way of letting you know of their needs. And those needs include things like food and companionship. Babies under a year old (and plenty of them over a year old) cannot be expected to understand the abstract concept of their room or their crib being a safe, comfortable place. Nor can they be expected to understand that even though mom isn't with them, she is there, but at a distance, to keep them safe.

The only reality to a young baby is body comfort: a full stomach, the warmth of another body close to hers, and arms to hold her securely. That kind of security is only effective for babies when it comes consistently from a primary caregiver. Another baby in the same crib, or in the crib next door, does not provide the same kind of comfort.

Studies have shown that babies who evoked a consistent, predictable response from their caregiver were less clingy to their parents later, and more self-confident in striking out on their own in their toddler years.

It is important that you learn to discern the difference between "crying it out" and letting your babies find their own way of falling asleep. Babies are much more likely to cry at least a little when they are falling asleep than they are upon awakening. One or both of your babies may need to fret for ten minutes before falling asleep each time you put them down. But that's very different from thirty minutes or an hour of hearty screaming; or even from fifteen minutes of truly distressed wailing.

The fact is, babies sleep through the night when they are ready to. You can help them learn that skill by giving them a consistent schedule of care that acknowledges and meets their needs most of the time.

Many babies will sleep for a four- to six-hour period when they are three months old. Some won't.

While it may be comforting to try to pinpoint a time when your babies will do it, by expecting them to sleep through the night by a particular day or week you may be setting yourself up for disappointment. Remember, for many babies, stretching out the time they are able to sleep uninterrupted by inner hunger clocks—or anything else—is a process, not a feat. Little by little they increase their sleeping time. You probably won't notice it much until one night, *you'll* awaken with a jolt at 5 A.M. and realize you haven't gotten up since 11 P.M. And just as millions of mothers before you have done, you'll rush to be sure the babies are still breathing.

DOES ALL THIS MEAN THAT IT'S USELESS TO TRY TO GET THEM TO SLEEP?

Even though sleep patterns are so individual, and even though many of us come equipped with tendencies to sleep soundly or restlessly, there are things you can do to shape your babies' sleep behavior. As with all sleep hints, none is foolproof. All can be adjusted to fit the individual baby. And this list is just the beginning—it may spark your thinking to give you ideas about similar methods that will work for you and your babies.

1. *Soothe.* Try the soothing methods listed earlier in this chapter, especially if you don't think the babies are hungry. Sometimes, even though their tummies are full, they just need to be held a while longer.

2. *Reduce stimulation.* While soothing reduces stimulation the babies may be receiving from themselves, you might find it useful to reduce stimulation that comes to them from other sources. If background noise seems to be a problem, you might consider soundproofing their room by covering the walls with quilt batting under decorative fabric or sheeting. A store specializing in home-improvement materials could supply directions for this relatively easy project.

Another way to combat background noise is by replacing it with "white noise," or consistent, nonstimulating noise like that from a running hair dryer, vacuum cleaner, or vaporizer. Some stereo stores and catalogues offer sound machines that also produce white noise.

Magazines aimed at parents of young children often have advertisements in their back pages for small companies that sell recorded music meant specifically for calming infants and toddlers. Some also offer recordings of sounds the infants heard inside the womb that are calming to many newborns.

Some parents swear by methods that reduce outside stimulation. But others point out that if newborns live in a home where there is background noise, say from siblings, then they should learn to sleep with that since it is part of the environment. Taking both sides into consideration, you can decide if your newborns need to learn to sleep with noise when they are very young, or later on.

3. *Provide company.* Sometimes the problem with restless babies is simply that they are lonely. The company of another baby, either in the same crib or the crib next door, might be comforting during playtime, but usually isn't during the night when the babies are very young. To save yourself and the rest of your family too many sleepless hours, you might consider setting up a family bed.

While the idea of families sleeping together is foreign to many people in our culture, it has been the norm for cultures around the world for centuries. If you ask a family who has used a family bed, they will tell you:

- it doesn't call a halt to the parent's sex life,
- it doesn't make the children unreasonably attached to their mother or father,
- and it doesn't mean the parent will roll over on the child and kill him.

What it does provide is a snug, safe place to cuddle and sleep. Creative parents find other places and times in their homes for intimacy.

The family bed can be helpful, too, for families with toddlers who continue to waken at night. Those who have slept in a family bed also find that just because you sleep with your children during some period in which it is useful to all of you, it doesn't mean that you will also have them in bed with you when they are sixteen. Many children, when they have gained the maturity to want to sleep alone or to have friends over to spend the night, for example, will suggest they move into their own rooms themselves.

If you want to try having infant twins in bed with you, you might want to plan for it a little more carefully than you would with a single baby. If your bedroom is big enough, you could move one crib up flush to the side of your bed, and lower that rail of the crib all the way, or remove it. When you put the babies to bed for the night, you can place them perpendicular to your bed in the crib. Then when they waken, you only have to roll over to pull one or both to you to nurse. Or have your husband bring the bottles, and you can both bottlefeed in bed. Many parents feel it's a lot easier for all concerned to get back to sleep if you can minimize the amount of running around the house for night-time feedings.

If your bedroom isn't big enough to put the crib next to the bed, consider using a cradle or bassinet for one baby while the other is in your bed. You can switch babies easily to feed or comfort them.

When your babies are newborns, there is little danger of them falling out of your bed, since generally they can't roll over yet. When they are able to roll over, you can avoid problems by pushing your bed against the wall, or placing the mattress box springs directly on the floor.

As with all the other routines you will establish with your multiples, you don't need to see the family-bed idea as an either/or choice. Many families get through difficult times by sleeping with their babies, and then slowly "weaning" them back to their own beds. For example, you could let them share your bed after the nighttime feeding until they are asleep, then put both babies in their own beds.

The point is, each family has to find the combination of ideas that works best for them. Your tailoring of these ideas can fit you like a glove, but would probably hang like a bag on another family.

4. *Keep it calm.* This is another way to keep stimulation at a minimum, especially for babies who continue to wake many times in the night. Some mothers have found that if it isn't as much fun for the babies to get up at night, some babies stop doing it. For example, if one of the babies cries, instead of turning on the light, picking up the baby, and talking to him, you would leave the lights off (this is where a good nightlight comes in handy), and try calming him by putting him back down if he is standing, and patting him on the back. Don't talk or interact

Getting Babies to Sleep, Try:

1. *Soothing*
2. *Reducing stimulation*
3. *Providing company*
4. *Keeping baby calm*
5. *Planning ahead*

with him, other than the gentle patting. If that doesn't work, offer him water, again without lights or voice, as a next step. If you really think the baby is hungry, feed him, but again, without making it a social event. Babies who are a few months old, and who have already been exposed to a routine, may react well to this, since they are more used to taking cues from you during their waking hours.

5. *Plan ahead.* If your babies seem quite wakeful at night, you might be able to shape their behavior by changing what you do during the day. For example, if they take fairly long naps, you might want to gently change their schedule by waking them a few minutes earlier each day. Theoretically they will be more tired by the evening and, therefore, more likely to sleep longer at night.

For breastfed babies, if it seems like they're nursing all night long, try nursing them more often during the day. For some mothers, this won't be possible, or won't be appealing. But if you are at home, it might be worth it to help the babies shape the habit of eating during the day and sleeping during the night by offering to nurse them every two hours or so. Sometimes, as babies become more aware of the world around them and of each other, they can be distracted from eating during the day. While the extra free moments for mom might might be nice, it also might mean more feeding at night.

BUT THEY'RE TWINS—WHY DON'T THEY SLEEP AT THE SAME TIME?

Your multiples are bound to be as individual in sleep habits as they are in their feeding habits. If you have identicals, they are more likely to have similar schedules, but they are not guaranteed to. If your multiples are fraternal, they will probably have sleep habits no more similar than those of any non-twin siblings.

You may be wondering if you should waken a sleeping baby if his brother wakens to be fed. There's no set answer to that, but as you begin to discern the sleeping and eating patterns of your babies, you will know if it is worth it for you to waken one if the other is up. It may be that the sleeping baby would get along fine without the nighttime feeding, if he were given a chance to try it. For other babies, the mother may learn that the sleeping baby will usually be up in a hour anyway, so waking him makes sense.

SOLIDS—FEEDING THE MASSES, PART 2

During this century, the pendulum has swung from one extreme to the other on what is considered to be the best time to start solid foods. According to the American Academy of Pediatrics, until about 1920, solid foods were seldom offered before babies were a year old. Then in 1924, a Swedish pediatrician began experimenting with solids (including minced meat, fish, and scrambled eggs) for infants, and by the 1940s some pediatricians were recommending that solids in the form of thickened farina (a wheat cereal) or oatmeal be routinely begun on the third *day* after birth.

All of this experimentation has led to one conclusion voiced by the Academy's Committee on Nutrition: that babies are extraordinarily resilient in enduring the whims of their caretakers.

Today, rather than adhere to a set age at which solid foods should be introduced, the academy and most dietitians and nutritionists recommend that the individual infant's development be the guide for when to begin solids. For example, before being given solids, a baby should be able to:

• sit up
• have enough head and neck muscle control to indicate when she's had enough to eat. (In other words, she can turn her head away.)
• swallow well. This means that the instinctive tongue thrust that

comes with sucking is left behind when a spoon is put in her mouth. If you've ever seen a very young baby (roughly under three months) being fed cereal, you might have noticed that at least half of every spoonful of cereal that went in came back out again because she pushed it out with her tongue. This is an indication that the baby has not developed her swallowing reflexes well enough to eat solids. If your babies can only swallow cereal well when fed through a bottle with an enlarged nipple opening, you should consider carefully whether you are feeding them this solid food too early.

Your babies may also be ready for solids if they are bottlefed and they drink at least a quart of formula a day, still seem hungry, and are fast-growing. Frequency of feeding is not an indication to start solids for breastfed babies, since compared to bottlefed babies, it is normal for them to feed more often.

Many babies will reach the developmental stage and the size to need solids when they are around six months old. But just as with sleeping and early feeding, it is very individual. And there are reasons not to push solids on a baby who is not ready.

1. *Allergies.* An infant's digestive system continues to mature during the first months of life, as explained in the chapter on breast- and bottlefeeding. Some solid foods fed too early can provoke an allergic reaction or an allergy that can stay with the child for years. Other solid foods are just too difficult for babies to chew or are perfectly sized to get stuck in a little throat. To avoid allergic reactions or choking, these foods should be avoided until your babies are 8–12 months old:

egg whites	peas	cereal flakes
citrus fruits	shellfish	corn
berries	raisins	cinnamon
buttermilk	fruit skin	artificial colors
mushrooms (whole)	whole grains	

Of course foods like nuts, chocolate, and colas should not be fed to children anyway. Eating these foods is a bad habit to get your children into, and nuts (including peanut butter) pose extremely serious choking hazards, to say nothing of the allergic reactions all might provoke.

Symptoms of allergy can include runny nose, coughing, wheezing, rashes, diarrhea, vomiting, and sometimes noticeable behavior changes.

2. *Obesity.* Babies who are fed solids before they are physically able to indicate they don't want any more are in a sense being force fed, according to research reported in *Pediatrics,* the journal of the American Academy of Pediatrics. That may interfere with establishing sound

eating habits and, of course, may contribute to overfeeding and consequent obesity in later life.

Members of the academy, and many other health-care practitioners, agree that iron-fortified commercial formula or breastfeeding supplemented with iron, fluoride, and vitamin D provides a complete and "highly desirable total diet for the normal full-term infant until 5 or 6 months of age."*

But that's not the way it happens in practice. The academy acknowledges that "most infants in the United States are fed some solid foods by the age of two months, largely due to social pressure, aggressive marketing by the infant food industry, and by the belief that feeding of solid food will help an infant sleep through the night."

Interestingly, another study noted that cereal and milk both stay in the baby's stomach for roughly the same length of time (about two hours and forty-five minutes), so one is not more likely to give the child a feeling of fullness than the other. In addition, cereal mixed with water has the same number of calories as an equal volume of breast milk. But the academy points out that cereal mixed with formula provides more calories than a baby under five months needs at a time—and that it therefore contributes to overfeeding.

If you're not convinced that overfeeding babies is undesirable, consider the recent research that shows fat cells formed during infancy (from overfeeding) may be emptied of fat temporarily during a person's life, but the empty fat cells are *always* there, just waiting to be filled with fat again. Some research has also shown that those fat cells tend to get filled even before other digestive functions take place, instead of being the repositories of what's left after the body takes what it needs from food. What that means is that people who have a lot of fat cells deposited during their infancy may actually regain lost weight more easily as adults than will those who were not overfed.

Convenience. The last thing you need, as a parent of multiples, is to make hassles for yourself. Why mess with propping three-month-old babies up in infant seats, making cereal for them, and shoveling it into their unwilling mouths three times a day? You don't need it, and neither do they. You'll be dealing with meals soon enough. Enjoy the convenience and ease with which you can exclusively breastfeed or bottlefeed your babies while it lasts. If you think they're hungry, give them more milk, until they are at least five months old. It will be easier on their digestive systems and easier on your schedule.

---

* However, many other health-care practitioners believe that a mother with a healthy diet and normal-term babies does not *need* to give vitamins or iron supplements to her breastfed babies under the age of six months.

WHEN YOU DO OFFER SOLIDS, WHAT COMES FIRST?

As with most things, there are varying theories about what should come first. But no matter which food you choose, the rules of thumb are:

- you shouldn't give your babies a lot of it to begin with,
- and you don't have to worry about offering a wide variety of foods until after your babies are about a year old.

The consensus on first foods is that you should offer something that is easy to digest, easy to swallow, and not likely to upset small tummies. For many health-care practitioners that means rice cereal, preferably fortified with iron. For others, particularly La Leche League counselors, that means mashed banana. All sides agree that a first "meal" means offering about a teaspoon of the food. That's it. For babies who are going to be sensitive to the food, that's enough for the mother to tell, but not enough to provoke an enormous and long-lasting reaction.

You can increase the amount by about a teaspoon or two a day. And in the early days of feeding solids, offer the cereal after the breast or the bottle. At this point, solids are extracurricular, and the milk feeding is the main event. Later, the roles will be reversed. These little teaspoonfuls of cereal or banana are just practice sessions.

Here's how your feeding schedule might look for the first year of your babies' lives:

1. Up to five or six months, breast milk or formula only. For normal term babies, you may choose to add iron as a supplement to breastfeeding, or for bottlefed babies use iron-fortified formula.

2. Around five to six months, begin rice cereal or banana. Once a day, offer one to three teaspoons to each baby. Be sure to breastfeed or bottlefeed *before* offering solids.

3. Increase amount of solids during the next month. Don't worry about your babies becoming bored with only one kind of solid—they've only had one kind of food (milk) at all to this point.

4. Between seven and eight months, begin adding puréed fruits, vegetables, cooked egg yolk. Puréed unseasoned table food is fine. Introduce one new food at a time and go slowly. It's much harder to identify which food is making which baby sick if you've given three or four new items at once. Some pediatricians believe that at this point,

you should offer vegetables instead of fruits, because few people have problems getting their children to eat sweet fruit later. That may work with some children, and it wouldn't hurt to try it. But when you consider that breast milk (and some formulas) taste extremely sweet, you may have already canceled out the advantage of avoiding sweets until the savories are tried.

5. At eight or nine months, you can increase variety. Add puréed meats and yogurt, but wait on other dairy products. Many health-care providers recommend that because of potential allergies and digestion problems, all cow's-milk products be avoided until age one. (The exception is plain yogurt because of its friendly bacteria, which it contains only if you buy the kind with real cultures. Some brands use thickeners that make it look creamy like the real thing, but it isn't. Read the label.) You can also add some soft finger foods now (see list that follows). And this is the time to begin offering solids first, and bottle or breast *after*.

6. By the time your babies are a year old, the emphasis will probably be on unseasoned table food and finger foods. For many babies the interest in the breast or the bottle as primary sources of food may be dwindling. They may, however, still want either or both of those for other reasons, such as comfort or help to sleep, but some babies can begin to learn to accept substitutes (if they haven't before). When you first offered solids, you began the weaning process in a small way. Now, the process can be accelerated for babies who are losing interest in, and the need for, the bottle or breast.

As you can see if you have had other children before your multiples, the process of going from a milk-only to a solids-primarily diet during the first year of life is just about the same for everyone. But there are a few tips that apply specially to parents of multiples:

- Before you begin offering solids, figure out where you will feed your babies and what equipment will really help you. If your babies cannot sit up well enough to use highchairs, you should reconsider whether it is time to begin feeding solids. If they are sitting up well enough, you can choose between using two highchairs or two of the little seats that hook on to a table edge.

- If you plan to use hook-on seats, remember that you will be sharing your table with two little ones who, when seated, have arms that magically become about three feet longer than you thought they were. You either need a table big enough so that everyone else can sit a safe—and that may be a considerable—distance away from the babies, or you may need to always feed them at a different time from the rest of the family. Separate feeding times may work until they are old enough to realize they are being "left out" of a family gathering. That may occur before they are civilized enough to eat relatively neatly.

• If you plan to use highchairs, floor space can be a consideration. They take up a lot of room, and you do have to be careful not to position them too close to each other (definitely not within reaching distance for food-grabbers), or too close to a table or counter (from which those sturdy little baby legs can push off for backwards crashes). If your kitchen really isn't big enough for two highchairs, consider using an old shower curtain as a floor protector, and feed the babies in the dining room or any other room adjacent to the kitchen. You might then also consider using foldable highchairs that you can hang on a broom-closet wall when the meal is over. This can serve two purposes: It gets the things out of the way, and it keeps little ones from using them as personal step-stools to climb wherever they will.

• Try to arrange for help with early feedings of solids. It can be harrowing for you and the babies as you figure out a new rhythm for feeding times. Feeding solids can mean that one or both babies have to wait more than they did with breastfeeding or bottles. A helping hand from a friend or your husband can maintain order.

• Do use just one spoon and one dish, unless you really can't stand the idea. Even when one baby has a cold, it's unlikely the other one will avoid catching it anyway. And there's something to be said for simultaneous instead of sequential illnesses.

• Since keeping life as simple as possible is the byword for parents of twins and triplets, offer your babies safe finger foods as soon as you can. The more they can feed themselves, the less you have to do and the more patient they will be. For example, cooled steamed chunks of carrot are soft enough to avoid choking, but sturdy enough to be picked up. Some other ideas for soft finger foods:

> large-curd cottage cheese
>   (wait until almost age one)
> bananas
> Cheerios
> cooked noodles
> squashed peas
> scrambled eggs or slices
>   of hard-boiled eggs

Finger foods like raisins and toast are best saved until babies are nearer to a year old because of choking possibilities.

• For do-ahead, homemade baby food, you can steam various vegetables (like carrots and green beans), purée them, and freeze them in ice-cube trays. Or you can boil a whole chicken, purée the cooked meat, and freeze it the same way. But you'll still be a good mother if you choose carefully among the commercial baby foods offered. Most no longer use added salt or sugar (with the exception of desserts, which no baby needs anyway), and a careful reading of the labels will tell you which to buy and which to leave on the grocery-store shelf.

• A microwave oven can be a lifesaver for parents of multiples, but be very careful how you use it for baby food. Many foods can have hot spots inside, where it is difficult for you to detect them before they hit baby's tender mouth. And commercial baby foods with meat in them can explode in the jars because the microwave heats the water particles within the meat faster than the meat solids.

HOW IT'S ALL DIFFERENT FOR PREMATURE BABIES

Nearly half of all twins are born prematurely, judging by birth weight (under 2,500 grams or 5.5 pounds). Many of those—either one twin or both—will spend time in the hospital after their mother has gone home. While most parents long for the day their babies will be able to come home with them, the transition from hospital nursery to home can be a scary and overwhelming one.

If your babies are premature, or if one of your babies has problems that must be dealt with in the hospital soon after birth, you will probably want to learn as much as you can from books that deal exclusively with the care of premature and special-needs babies. For example, *The Premature Baby Book,* by Helen Harrison (St. Martin's Press, 1983), defines and explains clearly every medical term you'll hear used to describe your babies, and explores the full range of physical and emotional realities of premature birth for parents and babies. In the meantime, as you plan for your babies' homecoming, you can make preparations that suit your situation.

1. Instead of establishing a workable routine at home, you will be setting up a routine at the hospital first. As you understand your babies'

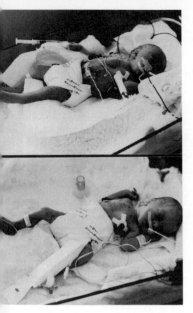

conditions, and as you feel comfortable with them, you may avoid last-minute homecoming panic by seeing yourself as the babies' parent instead of as a visitor. You can do that by participating as much as possible and as early as possible in the babies' care, and by learning to do the special things you will have to do at home—like administering medicine or physical therapy. You may not feel comfortable at first jumping right in to care for the babies, and some of the care early on might have to be done by the nurses. But the more you can make the transition from visitor to caregiver, and the earlier you can do it, the better you will all feel when you do go home.

2. You may be feeling nervous or scared about leaving the nursery and assuming full responsibility for your babies. Many parents of premies feel that way. But you may be able to assuage your fears by having your questions and concerns addressed at meetings with the babies' doctors and the nurses who have cared for them. You might want to have more than one meeting concerning their discharge from the hospital, and you might want to have those meetings several days before the discharge, when you will probably be feeling a little calmer than you will be on the Big Day. Carry a notebook with you, particularly at these meetings, so you can note your questions and answers.

3. Have your babies' physician write down all instructions for care, and all medications you will be giving your babies. Care instructions can be confusing for parents of a single-born premature baby, but with two babies' care to keep track of, you will need written instructions for each. A calendar for each baby with squares big enough to record daily medications and dosages, along with reactions and behavior, might be helpful and simple to keep up.

4. Try to arrange it so that no special medical procedures (like transfusions or medical tests that can be stressful to infants) are scheduled for either of your babies on the day before they come home. For most premies, tests and other procedures can be upsetting and leave them exhausted and fussy for a day or more afterward. If the day before homecoming has been routine and quiet, you have a better chance of a less-than-chaotic first few days at home.

5. Some hospitals will arrange for one or both parents to sleep at the hospital or room-in with their babies for a night or two before the babies go home. Just living the whole daily routine with them, and doing all the things you will need to do at home under the supervision of the nursing staff, can give some parents the confidence they need to feel good about taking their babies home.

In hospitals where rooming-in isn't possible, they may have a "home pass" program, in which parents take their babies home for gradually lengthening periods during the day, perhaps accompanied by a member of the nursing staff at first.

6. Be aware that in many towns there are community-based medical services to replace those of the hospital on which you have relied for weeks. Many parents of premature babies find they need some kind of ongoing help to provide special kinds of stimulation their babies may need. Infant stimulation programs also focus on the needs of mothers who may feel trapped at home with demanding infants, and on the needs of fathers who may feel overwhelmed by the responsibility of care for two or more babies with special needs. See the Resources list in the appendix for how to contact a program of this sort near you. You can also plan ahead by asking the nursing staff in the intensive-care nursery about community-based help after discharge.

7. If help and support from friends is important for parents of term multiples, it is many times more importnat for parents of preterm multiples. Don't underestimate the stress of adjusting to the idea of having delivered preterm babies, or of worrying about their health, your health, the well-being of the rest of your family, and of your pocketbook. Most friends and relatives are more than willing to come to your aid, and you will help them do that if you can tell them what you need —from simple companionship to running errands and supplying babysitting. Chapter 2, Transitions, and chapter 5, Mothercare, will give you ideas on how to do this.

Perhaps one of the most important facts for parents of premature babies to know, and one that can help them form a good attitude toward their babies, is that you needn't compare your premature babies by chronological age to full-term babies. You should always correct for the number of weeks premature they were. For example, a baby who arrived ten weeks early (born at thirty instead of forty weeks gestation) cannot fairly be compared at three months with a three-month-old full-term baby. To make an equal comparison, you need to subtract the number of weeks early she was from her chronological age. So three months after she was born, a baby who was ten weeks premature is developmentally about two weeks old.

Some pediatricians suggest evaluating children who were premature by this corrected age until the children are about two and a half years old, when many of the effects of prematurity begin to disappear.

Basic issues like crying, sleeping, and feeding are also different for premature babies. For example, when they are first born, many premature babies don't cry much, mostly because crying takes so much energy, and they have little to spare when most of their energy is being used to stay alive. As premies get bigger and stronger, their crying becomes more like that of term babies, but there the similarity ends. Studies have shown that many premature babies tend to be more fussy and cry more as they get older (most studies of this sort have been done on babies up to eight months of age), instead of crying less, as term babies do. It has also been shown that premature babies are distinctly more fussy just before a developmental breakthrough, such as learning to roll over or crawl.

Premies often have even less in the way of rhythm or organization at birth than do term babies. It may be difficult to read their "signals" for feeding or other needs, because it may be equally difficult for them to decipher their own feelings and get the message to you in an organized fashion. As you help your babies to acquire a rhythm that suits your life-style, it might help you to keep a chart of feeding times on the calendar you may be using to record medications. Even though it looks like there is no pattern to life as you're living it, you may see patterns of progress emerge as you look back on the calendar. Although this kind of record keeping doesn't necessarily help the babies, it might help you to feel less like time is standing still.

Sleep may come in large chunks for your premature babies—they sometimes sleep a good deal more than term babies at first—or it may be fitful and come in short bursts. Premies are as individual as term babies in their sleep preferences, but they may have less ability to calm themselves and find their own pattern to sleeping/waking cycles. You will need to find—probably by trial and error—what stimulation or lack of stimulation level best suits each of your babies. After the light and activity of the intensive-care nursery, it may be difficult for some babies to become accustomed to the dark and quiet of home. Others may be relieved and quite at ease with the calmer home atmosphere. Your best guide is to be sensitive to the number and kinds of changes your babies have gone through in their short lives, and try to accommodate their needs as you see them.

If you are bottlefeeding your babies, you will probably be using a formula specially made for premature babies to be sure they can easily digest it. You may also want to use a special nipple made for premies, which is softer and generally easier to suck from, to minimize the effort (and therefore the energy) they have to put out to get the formula. Since premature babies don't have the larger iron stores that term babies do, you may want to start an iron supplement at about two months corrected age or earlier. Do not add iron to a premature baby's diet unless your pediatrician or a pediatric opthamologist has checked the baby's eyes to be sure the retinas are mature and there is no unresolved retrolental fibroplasia—a condition of the eye seen in some premature babies that can result in detached retina and blindness. Iron supplements may contribute to a vitamin E deficiency in premature babies, and vitamin E plays a role in eye development.

If you are supplementing your babies' diets with iron, you can use an iron-fortified formula suitable for premature babies, or if you are breastfeeding, you can use multivitamins with iron. Fluoride supplements (which are recommended by the American Academy of Pediatrics Committee on Nutrition at two weeks of age for all breastfed babies and for bottlefed babies where the water supply is not fluoridated) may be started when the babies reach forty weeks gestational age.

Solids for prematures can be introduced the same as they are for term babies, and on the same schedule, using the premie's corrected age as a guide.

Premature babies can use most of the same equipment that full-term twins can, but you may need to adjust your equipment somewhat to fit them until they get bigger. For example, car seats and infant seats usually seem gargantuan with a tiny baby in them. Some infant clothing stores have cloth inserts for these seats with a U-shaped rolled edge to help steady a small baby's head. If these are still too big for your babies, try rolling a receiving blanket or a couple of diapers into cylindrical shapes to place on either side of each baby's head to keep it from flopping to one side or the other. You might want to use a twin stroller that allows the babies to lie down at first. Infant swings may be too stimulating for some premature babies, but if one or both of your babies seem to like that kind of motion, you might want to try the swing that has a cradle instead of a seat at first, so the babies can lie down instead of being propped to sit.

DETAILS, DETAILS

No matter when your babies arrive, and no matter what size they are, they all need the same basics: diapers and clothing. Here are some guidelines for making choices:

Diapers. As with most baby products today, diapers are no longer *just* diapers. Any parent worth his or her baby powder figures out soon enough that options are the name of the game. You can choose:

Do-It-Yourself Cloth Diapers. According to recent surveys, no matter what kind of diapers they chose, mothers report using an average of ten diapers a day per baby; a few more for newborns, a few less for older babies. If you choose this option, you will need to buy about eight dozen cotton cloth diapers if you plan to wash diapers every other or every third day. You can choose either the prefolded type or flat, unfolded diapers and fold them yourself. Most mothers who wash their own diapers give themselves a break and buy the prefolded type (64 percent). Unless you really love to do laundry, you might consider giving yourself an even bigger break and choose a diaper service or disposable diapers.

If you use cloth diapers, either from a service or home-laundered, you will need about ten pairs of rubber pants (they are actually usually either plastic or nylon, which is less irritating to some babies, but also less waterproof), and three or four pairs of diaper pins or clips. (Store pins in a bar of soap still in its wrapper to keep in the soap flakes. Be sure to keep clips away from babies—they are just the right size to swallow.)

COST: Buying your own diapers and washing them yourself may cost slightly less (about a dollar a week less, according to some estimates) than a diaper service. To find out what the cost will be for you in your area, add the costs of buying the diapers and rubber pants, and the presoak, detergent, bleach, softener, water (about forty gallons a week), and energy costs (like electricity costs for running the washer and dryer). The average weekly cost for doing your own diapers (140 diapers or about five loads of wash) in one part of the country is about $12.50. The cost may be different in your area.

PRO: Cotton diapers are nonirritating to most babies. Home-laundering allows you to know which washing products may affect sensitive skin. There is little or no environmental impact, depending on laundry products used.

CON: You have to rinse and wash them yourself.

Diaper Service. This is a great gift suggestion for relatives and friends who know you don't need any more receiving blankets. Several people can contribute, and you can end up with months of paid-for diaper service. Even if you don't receive this as a gift, it may be worth it to you if you are committed to using cloth diapers and don't want to invest the time and energy it takes to wash them yourself. And most diaper services are keenly aware of competition from the disposable-diaper industry—enough to make their prices competitive.

Don't count on a price break for two (or three or more) babies. Most businesses—including pediatricians—no longer offer those kinds of two-for-the-price-of-one deals because of the influx of multiple births (a 6 percent increase in twin births and a 1 percent increase in triplet-or-more births in 1985 over 1984), but it never hurts to ask. Many services have a recommended number of diapers to order for newborn twins, and a refund system so you don't pay for unused diapers. You can usually also adjust the number of diapers ordered per week and the size of the diapers you use as your babies' needs change. And most services are responsive to problems your babies may have with diaper rashes, and offer to adjust washing solutions to help solve the problem. Most also provide a diaper pail.

COST: If you choose to use a diaper service, you will still need about ten pairs of rubber pants and about four pairs of diaper pins. For 140 diapers a week (ten diapers a day for each baby), an average cost for diaper service per week is about $13.50. Prices vary, so check with each of the services in your area.

PRO: You can get the benefits of cloth diapers without the effort of washing them yourself.

CON: May be slightly more expensive in some areas than washing them yourself. May have more environmental impact than home-laundering, depending on washing products used.

Disposable Diapers. Nine out of ten expectant and new mothers in one 1984 survey reported that they used or intended to use disposable diapers. Currently, 92 percent of all mothers use disposable diapers, compared to 83 percent in 1980. (Cloth-diaper-only usage is down from 17 percent in 1980 to 6 percent in 1984. About 7 percent of new mothers use a diaper service exclusively, while combined usage—diaper service and disposables—accounts for the greatest percentage.) In terms of sales, there are three leading brands (Pampers, Huggies, and Luvs) and various store brands available. Mothers report differences in absorbency and fit among the brands, and trial-and-error usually guides them in finding the right one for their babies.

COST: Figuring an average ten diapers per day per baby, the average cost of newborn-size disposables for twins may be about $15 per week, but prices vary widely in different parts of the country and from store to store. Prices also go up as the size of the diaper goes up. Toddler-size or overnight-size diapers may cost nearly twice as much for the same number of diapers as newborn size. Some mothers believe they use fewer disposable than cloth diapers a day. Surveys show they do—about one fewer diaper per baby per day.

You may be able to slightly reduce the cost of disposable diapers by using coupons, taking advantage of sales, buying store brands, and buying diapers in bulk or from a consumer club–type warehouse.

Clothing. When you're buying the basics, keep in mind that a few more of anything may mean that you don't have to do laundry as often, but

The issue is: What does dressing your children alike say about your attitude toward them? What does your dressing them alike say to the rest of the world about who your children are and how you think they should be treated?

more may also mean that you have more to organize. With two or more babies you will soon feel like you're running a retail outlet for children's clothing anyway, so for the sake of your pocketbook and your sanity, fewer pieces of clothing might be better.

Here are the basics you will need for two babies:

• *8–10 undershirts.* The snap-type instead of the pullover-type may be easier for you to get on and off of very young babies.

• *10–12 sleeping outfits.* Stretchy one-piecers can double as playsuits. Kimonos that open in the front are useless for keeping a baby's feet or body warm. Two-piece sacque sets are nice for summer babies. Be sure to get different colors for each baby so when you get up with them in the night, you know who you're cuddling.

• *2–4 blanket sleepers for winter babies.* These can go over one-piece pajama/playsuits for extra warmth.

• *2–4 hats.* Premature babies, and newborns under eight pounds, generally could use some help in keeping warm, particularly if they are born in the winter. Knit caps (not just for outdoor wear) can cut heat loss from the head, which is where the greatest heat loss occurs.

• *2 cold-weather suits.* Be sure to get the kind with legs instead of the duffle-bag-type pram suit if you will be taking your babies out in the car much. Most car seats have a center belt that goes between the baby's legs. It's almost impossible to fasten it if you have to pull the belt over the thick, bunched-up fabric of a legless pram suit. And hoods are usually warmer than hats—they cover the back of the neck better —and you can't lose them.

• *2 each, sweaters and booties.* These are optional for very young babies. If you have one-piece playsuits, you probably won't need booties. Sweaters are a pain to put on small babies. A blanket sleeper over their one-piece playsuit would keep them warmer.

• *8–10 receiving blankets.* These are very useful when your babies are young, but they do outgrow the need for them in a month or two.

Miscellaneous. You may also want to have hooded baby towels and washcloths (two for each baby), but if finances are low, they aren't essential. Any soft, large towel will do. You may want a bathing sponge (a large sponge the size of the baby for her to lie on while you bathe her) or similar product to help with bathing, but while these are helpful, they aren't essential. People were giving babies baths long before these products came along. Until your babies are big enough to sit alone, you will be bathing them one at a time anyway, just like parents of single-born babies. An infant seat or a bouncy chair might be more helpful at bath time, since one baby will have to wait his turn.

Planning how much bedding to buy means deciding how many cribs you will use and multiplying by that number for fitted crib sheets, bumper pads, quilts, waterproof sheets, and waterproof lap pads (if you use them).

Dressing Alike. Any prospective mother of twins can find a list of what to buy for a layette and double it. But what that mother really has on her mind is not how many crib sheets and undershirts to buy, but whether clothing for her twins or triplets should match, and what to do about all those gifts of matching clothing she's bound to get whether she wants to dress her children alike or not.

Everyone debates whether it is harmful to dress twins alike. But many grandparents, parents, and friends of the family can't resist coming up with those matching outfits, especially when the twins are infants, reasoning that the little ones will never know the difference if they are dressed alike "just for now." That's true. It's doubtful any twins' lives were ruined because they were dressed alike as babies. And they do look cute.

So the issue is not really whether it will harm the infants if they are dressed alike—they don't know or care what they are wearing, so long as they are warm and comfortable.

These issues deserve careful consideration before you act, because you have the power to design the atmosphere in which your children will grow up. For example, if you choose to dress them alike, even as infants, you may have a hard time convincing other people that you see your twins as individuals. You may have a hard time yourself remembering that you want to see them as individuals. And you may be sending the world (and more subtly, your children) an ambivalent message about whether these children are two distinct personalities. If you think that how any of us dresses has little or nothing to do with how we act or how the world sees us, consider how dress codes affect behavior in schools, how dress-for-success theories affect hiring practices, or how you react when you meet a new person who is shoddily dressed compared to how you react when you meet someone who is well-groomed.

We all use the way we dress to tell the world who we are. If you develop the habit of telling the world (for your children, when they are infants) that your twins are a matched set, you may find it difficult to break that habit even if you want to later. And you cannot expect others to treat your children as individuals if you have "told" them your children are a matched set.

From a purely practical point of view, children who look alike are hard to tell apart. You don't make it any easier to distinguish one twin from the other if you dress them alike. Conversely, you can create the opportunity for others to discern personality differences in your twins

> **Whether you decide to dress your multiples alike or not, be sure you know what you are saying to the world about your children by the way you dress them, and be sure what you are saying is what you mean.**

"I used to trade shirts with the boy next door before I went to school, so my brother and I wouldn't be dressed alike."

if you dress them differently. At least others will have a fighting chance of learning how to tell your twins apart.

So what do you do with all those gifts of matching outfits? If you don't want to dress your children alike, you can avoid receiving some of them by telling people how you feel. Rest assured that the topic will always come up. Some people will give you matching outfits anyway, but that doesn't mean you have to put them on your children at the same time.

Obviously, you have plenty of control over what your children wear when they are infants. The same is just as obviously not true when they are older. Sometimes, twins who are older choose to dress alike for a time. My identical girls were the most interested in being twins when they entered kindergarten and they realized for the first time what a plus it was to have someone to start school with and to have something special about them that made them stand out. Although they didn't have any matching outfits, they did their best to wear similar styles, the same hairdo, and close to matching colors. As they felt more secure about school, dressing alike stopped being an issue.

Many mothers of twins report their children have similar patterns of rising-and-falling interest in acting and dressing like twins. It seems the best way to deal with the dress-alike-or-not issue is the simplest: Let your children decide, within reason, whether or not they will dress alike. (Keep in mind that if you have always dressed them alike as infants and toddlers, they may not know it's an option for them to dress differently when they are old enough to decide for themselves—say three or four years old. And if they have always been dressed alike, they may feel they are "going against your wishes" by choosing to do otherwise, which is uncomfortable for some children.) You can know that just like every other pattern they ever develop, this one, too, is likely to change.

If you're still not sure about dressing your multiples alike, find one or two adult twins who were dressed alike through their childhood, and ask them how they feel or felt about it.

OUT AND ABOUT

Getting out of the house can be a lifesaver for cabin-feverish moms. But sometimes the thought of packing up two or more babies (and siblings, for some moms) and remembering all the requisite toys, diapers, snacks, etc., looks worse than suffering the claustrophobia of cabin fever. Actually, if you plan for it and practice it until you are good at it, going out with your multiples can see you through many a tough day and can simply enrich your life on good days.

For many parents of twins and triplets, there are three obstacles associated with going out with their little ones:

1. *Fear.* They are afraid they won't be able to handle all of the babies or, for older children, parents are afraid their attention will be so divided they can't safely care for all of them. There is also a fear of being embarrassed by, for example, two or three babies who launch into uncontrollable screaming and thrashing while you're trapped in line at the grocery store.

2. *Logistics.* Just how does one person juggle two or three babies and groceries into and out of cars and grocery carts? Even getting more than one baby from the house to the car solo, without leaving any babies alone, is impossible. And what happens if you've ventured out alone with your two toddlers to a restaurant, and one has to go to the bath-

room just as the other finally stops throwing crackers, spoons, and the toys you brought on the floor and begins to eat his meal? Do you tell one to wait so you can keep the other quiet, or do you interrupt the quiet one (risking a reenactment of the throwing scene) to accommodate the one who has to go to the bathroom? These are legitimate concerns and need to be planned for.

3. *Attention.* Some people just can't stand the kind of attention that comes with going out with multiples. Particularly when your children are easily identifiable as twins—when they are infants and in a twin stroller, when they are dressed alike, or when they are identical— almost everyone walking down the shopping-center mall will stop and talk to you. Even if you don't mind the attention, getting errands done in less than five or six hours may be impossible because of all the people who want to ask you if your boy-girl twins are identical.

There are ways to handle each of these concerns, and there is special equipment that can help you. But your biggest aid in getting out with your multiples will be your ability to anticipate your needs and the needs of your babies in any situation. The keys to getting around happily with multiples are:

> Plan Ahead
> Bring Supplies
> Relax and Be Flexible

Weather permitting, you can start taking properly dressed, normal-term babies out for walks within ten to fourteen days of their birth— providing you are well and feel energetic enough to walk. It is a good idea to avoid contact with a lot of strangers until your babies are older —some say two or three weeks; others say as much as four to six weeks, depending on the babies and their conditions at birth. Your babies are likely to have much more contact with strangers than will most single-born babies. Well-meaning people you have never seen before may lean to within inches of your babies' faces to see if they really are identical. They may touch your babies or even ask to hold them. Be prepared for these overtures and with your responses to them. To make life easier for you and your babies at first, you may want to avoid places where people gather, like shopping centers. You'll avoid strangers who like to touch and have a chance to practice your getting-out skills without an audience.

Here are some ideas for overcoming basic obstacles:

1. *Fear.* The two best solutions for dealing with the fear of taking your little ones out are practice and company. Most mothers or fathers

of twins feel at least a flutter of the heart when they first venture outdoors alone with two babies. It's only normal. Outside the familiar and protective confines of your own home, you can suddenly feel the responsiblity you bear for these two little ones more acutely. And if your babies are very young, you are still in the learning stages of caregiving yourself. So give yourself a break, and plan your first trips out into the world at a time of day when both babies are usually calm, and at a time when you are not at your wit's end. Later you may find getting out and walking with fussy babies a godsend, but for your first effort, try to do it during a calm time of the day. For many babies and parents, that happens in mid-to-late morning.

Probably the simplest thing you can do is get them both dressed appropriately, strap them into the stroller (which you have already brought into an entry area inside your home, so one baby isn't left alone outside in the stroller while you go back inside for the second baby), and go for a stroll. You can go around the block and come home, but if the weather is nice and the babies fall asleep, you probably won't want to. That's fine. Just try to come home before you feel exhausted, which might be considerably sooner than you would have in pre-babies time, or even during your pregnancy, if your babies are quite young.

The more times you can do this, the easier and more familiar the routine of dressing and strapping-in will become. And that removes the fear for most people. As you get to know your babies, you will be able to gauge their reaction to different kinds of weather and different times of day for strolling. For your well-being and theirs, you should try to get out once a day, even if it's only for a few minutes. If nothing else, getting out reminds you that even if your world feels upside down and hopelessly chaotic, the rest of the world still exists more or less as you remember it. Life is going on, and you will rejoin the mainstream soon enough.

If your neighborhood doesn't have suitable sidewalks for twin strollers, or if you don't think it is the best place to walk your babies, you can accomplish the same thing by adding one step to your early going-out routine. Have someone else put the stroller in the car for you, or put both babies in their cribs and run the stroller out yourself. (This is where a foldable twin stroller comes in handy.) Then dress both babies, put one back in her crib or strap her securely into an infant seat on the floor, and take one baby out to the car. When she is securely strapped into her car seat, retrieve the other baby. Then you can drive to a park or an area you'd like for strolling. With the stroller unfolded right next to the car, you won't have the same back-and-forth baby-retrieval process you have at home.

The other way to handle fear of taking your babies out is to arrange for company. This is where getting to know other mothers comes in.

While you may feel less free now that you have twins or triplets, remember that many people see freedom not as the absence of responsibility, but as the availability of options.

For most mothers it doesn't really matter whether they have twins or not—in fact sometimes it helps to hang around a mother of one; she'll have an extra hand to help you. Sometimes simply having another adult with you takes the pressure off, and you manage just fine with little or no help from the other adult. But sometimes you legitimately need another pair of hands and eyes. That's when you need to either hire a baby-sitter (like a high-school girl who can come for an hour or two after school) to help, or you need to ask a friend to go along. If you have older children, say, toddlers, and you are sincerely concerned about your ability to safely supervise both your twins and their siblings, trust your instincts and arrange for someone to help you. You won't enjoy yourself, and neither will anyone else, if you are constantly afraid that your children will fall into a swimming pool, off a cliff, or into the lion's den at the zoo. You put out a fair amount of effort to get out so you'll have a good time. Plan ahead, and arrange it so you all can, and your fears will most likely vanish.

Having another adult with you can also help get rid of the fear of being embarrassed by having several uncontrollable babies in a public place. At least you know there is another pair of arms to help comfort a crying little one or to help you make a quick escape if all babies become inconsolable. For early excursions, you might feel more comfortable limiting your outings to places where you are not likley to be stuck alone with two or three crying babies and a gaggle of onlookers. Later, when you are more in tune with what your babies can handle and what they can't, plan ahead. Some babies never like being in places where there are a lot of people; others learn to love it and the distraction of all the action around them keeps them calm. As you get to know your babies, try to respect their limitations—don't go places you know or suspect they won't be able to handle, especially at times of the day that are difficult for them.

But no one's life is perfect, and sometimes it's just not possible to avoid those situations. Sometimes you just have to run to the grocery store, alone with all the little ones, or there won't be any dinner on the table. When that happens, bring supplies. You may want to keep a packed diaper bag or tote bag in the car or coat closet to making getting out at any time a little easier. Keep it full of little toys and books your children don't see every day, and of course diapers and disposable wipes. At the last minute, you can throw in portable snacks (if your babies are old enough) like crackers, raisins, etc. If your going-out gear is already half-assembled, it makes any trip easier.

Once you've done all you can—planned ahead as much as possible and brought your supplies—then you need to relax a little bit and remind yourself that all those people you see in the store (many of whom *are* mothers) know most mothers have trying times with one baby. They also know that trying times can be par for the course with two or more. And if they don't understand that, who cares? You'll probably never see them again in your life anyway.

2. *Logistics.* Worries about logistics can also be eased by practice, planning, and using the right equipment. Choose the equipment that will work best for you from the list at the end of this chapter. There are several kinds of strollers for twins and triplets. Some are lightweight and fold easily for stashing in a car trunk; others are heavyweight, nonportable styles for concentrated city walking. When your children are small, you can use combinations of front or back packs or carriers and single strollers, especially if you want to minimize the amount of attention you receive when you go out. Whatever you choose, be sure it works for your particular life. You may find that having inappropriate equipment limits horizons that may already seem considerably smaller than they were before your multiples were born. For example, if you have to struggle to get a heavy stroller into the car every time you want to go farther than your own neighborhood with your children, you may find you just don't go on those trips. It may be worth it for you to spend the extra money (or to borrow one or search yard sales and newspaper ads) for a lightweight, portable stroller that will allow you more options.

You can always cultivate your options. To be sure, your options will be different from those of someone who had one baby at a time, but you still have options. You have to find different ways of discovering them and using them. Getting out with two or more babies may be more complicated to begin with, but as you create the process that works for you, you may find yourself no more tied down than many mothers with small children.

The same kind of planning that helps diminish parents' fear of taking their multiples out can help you work out the logistics. Know your children and how far their good nature can go. For example, some twins will in fact amuse one another somewhat quietly at a restaurant while waiting for their meal, particularly if they are supplied with things like crayons and paper, books, or snacks. Very young babies are actually rather easy to take to a restaurant, especially if you sit in a booth and can let a baby lie on a blanket on the seat on either side of you. But some children will never be quiet, calm, or fun to be with in a restaurant. Sitting quietly for twenty minutes while the hamburgers cook is just not possible for them, and you may be setting yourself (and them) up for a miserable time if you expect it of them.

A certain amount of trial and error is part of learning what kinds of

outings will work best for you and for your children. There is no one way to do it. Allow yourself the latitude to learn your best methods. As you understand the needs and moods of your children better, you will probably find that you have fewer difficult outings and more variety in what you can do with them.

3. *Attention.* The attention parents of multiples get when they are out with their children is a blessing to some and a curse to others.

If you enjoy the attention you and your twins or triplets get when you go out with them, by all means indulge yourself while they are small. As multiples get older it is less obvious to the casual observer that they are twins or triplets, unless they are dressed alike. So you really only have the few years that they are confined to a stroller during which their twinship will be obvious to everyone.

The fact that those years are few can also be a comfort to you if you can't stand the attention that comes with being a parent of multiples. You can console yourself with the thought that you won't always be stopped by strangers in the grocery store who want to know if you took fertility drugs. In the meantime, there are a few ways you can minimize the attention you'll get while your twins are young.

- Try using a Snugli or other front or back carrier for one baby and a single stroller for the other. Although you still have two babies, mothers who use this method report that somehow the twinship is not so obvious and they don't get stopped nearly as often as they do with a twin stroller.

- Try taking one baby at a time with you when you do errands. It means arranging care for the other baby, but you will get a taste of how relatively easy it is to get around with one baby (if you haven't had children before), and it might also make you feel better to be giving some individual attention to one of the babies.

- Try using two single strollers for your babies when you go out with a friend, instead of a twin stroller. If you have the kind of foldable strollers that can be fastened together or used separately, it might help to undo them when you have someone with you. When you each have one baby, who will know they are twins?

- Try dressing your babies very differently—not even in coordinating colors or different colors of the same outfit (which are the compromises many mothers make who don't want to dress their children exactly alike). The less alike they are dressed, no matter what kind of stroller or carrying arrangement you use, the less strangers will assume they are twins. (This also offers more food for thought about dressing them alike—even in different colors of the same outfit—and the amount of importance that attaches to the twinship instead of the individual.)

• Try pretending someone else is their mother. One mother of triplets who couldn't stand the attention she got would bring someone along to help and have her push the stroller while the mother browsed peacefully through stores away from the group. The helper didn't mind the questions, and by telling those who asked that she wasn't the mother, she ended most conversations before they began. When that mother got more used to being out alone with all three babies, she sometimes used the same technique, simply claiming that she wasn't the mother.

Even parents who don't mind the attention cringe when strangers always exclaim over the babies, ignoring an older sibling completely. Some mothers solve that problem by attaching a sign to the stroller that tells well-wishers the babies don't mind if you talk to their older sister or brother first. The sign works particularly well if the older sibling is too young to read—which may also be an age (two to four) when they are especially sensitive about all the attention given to the new babies.

Other mothers, tired of hearing the same questions over and over, have considered having T-shirts printed up with YES, THEY ARE TWINS printed on the front and YES, I HAVE MY HANDS FULL, printed on the back.

WHERE CAN YOU GO?

Once you have the basic routine figured out that allows you to get out of the house relatively easily, you might wonder where you can go besides around the block and to the park. There are lots of options. Some will seem more possible to you than others. And don't think of this as the complete list. It should spark your thinking so you can make a list of your own. Keep it in a handy spot so when you feel the walls closing in and can't think of where to go, you can consult it for ideas on how to save the day.

• You can do errands with the babies. Everyone has a certain number of mundane trips to make, like picking up clothes at the cleaners or going to the bank. Plan your route carefully, and decide if you can do it all on foot with the babies in a stroller more easily than you can in a car. If you make a point of using services, like a bank or the cleaners, that are within walking distance of your home, you might have better luck getting errands done with babies. If that's not possible for you, try to

"When my twins were babies, any time I felt down or overwhelmed by them, I would dress them in something cute and go to the nearest shopping mall. The attention we would get from all the people we'd meet would inevitably lift my spirits, and I'd be reminded that it really was a miracle to get two healthy babies at once."

"One of the hardest things for me was the attention we'd get when my triplets were small. Not only could I not get anything done very quickly when we went out, but I felt like a freak with all those people asking personal questions about me and my babies. I dreaded going out with all three babies so much, I really avoided it."

use businesses that have drive-up facilities to minimize the number of times you have to load two or three babies into and out of the car. Or group the errands (and the businesses you use) in one area to which you can drive and unload the babies once, and then walk to complete your errands.

• You can take your babies to the supermarket with you. There are several ways to accomplish this feat:

—If they can sit up well, try seating them facing one another in the cart seat each with one leg bent and one leg sticking out a leg hole provided for one child. They can amuse each other, and you still have room for groceries in the main part of the cart.

—If they are too large for the seat, put both toddlers in the main part of the grocery cart, and stash groceries in a cardboard box (one you keep in the trunk of your car for this purpose) on the lower level of the cart. This obviously limits the amount you can buy at one time and may therefore not work for major shopping trips, but it can serve a purpose in a pinch.

—If you don't want children in the cart, you can take your twin stroller with you and pull it behind you while you push the cart ahead. Some mothers get two grocery carts and pull their children in one, while pushing the groceries in the other.

—If your stroller wouldn't work this way, you could wear one baby in a front or back carrier and put the other in the grocery cart seat. Or you could carry both babies in front-and-back or double-front packs if that is comfortable for you.

—You might want to leave the babies home. For some mothers, grocery shopping can actually be a pleasant, peaceful time alone. And for some children, it is never realistic to expect them to sit quietly in a cart or stroller while you shop. Some young babies get fussy; some older children only want out of the cart; and those who can walk have been known to help their mothers select items from grocery store shelves all too well.

• You can take classes with your babies. Many community centers offer swimming classes or gymnastics classes for infants with their parents. You can participate in those, too. Of course you need another pair of adult hands, and some fathers are able and willing to provide those. If that's not possible, you can ask the people who provide the class if they have helpers you can use.

• You can participate in parents' groups with your babies. Churches, community centers, the YMCA, and the YWCA often offer classes for parents on issues of interest. Some are evening classes and focus on both parents; some are for mothers and are scheduled during the day. All offer an opportunity for parents to meet other parents, and since they are for parents, they often also offer baby-sitting and a chance for children and parents to socialize together. Check your local newspapers or the yellow pages of your telephone book for these kinds of groups near you.

• You can participate in a parents-of-twins group. Some groups offer meetings for parents and babies, and separate meetings for parents only. Groups are usually listed in the white business pages of your telephone book. Often notices about meeting times and dates are posted in pediatrician's offices.

• You can participate in La Leche League meetings. If you are breastfeeding your babies, this is a way to meet other breastfeeding mothers. La Leche League, too, is listed in the white pages of the telephone book.

• You can work out at a health club or a recreation center. Once you feel comfortable resuming your workout routine, and you feel comfortable taking your babies to a nursery, you can go to a health club. A less expensive alternative may be a community recreation center. Both often have baby-sitting available, and you can call ahead to make sure they have room for two or three babies.

• You can jazz up your walks to the park by bringing a picnic and some friends. Get another mother to walk with you, and pack a whole lunch or just some snacks. Even if your babies are very young, you can spread a blanket on the ground in the shade, and they will enjoy the change of scenery as much as you do. If there is no suitable park near you, do this in your own backyard. And if you and your toddlers are sick of winter, spread the blanket on the living-room floor, bring out the snacks, and pretend it's summer. Then fold up the crumbs in the blanket when you're done, and shake it out the back door.

• You can take your multiples on special outings. The zoo, a children's museum, a theater production for children are all possibilities for you as they are for parents of one. You may need to plan a little more carefully, and you may need to have help with you, but there's no reason why you need to avoid these things just because you had two or three babies at once. Check your local newspaper entertainment section (often in the Sunday edition) for special children's activities.

• You can substitute some shopping centers for playgrounds when the weather is bad. It's easy to get cabin fever when the snow just won't quit and you're stuck inside with two bored, cranky toddlers. Try loading them into the car and going for a walk in the nearest shopping-center mall. Have a friend meet you. You can have coffee and stroll the mall while your children get some exercise too. You don't have to go into a single store if it doesn't seem possible. Your children won't care. They need the change of scenery as badly as you do, and the chance to stretch their legs.

• You can start a playgroup. Call up a few of the mothers you've met through other activities, and see if two or three of them might want to get together once a week. You can rotate the house you meet at, so you can mix practice getting out with practice having people in.

WHAT ABOUT TRAVELING?

For some families, getting out with their children means more than a trip to the corner grocery. Many families have grandparents or friends who live at a distance, and trips of larger proportions happen once or twice a year.

For many babies (and parents) traveling by car is the least painful way to go. Lots of babies fall asleep within blocks of their home and tend to be lulled by the motion and the sounds of car travel. But there are also those babies who don't like it; they may scream their way through mile after mile of the miserable trip. The saving grace about traveling by car, even with screaming babies, is at least you don't have to think about the disapproving stares from fellow travelers you can get on an airplane.

The other, perhaps most important, aspect of car travel with babies or small children is that you can control the pace. The best rule of thumb is to travel when *they* are ready and stop when *they* want to. If you will be traveling by car, try to arrange your schedule to allow for plenty of stops. You'll probably all be happier for it. Where can you stop with small children when you're whizzing along the interstate? In order to know that, it helps if you do some research ahead of time. Check a map for small towns you can easily pull into from the highway. Check for state parks with rest areas. Visit your library and check the yellow pages in out-of-town telephone books for ideas in towns you may be passing through. Here are some places to look for:

• Public libraries. Many have special children's rooms, which can be a godsend for crawling babies and toddlers (or older children). An hour of crawling around, a story or two, and a snack on the grass outside can refresh a cranky little one for another few hours on the road.

• Public recreation centers or community centers. Many communities have these, and they are not usually hard to find. Children of any age would love the activity break.

• The YWCA or YMCA will have similar facilities.

• A school playground.

• Museums or galleries in a larger city may offer some quiet time and carpeted floors for crawling babies.

• A college or university campus. You'll find open grassy areas, a cafeteria, and a gym at most of them.

• A hotel or motel isn't just for spending the night. Of course you don't want to add to the cost of your trip without reason, but you might be able to change an unbearable twelve-hour drive into an enjoyable one by stopping midway in a motel. A bath and a nap in the middle of the day, with quiet time to nurse or feed the babies, can be a lifesaver.

Generally, it works best for many families to plan to drive during the times their babies usually nap, and stop during the times the babies usually play. As your children get older, it doesn't necessarily mean you have to drive less because they sleep less. Older children can usually tolerate nonsleeping time in the car better, especially if they have car games (check your local toy stores), books, and other activities to keep them busy. And some mothers have reported that their infants travel better if mom sits between the car seats in the back of the car where they can reach her, and she can reach toys and snacks for them.

You might also make life easier with young babies if you plan to feed them (and yourselves) in the car or outside on a picnic blanket. If your children are the kind you love to take to restaurants, you don't have to do this. But if restaurants always set you up for a tense and terrible time with your children, don't think it will be any different on the road.

With some planning ahead and plenty of stops along the way, you may find that you arrive a little later, but more refreshed than you would if you drove straight through.

If you will be traveling by air, you can still do some planning ahead.

• Most airlines require that infants for whom you have not purchased a ticket be held by an adult at take off and landing. That means they won't let you strap one into an infant seat or other apparatus during these times. Check ahead of time with the airline to see how you will be expected to handle the babies if you will be traveling alone.

• Whether you are traveling alone or not, enlist the help of a friendly looking stewardess or a seat-mate as early as you can. Most airlines allow travelers with children to board early, so you will have time to get settled before the aisles are too crowded.

• Try to schedule the departure to coincide with when your babies would normally nap. Sometimes midday flights are less crowded than those in the late afternoon. Early morning flights, when your babies might be willing to play calmly, are sometimes less crowded, too. At holiday times, everything is crowded.

• Reserve seats in the bulkhead for extra legroom and a small space for babies to play. If you're lucky enough to be the only one in the bulkhead, put a blanket on the floor during smooth flying, and let the babies play there with toys you've brought. If you're sharing the bulkhead with one other adult, see if you can have the aisle seat while the other person has the window seat. The babies can play on the floor between you, and you can block their way to the main aisle. If you're sharing the bulkhead with two other adults, floor play for the babies is out.

• Most airlines offer a baby meal. Usually it is a small selection of baby food from jars, juice, and a cracker or two. Call a couple of days ahead if you want to order it. It might be better to take your own nongloppy finger foods. Trying to restrain both babies and feed them mushy food from a jar may be more trouble than it's worth. Even though your little ones may produce a lot of crumbs and leave more than a few raisins behind, finger foods can be easier to eat, more entertaining, and just as satisfying to small tummies.

• Nurse or offer a bottle at takeoff and landing. Sucking will help the babies' ears adjust to differing air pressure. And if you are flying during nap time they may fall asleep and stay that way for part of the trip. If one or more babies fall asleep in your lap, ask the stewardess to give you a few airline pillows to prop them and leave your hands free to read or eat. Use the tray table for the seat next to you (if it's empty).

• Unless you know from experience that they work for *your* babies, don't use drugs to make them sleep. Some doctors will prescribe mini doses of tranquilizers for babies who will be traveling. But some babies become agitated rather than sleepy after taking them. And if your babies haven't had such drugs before, what you don't need is to have to deal with a surprise reaction at thirty-five thousand feet halfway between Chicago and Miami.

• Always take a goodie bag of books, blankies (if your children use them), quiet toys (old favorites spiced up with some special new items), snacks, diapers, disposable wipes, and a change of clothing for each baby.

A WORD ABOUT SAFETY

Many parents who have active, adventurous children find that their biggest medical expense occurs not at the pediatrician's office for well-child checkups and immunizations, but at the hospital emergency room for stitches and casts. You don't have to be a parent of multiples to know that for those active kids, a lot of those emergency-room trips happen before the little ones are even in school. In fact one study on injuries to twins showed that more injuries happened in the home than at school, until children were old enough to participate in sports, when school-related injuries increased somewhat.

In the same study, the most common injuries to preschoolers were found to be blows to the head (sometimes injuring teeth also), and the next most common were cuts or fractures that were the result of children falling off of or running into objects. Interestingly, this study showed poisoning and automobile-related accidents to be at the bottom of the list. Either all the public attention these two receive is working, or they aren't that real a threat to many preschoolers.

Some parents of twins believe that their twins, compared to their single-born children, are more injury-prone. The conclusion of the only study that has been done on the topic (part of the Louisville Twin Study in Kentucky) is that there is the "impression" but not the absolute proof that twins may be more prone to injury than their single-born siblings. But then, parents don't need absolute proof to know how distracted they are when they (the parents) are tired at the end of a demanding day, their multiples are fresh from their afternoon nap, the house is a mess from earlier escapades, and the older children are just getting home from school and want to tell them everything that happened during the day. Under these conditions, which happen every day for many families with multiples, it's not hard to see how those little toddler twins can help each other climb over the gate to the basement stairs (something they could never do alone), and land on their heads on the concrete floor at the bottom.

Since you can't change the number of children you have now, and you can't change the kinds of demands there are on you as a parent, you'll have to focus on what you can change to make your house safer. As a parent of multiples, you probably need to be at least twice as careful about potential hazards as do parents of single-born children. That's because your multiples have each other to help figure out how to do things single-born children would never dream of. Not only do they have the extra pair of hands it may take to get over the fence and escape from the backyard you thought was safe, but they have the (false) confidence that comes from having a partner in crime. It's one thing to flee the backyard for unknown territory when you're three years old and alone. And quite another when you're three years old and your best friend is backing you, and perhaps even egging you on.

So you need to reexamine your home with the most critical of eyes. You probably already have the obvious poisons and harmful household products out of the way, you don't let your little ones outside in areas where they would have access to a street, and you've long since gotten rid of all the poisonous houseplants. You have ipecac syrup in your medicine chest to induce vomiting in cases of poisoning that require it. Very good. But remember that the largest number of injuries to preschoolers are head injuries, followed by cuts and fractures—all from falls of some sort. Here are some things to check:

• Do you use walkers? Many little ones love them, but walkers are responsible for thousands of head injuries to young children a year. And they have not been proved to be especially beneficial to leg development or walking skills in young children—the reason many mothers give for using walkers. Some newer walkers feature braking systems, but they have not been on the market long enough to see if they really eliminate hazards. If your children like to be upright, try a jumper, which is a canvas seat into which you strap the child. It hangs from a doorway and allows the child to use her legs to jump and bounce.

• Do you use gates to block entrances to rooms or stairs? They can be very helpful, but remember, with two little ones to work on them, they are not necessarily impenetrable. Some children aren't interested in climbing and others seem to be born with a fierce desire to scale mountains. Check your gates to be sure there are no tiny foodholds or handholds that would work for your children. Turn gates so the cross-bar (if there is one), or any horizontal part, is away from the side the children are on. And don't trust the gate alone to protect your children from whatever is on the other side. Your best effort at supervision is the only way to ensure they are safe.

• Do you have stairs in your home? If you do, you can't keep your children off them forever. When they are able to crawl well, or when they are in the early stages of walking, some mothers teach babies how to go up and down the stairs. One mother of seven children swears by this method. She has spent the better part of a day or two with each child, as the child was ready, showing her how to crawl up the stairs facing upward, and how to crawl down the stairs, still facing upward. Many babies try to go down head first, which doesn't work—not safely anyway. If your stairs are uncarpeted, you might consider carpeting them, since a fall, however minor, is almost inevitable. Carpeted stairs are a lot kinder to little heads than are bare wood stairs.

• If you use highchairs instead of seats that attach to the table, and if your children love to climb, you will need to lock the highchairs in another room or somehow make them inaccessible when not in use. Children learn how to climb into highchairs—even when the tray is attached—at a remarkably early age. Once they can do that, the world of countertops and stovetops is open to them.

• Your babies are ready to leave their cribs behind when they are about thirty-five inches tall or they can climb and/or fall over the side. If they share a crib, they may be ready for separate cribs or beds earlier, because they may be able to help each other out of the crib.

• If you use hook-on seats that attach to the table, be sure there is a seat belt to hold each child in the chair, and don't leave them alone in their chairs. The tabletop is inviting to little ones, and for some, even the chair's seat belt won't really restrain them, given some time alone to work on it. Also, be sure to place the chairs on opposite sides of the table to balance the weight.

You will have to look at your own home to judge the opportunities for falls and at your children to judge how likely they are to climb to dangerous heights. But remember, sometimes you don't know your children are capable of certain feats until they perform them. So don't wait for the fall to happen. Try to anticipate, and keep the doctor's telephone number handy.

EQUIPMENT YOU MAY NEED

As you assemble special twin or triplet equipment for the multiples you are expecting, or as you reevaluate what you have, you may find this list helpful. Products change all the time, but this will give you an idea of what's usually available:

Strollers

Some position the babies one in front of the other, some side-by-side. Be sure when you choose a stroller that it fits easily through standard store doorways and aisles (test it at the store that stocks it), that it folds smoothly to a manageable size, and that it is light enough for you to lift into your car if that is how you'll use it.

Prices change, but most twin strollers range from one hundred to three hundred dollars. If you buy two inexpensive umbrella strollers (about twenty dollars each) and hook them together with the device made for that purpose by Gerry Products (about four dollars), you can bring the total cost down. But while that arrangement is handy, it may not be as durable as a stroller made for two children.

Be wary of trying to modify a single stroller to accommodate two babies or toddlers. It was not made or balanced to hold the extra weight, and could tip or otherwise be unsafe.

Here are the manufacturers and model names of some strollers for two, and one for three.

—McLaren Royalty Double Stroller (umbrella style)
—Bebecar of America, Superstar Twin Stroller
—Bebe Mate, Galaxy II (model #2002)
—Cosco/Peterson, Tandem Stroller (model #58)
—Silver Cross, Twin Ranger (umbrella style)
—Silver Cross, Twin Trident (carriage style)
—Hedstrom, Totliner Twin Stroller
—Perego, Duette
—Strolee, Limousine Stroller
—Welsh Company, Duchess Gear Stroller for Two
—Baby Furniture Outlet, Little Wheeler Limousine
—Octagon, Model No. 9901
—Perego, Triplette—a triplet stroller

Packs and Carriers

You can use two of the type made for single-born babies if you will be sharing the load with a friend or your husband. There are scores of single-baby packs and carriers made, by many manufacturers. One made especially for twins is the Twin Matey. It works like single carriers, holding babies in a soft fabric pouch against the adult's body. Both babies can be carried on the front, or you can carry one front and one back. Extra straps sold separately allow the two pouches to be separated so babies can be carried by two adults. The Twin Matey is available through mail order for $82 (extra straps $14.50 and postage $2.50) from Kidpower Unlimited, P.O. Box 12045, Overland Park, Kansas 66212.

Other Getting-Out Equipment

Double Kid-Kuff harness: adjustable harness and leash for two children. About ten dollars, from Zelex, Inc., 507 South Federal, Riverton, Wyoming 82501.

Kart-Kuf: safety strap for grocery carts, about six dollars, also from Zelex, Inc. Some supermarkets have similar devices for you to use while you are in the store. Ask at the service desk.

Twin View Mirrors: fits over the rearview mirror in your car so you can see what's going on in the back seat and still see rear traffic. About nine dollars, from Perfectly Safe, Dept. 401, P.O. Box 988, Stevens Point, Wisconsin 54481.

Blue Sky Cycle Carts: double-size bicycle cart with rain canopy for pulling up to 150 pounds of children or groceries, etc., with your bicycle. Available from Blue Sky Cycle Carts, 29976 Enid Road East, Eugene, Oregon 97402.

For a complete listing and evaluation (of safety, performance, etc.) of other, non-twin-specific baby gear, see *The Baby Gear Guide,* by Taree Bollinger and Patricia Cramer (Addison Wesley, 1985), or a similar baby-equipment book.

5 | Mothercare

"The hardest thing for me about being a mother of twins is that my needs are *always* dead last. I use up all my energy caring for the babies and their older brother, and when my husband comes home, I find myself looking after him, too, or feeling I ought to. I may sound terrible, but sometimes I resent everyone and the care they get from me. I wish someone would give me that kind of care."

You take care of your family, but who takes care of you? After the initial postpartum help has gone home, it might be nice to have someone who always has the time and sensitivity to understand your needs and help meet them. But don't plan on it, because that person doesn't exist. It's certainly not a bad thing to depend on others for tender loving care, but if that's the only way you ever get that TLC, what will you do when your best friend's children come down with chicken pox and she can't come over to help you get through that long, hard afternoon? What will you do when your mate is out of town on business for days on end? What if you're a single mother? And even if you're not, as much as most spouses want to help, sometimes it's enough for them to struggle to adjust to this new life themselves.

That leaves you as your own most stable resource. Of course no one expects you to comfort yourself and take care of yourself to the exclusion of all others in your life. But when the going is tough for you, there are some ways you can plan to brighten you own life, instead of waiting for someone to rescue you.

You can learn how to make your own life better by seeing how you can plan for changes, how being optimistic can change how you live your life, and how you can make time for yourself. You can learn how to feel better by treating your body well, learning how to relax, and by re-charging your body and your mind in ways you may not have considered before. You can choose some of the ways suggested in this chapter— or use these to help invent some of your own—and smooth the jagged edges you may feel in your life, whether your multiples are two years old or twelve years old.

PLAN AHEAD

You may be feeling like a Girl Scout with all the Being Prepared and Planning Ahead that being the parent of multiples seems to require. But experienced parents agree that, particularly with small children, the more you can anticipate, the more smoothly life will flow for you and your family.

If you are expecting multiples, you have a chance to look ahead and think about ways in which you might want to be sure you are taking care of yourself. If your multiples are already here, it's never too late to learn how. All of the information in this chapter can help you plan, or help you make changes in your life now. But if you're uncertain about the value of planning, it might help you to know about one study in which a group of prospective parents was encouraged to plan specifi-cally for the months after the arrival of their baby. Their reaction to parenthood was compared to another group that was not given specific instructions on planning for the changes ahead. During their prenatal classes, the prepared group was encouraged to do ten things:

1. Understand that parenting is a learned skill, and that everyone needs help and advice.

2. Make friends of other couples who are experienced with young children.

3. Avoid overloading yourself with what you consider to be tasks of low importance. (Which of course means deciding first what is of high importance to you.)

4. Avoid moving to a new home within a few months after the baby arrives.

5. Try not to be concerned with appearances (home and yourself) when other things are more important (sleep and feeling loved).

6. Get as much rest and sleep as you can.

7. Talk to husband, family, and experienced friends, and discuss your plans and worries.

8. Cut down outside responsibilities, but don't give up outside interests.

9. Arrange for baby-sitters in advance.

10. Learn to drive a car, if you don't already know how.

After six weeks, only 2 percent of the mothers who were encouraged to do these ten things reported they felt depressed, compared to 28 percent of the mothers in a control group not given these suggestions. The mothers who judged themselves (and were judged by the researchers) to be feeling good about their adjustment to motherhood:

1. had made more friends of couples with young children (many from their prenatal classes).

2. had given less emphasis to tidiness in the home.

3. had gotten more experienced help with the baby.

4. had husbands who became more available in the home and reduced their outside activities.

5. had continued to socialize with their husbands outside the home, although less frequently.

6. had made sure that they (the mothers) continued their outside interests, but limited their responsibilities.

TAKE RESPONSIBILITY AND CHANGE YOUR LIFE

While this study was done with parents expecting one baby, the same principles apply whether you are expecting two or three babies, or whether you had your babies years ago and just aren't satisfied with your life. You don't have to be a new mother to feel unsatisfied or even depressed when you are in a situation where:

1. You feel you have no control over what happens to you.

2. You feel isolated—physically, mentally, and/or emotionally.

3. You feel tired because of the physical demands of your life.

There is a key to taking control, relieving isolation, and regaining energy—the basics of taking care of yourself. It lies in taking responsibility for your life, seeing change as positive and possible, and then creating the reality—the kind of life you need.

Since you didn't choose to have twins, you might wonder how you can take responsibility for that. Well, you can't, but you can take responsibility for how you react to the change.

Some people have suspected for years that, responsible or not, we each create our own realities. Even your mother told you if you smile the world smiles with you. Now psychologists are finding there is more than a grain of truth to those old ideas.

What they have found is that by changing the way we think about hardship, we may be able to boost our moods and even our physical vitality. That's what one psychologist, Martin E. P. Seligman, told a 1986 meeting of the American Psychological Association, based on research he had done with psychologist Christopher Peterson of the University of Michigan and Dartmouth College psychiatrist George Vaillant. The psychologists analyzed the words used to describe their experiences by ninety-nine World War II survivors with similar backgrounds and similar wartime situations. The psychologists then discerned which of the group were optimists and which were pessimists. As a group, the optimists had returned from the war to lead healthy, robust lives and the pessimists had led lives of disappointment and illness.

What may be important to you about whether World War II veterans were optimistic or pessimistic is how the psychologists spotted those qualities in the men's descriptions of their lives. Then if you can discern what your own outlook is, you are one step closer to changing it to make your life rosier.

Seligman believes that when a pessimistic person encounters hardship, he sees it as:

• *Ongoing* ("Having twins will *always* be a problem for me—it will be difficult to care for them when they are newborns, they'll be doubly bad as two-year-olds, it will be hard for them to separate in school, and they'll probably have trouble finding spouses.")

• *Global* ("Having twins will undermine *everything* I do.")

• *Internal* (If only *I* was a more patient person, this wouldn't be so difficult.")

On the other hand, an optimistic person sees hardship as:

• *Temporary* ("It will probably be difficult learning to handle two babies at once, but I'm sure I'll get the hang of it.")
• *Specific* ("I know it's hard for me at home alone with the babies, but at the office, I find their birth hasn't affected what I know.")
• *External* ("Sometimes those kids are really hard to handle. They would drive anyone up a wall.")

Others who do psychological research find example after example of the power that lies in how each of us perceives what happens to us. It all points to the idea that it isn't the specific event that shapes our lives (the birth of twins, the loss of a job), but whether we see that event as a good thing or a bad thing. Seligman even believes that pessimistic people run a higher risk of getting sick. "It's not reality itself that's producing this risk factor, but what you do with reality and the way you think about it," he said.

Physicians see the same thing in working with people who are ill. One study showed that patients with herpes have more flare-ups of the disease when they are depressed, and the rate of herpes recurrence overall may be linked to how those with the disease face problems. And physicians who work with cancer patients see enormous differences in recovery and remission rates between those who attach only negative meaning to their disease, and those who see its positive aspects.

For example, Dr. Carl Simonton and Stephanie Matthews-Simonton, who run a cancer clinic, see that, "the amount of stress and particularly the degree to which events make you feel hopeless and helpless are the result of the meaning you attach to the experience. You determine the significance of events."

They see that principle in action. Cancer patients who use a strongly positive attitude and behavior in their move toward health can create a "spiral toward recovery." Many of them go through these three steps, which you can adapt to your situation, as they become better:

1. They learned to rewrite the rules we all live by to fit their own lives. For example, the details of your life are very different when you get two or three babies instead of one. Let your eyes be opened to new ways you can deal with the difficulties you may see in handling multiples. It's the perfect time to be creative.

2. They learned how to change. If you don't like the way your life feels now, you may be more motivated than ever to make the decision to change it.

3. They learned that their bodies respond to feelings of hope. A positive, take-charge attitude in cancer patients often produces im-

Taking responsibility means understanding that the only changes we can ever make are in ourselves. And that means we are not helpless. We may not control other people, but we are controlling our lives every day by the choices we make.

proved health. But you don't have to be a cancer patient to see that. The principles of biofeedback show that mind, body, and emotions act as a system—mental changes affect physical changes and vice versa. If you can feel that you have some times when you are not at the mercy of your babies, you can feel more in control of your mental and emotional life, and that can show in physical ways. You may not feel so tired all the time, for example.

They felt "weller than well" after they put all of this into practice. You can make your life more than just bearable, even in difficult circumstances. And if you can learn how to change your attitude and change your life during this difficult phase, the skills can stay with you forever.

IF IT'S SO GREAT TO FEEL GOOD, WHY DO I HAVE SUCH A HARD TIME MAKING THE SWITCH?

For all the benefits of a positive attitude, sometimes it just doesn't come easily. If it is hard to see past your present difficulties—whether they are with caring for two demanding babies or dealing with two moody preteens, you might ask yourself what you get out of feeling bad.

For example, the Simontons' cancer patients have found that by succumbing to being ill they get more attention, and they may be able to behave in ways that would normally be unacceptable for them, or say things to people they would normally never dare. Mothers of twins have told me that by constantly placing the emphasis on how hard life is for them, they are sure to get their "red badge of courage" for surviving each day. What we each need to decide before we can make any positive change is whether ultimately it is more rewarding to remain a victim of our situation or to decide to take charge and change what we can.

That decision can lead to the next step, which is understanding what we can change and forgetting about what we cannot change.

As a mother of infant twins, you may not be able to change the way your babies scream to be fed in alternating shifts. As a mother of teenage twins, you may not be able to change the way they fight with each other constantly. As the wife of a husband who must work the night shift, you can't change his business schedule. In fact, it's safe to say that you can't change the facts of anyone's life but your own. You can't change their behavior, but you can change what you do about it.

For example, let your mind wander all the way back to when you first found you were expecting not one baby, but two or three or more. For most mothers, whether that day was yesterday or ten years ago, the memory is crystal clear. How did you react? Many mothers remember being thrilled, excited, and feeling special for being given two or more babies. Many other mothers remember feeling devastated, panicked, hysterical, resentful, and scared. And those mothers may have worried (and maybe still are worrying) about whether their negative reaction was a bad thing. No one can plan a spontaneous reaction—and that panic of the moment is not what is ultimately important to you or your children. It is normal for many people to feel extremely upset when faced with a dramatically different and unexpected turn of events. How you *act* on the news is more important than how you *react* to the news.

If you are to develop a positive attitude about your life with multiples, you need to first give yourself permission to acknowledge your feelings the way they are. Then you can see what changes you may need to or want to make in how you act.

Psychologist Susan Jeffers, in her book *Feel the Fear and Do It Anyway,* lists seven ways to begin making needed changes in yourself instead of expecting them to come from someone else. In parentheses after each one, I've added ways they apply to mothers of twins.

1. Avoid casting blame on anyone or anything for your bad feelings about life. Nothing and no one outside yourself can control your thinking or actions. ("It's my mother's [mother-in-law's, friend's, husband's, God's] fault I'm having such a hard time with these twins. If they would just [you name it], life would be easier.")

2. Avoid blaming yourself for not being in perfect control of your life. You are doing the best you can. (If only I were more patient [unselfish, intelligent, etc.] I wouldn't be having so much trouble with these kids.")

3. Be aware of those circumstances in which you play the role of victim. Learn to identify clues that you are not taking responsibility for your life. ("I didn't ask to be a mother of twins. It's not my fault I'm so unhappy.")

4. Practice replacing your internal chatterbox (that little voice that tells you you're incapable) with a loving internal friend. (Replace "See, they're crying again, I knew I'd never be able to take care of two babies," with "I trust that I am a loving person. I know I am learning how to mother. I feel this trust and love will be felt by my babies, too.")

5. Figure out the payoffs that keep you "stuck" in life. Once you identify them, you will probably be able to become quickly "unstuck."

(Not being able to find an easy way to exercise, get out, or eat well, can bring "poor you" attention. How much more rewarding to search for the ways to do those things and get "amazing you" attention.)

6. Determine what you want out of life and act on it. Stop waiting for someone to give it to you. You'll wait a long time. (You'll also wait a long time for your children to grow up. Figure out how to do what you want to *now*.)

7. Be aware of the many choices you have in any situation. Choose the path that contributes to your growth and makes you feel at peace with yourself and others. (Even with two or three babies, you always have choices. They may not be the same ones you're used to, but they are there if you look.)

DON'T FIND TIME, MAKE TIME

One of the most often heard complaints from mothers of single-borns or twins, newborns or teens, is that they can't find time for themselves. It is a legitimate complaint, since it is probable that no person in the world has as many demands to meet as does a mother. But it is equally probable that if you can't find any time for yourself, you might be looking in the wrong place. It's not just a play on words to say you will never "find" time, because there isn't any extra time just lying around. The only way to have time for yourself it to *make* time.

The difference between finding time and making time is like the difference between waiting for a rescuer and saving yourself. You can wait around for a free half hour when someone has volunteered to take care of your children during a time of day when you have a lot of energy and nothing else to do—and *then* go out for a walk or a jog. Or you can decide that you really could start making dinner when the babies are napping in the morning, arrange with a friend to trade a half hour of baby-sitting in the afternoon, and start your exercise program today.

Your best bet for making time for yourself is to reevalute all that you do, and decide what you can change. When your babies are very small, there may be less you can rearrange in your schedule, but there is always some small thing. And no matter what age your multiples, you know that even ten minutes for yourself, wisely used, can make a difference.

One way to start looking at your time is to make a list of everything you do, just for a day. It may seem a hassle to you at first to write down each thing and how long it takes (changing diapers: five minutes, dishes in dishwasher: ten minutes), but once you begin to see how many things you do each day, and how often the focus of your attention is changed, you might be impressed that you finish anything—and more understanding of yourself when you don't. If you are working outside the home, list what you do when you are at home, since that is the time from which you will carve pieces for yourself.

When you have completed a day's list, decide if this is a typical day for you. You might want to track another day or two, just to get a clear idea of what a normal use of time is for you. When you are satisfied that you have the picture, make a sketch of a typical day, using a pie chart like this:

Now you can easily see what takes most of your time. If your children are young, it might be child care. If you are working outside the home, it might be housework or cooking. If your children are older, it might be car-pooling. Some of those requirements are unavoidable. What you need to look at carefully are those that are changeable. For example:

• How many hours a day do you spend watching television? Even if you get some enjoyment from watching certain things, television can be a great time waster. If there are certain things you'd like to see, be sure you watch just those, and don't lap over to other programs just because you're still sitting there when the next program comes on. Many people find they can easily slice a half hour or an hour out of their viewing time and give it to themselves to spend on other things they've decided are more important. If you have a VCR, try recording programs you really don't want to miss and watching them at times that are low-energy times for you. For example, if morning is a high-energy time for you, figure out how to use it for yourself or to accomplish something important to you. Record your favorite daytime show, and watch it in the evening when you are too tired for other tasks.

• What time do you go to bed? Whole days can be lost because you are exhausted from staying up too late and then having to get up too early—for babies, for work, for children going off to school. Late at night may seem an easy time to fit in extra duties or to read a little, but is the price you're paying for taking *your* time at that time of day too steep?

• What do you do, and when do you do it? What is your most energetic part of the day? For many people it is the morning. For others it's late afternoon or early evening. No matter what time of day your energy peaks, that is the time you might want to target as a place to squeeze out minutes for yourself. If what you want to accomplish during that time requires a baby-sitter, find one to accommodate you. If you want to spend time with your family during that time, schedule activities as best you can to coincide. But at all costs, don't fritter away your high-energy time.

• Learn to say no. This doesn't mean you need to turn down all offers of activities that aren't family-oriented. It just means you need to limit your responsiblility where those activities are concerned. For example, you don't have to quit your bowling league because you had twins. You will no doubt want to wait until you and the babies are ready for the separation, and you are ready for the physical activity. But continuing to see old friends in familiar circumstances is a must; and you can enjoy yourself and limit your responsibility by being a participant instead of a leader for a while. You don't have to be your favorite group's organizer, president, or treasurer just now.

• Decide how important a perfectly clean/tidy house is to you and your family. Don't let this issue slide by without careful consideration, because as you have more children, the potential for mom becoming a full-time maid increases dramatically. You need to decide clearly how much housework must be done by you, how much can be delegated to family members, and if you have the money, how much can be hired out. If you don't establish boundaries for yourself, housework can eat up your time before you know it. Consider: grouping chores on certain days to leave other days housework-free; teaching young children to fold and put away laundry; letting children run the vacuum; giving each person a part of the house that is his or her responsibility to keep picked up and clean—then trading after a week or two; trading chores with a friend—her ironing for your windows might make both of you happy.

If you have been a mother for any time at all, you know that making time for yourself is never easy. But you can also know that it is possible. Remember as you carve these moments out that just as life with small babies always changes, so will your schedule change whether you have small babies or big kids. In any family, everyone has to make some accommodations for the others. You will find that the exercise schedule that works for you in the spring doesn't quite work in the summer, and summer's won't do for the fall. So try to be flexible in your timing, and don't be too upset by changes. But do be persistent in getting that time. There's always another way to get that half hour to go for a walk. It's there if you keep looking.

> **Besides cultivating a positive attitude about the options in her life, and developing her ability to mold her time to fit her needs, a mother of multiples has to learn to deal with a body that may feel and look very different from the one she was used to before her multiple pregnancy.**

WILL MY BODY EVER BE THE SAME?

The bad news is: probably not. The good news is: That isn't necessarily bad, and if you feel it is, you might be able to do something about it. Every woman's body changes with every birth. Women who have a multiple birth see the same kinds of changes as women who have a single baby, but the bywords for them seem to be "more" and "longer." Mothers of multiples may see those body changes as being more intense for them, and they may see their bodies taking longer to return to their familiar, prepregnant form. For example:

Body size: Some women gain fifty to seventy pounds during their twin pregnancy, and sometimes more for a triplet or quadruplet pregnancy.

It is normal for mothers to gain significantly more weight during their multiple pregnancy than they did (or will) during other single-baby pregnancies. It is also normal for them to gain more weight than other mothers who carried just one baby. Most obstetricians now advise expectant mothers to try for a twenty-five–to–thirty pound gain during a full-term normal pregnancy with one baby. It isn't unreasonable, then, to have gained twice that during your twin pregnancy. On the other hand, not every mother of twins gains twice what a mother of a single-born baby gains; and not every mother of triplets gains three times that amount. As you have probably noticed from talking to other mothers, whether they had twins or not, weight gain during pregnancy is an extremely individual matter. Everyone's metabolism is different. But you can know that it is normal to have had a much larger weight gain during a multiple pregnancy than during a single pregnancy.

It follows that all those pounds won't disappear in four to six weeks, as many of the pregnancy manuals directed toward mothers of single babies will tell you.

How long will it take? That depends on how much weight you

gained, how you eat after your birth, how active you are or are able to be, and how your metabolism reacts to the birth and to breastfeeding —if you do so. If you have never lost weight easily in your life, it is probably unreasonable to expect you will after your birth. Your body is more likely to return to patterns that are normal for you than it is to suddenly behave in ways it never has. You can look forward to losing the weight of the babies, their placenta(s), and the amniotic fluid right after the birth. And the reduction in tissue fluid and blood volume (it doubles with a single-baby pregnancy, and increases even more for a multiple pregnancy) to a nonpregnant state will result in a little more weight loss in following weeks. But you shouldn't expect to look like your prepregnant self at the six-week checkup.

Some people believe that breastfeeding mothers lose weight quicker than others, and that is true for some mothers. Indeed, some find they must struggle to keep their weight up while they are breastfeeding. But individuality rears its head again. Many mothers find that they remain five to ten pounds over their prepregnant weight as long as they are breastfeeding. Recent research shows that some breastfeeding mothers don't need to eat large amounts of additional calories in order to successfully feed their babies, because their bodies compensate for the calories used in milk production by becoming more efficient users of calories themsleves. That means their bodies store calories as fat rather than use them, which means they are probably not going to find that extra pounds vanish as their babies nurse.

Whether you are breastfeeding or not, it may be a good idea to try to forget about losing weight until at least two or three months after the birth. If you are breastfeeding, you can be sure by that time that your milk supply is well established. And if you are not, you will have given your body a chance to get all the nutrition it needs to help heal itself and rest after the tremendous amount of work it has done in carrying and birthing more than one baby.

Your abdomen. You already know that your pregnant belly was anywhere from a little to a whole lot bigger than those of women you know were carrying just one baby. But in the months after the birth, as you're waiting impatiently for your abdomen to return to something close to its prepregnant size, it might help you to know just how much bigger you were.

If you are still pregnant, ask what the fundal height of your uterus is each time, if your doctor doesn't tell you. If your babies are already born and you don't know your peak fundal height, ask your doctor—it's in your records. The doctor or an assistant usually measures the fundal height with a tape measure at each prenatal visit, especially if they know you are having a multiple birth. It is the distance from the top of your pubic bone (which is roughly where the bottom of the uterus sits), over your pregnant belly, to the highest point at which the doctor can feel a baby. Early in your pregnancy, that might be an inch or so above your navel. Later, it will probably be right up to your breastbone where your ribs meet in the middle. The doctor can chart the babies' growth (and the growth of the uterus) by measuring the fundal height.

The rule of thumb for fundal height is that it increases about a centimeter a week after four to six weeks of pregnancy, until the due date at forty weeks. So most women carrying one baby will have a peak fundal height of thrity-six to thirty-eight centimeters. (The fundal height drops slightly, particularly for first-time moms, when the baby drops lower in her pelvis during the last weeks of pregnancy.) If you know that you peaked out at forty-eight to fifty centimeters or more with your twin pregnancy, you might be able to be a bit more tolerant of your uterus taking more than the standard six weeks to return to it's prepregnant size—about the same size as your clenched fist.

Your skin: Considering the size to which your uterus and the abdominal skin that covers it must stretch to accommodate two or more babies, it's not surprising that many—but not all—mothers of multiples are left with plenty of stretch marks. They are usually the result of tears that develop just under the skin surface as the skin expands, and they usually look red or brownish. During the healing process, these tears form scar tissue and appear as stretch marks when the skin shrinks back. Then they often look silvery, white, or bluish. In some cases, the tearing can continue into the muscles below the skin, causing the lower abdomen to pouch out. This kind of pouching cannot be corrected by exercise because it's not possible to rebuild damaged muscle simply by doing situps.

While no one knows exactly why some people get stretch marks and others don't, the best guesses have it that stretch marks have more to do with heredity (did your mother have them?), how quickly your uterus grew, and how large you finally became than with how many times a day you rubbed your pregnant belly with vitamin E cream. Vitamin E may contribute to skin elasticity, and some mothers believe including extra doses of it in their prenatal supplements or using creams enriched with vitamin E during their pregnancy helps prevent stretch marks and may help heal them later. When skin is stretching while you are still pregnant, and you feel dry, itchy, and even numb because of that, creams certainly feel good, but there is no conclusive evidence that shows any of them (or anything else) can absolutely prevent stretch marks.

Since the easiest and cheapest way to make stretch marks less noticeable is to wait for time to fade them, the best thing for you to do while you wait is to concentrate on something you *can* actively change —like the overall shape and feeling of your body through healthy eating and gentle exercise.

Another skin change a mother of multiples is more likely to see is the extra skin she may be left with that hangs around her middle. The lengths to which your body has gone to shelter these babies before their birth may produce skin that just can't snap back to cover your frame as snugly as it once did. Some mothers actually have handfuls of loose abdominal skin, and some have crinkly "seersucker" skin. Others find loose or crinkly skin on their thighs and ankles too, usually noticing it soon after their birth, as all that extra fluid that produced perpetually swollen ankles makes its exit.

Time is the great healer here too. Some mothers of twins believe it has taken their skin longer—sometimes years instead of months—to become smooth again. Some say it never looks like it did before their multiple pregnancy. Others believe exercise and losing their pregnancy weight helped their skin regain its elasticity.

There is some consolation in all of these skin changes. And that is that you don't have to show these parts of your body in public. Some mothers are dismayed at the changes at first, then time fades some of the stretch marks and smooths out the seersucker tummy a bit, and eventually, time also fades the urgency of wearing a midriff-baring swimsuit.

Cosmetic Surgery as an Alternative

For other women, the loss of their prepregnant bodies remains an issue. For a woman with handfuls of excess flesh around her middle, it may be worth it to seek out a plastic surgeon who will help make the changes she wants to see in her body. Cosmetic surgery techniques change all the time, but some of the standard ones are:

Tummy tuck or abdominoplasty. Excess skin and fat are removed from the abdomen through a horizontal incision made low across the abdomen, usually starting at one hip, going across the upper level of the pubic hair and ending at the other hip. At the same time, stretch marks of the lower abdomen are removed (because they are on the excess skin), and if there was damage to underlying muscles that created a pouchiness in the lower abdomen, that can be corrected. If you have a vertical cesarean scar, this might be removed too.

Abdominoplasty typically is performed in a hospital under general anesthesia, with a day or two of bed rest recommended after surgery. An abdominal support garment is often worn for two or three months, and normal activities—including strenuous exercise—can usually be resumed after about six weeks, depending on how fast you heal and how you feel. Surgical fees range from fifteen hundred dollars to five thousand or more, depending on length and complexity of the operation. Additional expenses will depend upon where surgery takes place and the anesthesia used. As with all cosmetic surgery, most insurance companies will not cover any of the costs if the surgery is elective. But they may cover all or part of the costs if medically necessary repair is connected with the surgery, like reconnecting torn muscle tissue or repairing a herniated navel. You may also be able to deduct the costs as a medical expense on your income tax return.

Any surgery poses certain risks. Those associated with abdominoplasty are:

• Infection and blood clots. Can occur after surgery, and are treatable with medication.

• Poor healing, resulting in conspicuous scars. May necessitate a second operation to reduce scarring.

- Heavy smokers should be aware that nicotine can delay healing.
- Use of general anesthesia always includes certain risks.

Breast repair. Stretch marks on breasts form in the same way they do on abdomens—by tissue tearing under the surface instead of stretching as you grow. As with abdominal stretch marks, these do fade somewhat with time, but if you want to do more than wait for them to fade, and if you have loose skin on your breasts, surgery can be the answer. Silicone breast implants (*not* injections) can fill the loose skin, getting rid of the wrinkling, and pulling the stretch marks tighter too. The stretch marks will still be there, but since they are taut and flatter, they may be less visible. This operation also produces larger breasts, which may be a consideration for you.

Breast surgery offers just about any other change you may wish to make—uplifting, reducing, enlarging, or simply changing the shape. Be sure if you do opt for any of these that include enlarging your breasts that your surgeon uses silicone implants (a small bag of silicone—a chemically inert, nontoxic kind of rubber—filled with either silicone gel, saline solution, or a combination of the two). Silicon injections—injecting silicone directly into the breast—are not sanctioned by the Food and Drug Administration so medical-grade silicone is not available to surgeons, while researchers test its use further. The only silicone available to most surgeons is lower commercial grade that can cause breast destruction and infection. In addition, when silicone is injected directly into the breast, the body reacts by forming hard lumps. These are benign, but they are indistinguishable from lumps that are malignant, and that may mean that breast cancer can go undetected in a woman who had silicone injections.

The only way to remove injected silicone is by a mastectomy, which removes all breast tissue except the skin and nipple. Silicone implants can be used to restore the breast.

Breast surgery that uses implants is usually performed under general anesthesia, and can be done in the surgeon's office, in an outpatient surgical facility, or in a hospital, depending on the details of your case. In some cases, a local anesthetic along with a sedative are used instead of general anesthesia. During the surgery, an incision is made either in the lower part of the breast, just under the nipple, or in the armpit. From the incision, the surgeon lifts the breast tissue up and pulls the chest skin down to create a pocket either just under the breast tissue or under the chest wall muscle. The implant goes into the pocket.

If you were admitted to the hospital for the surgery, you will probably stay a couple of days. Surgical dressings are usually replaced by a supportive surgical bra in a few days, and sutures are removed within a week of surgery. There is usually some discoloration and swelling at first. Scars from the surgery often fade and most surgeons attempt to place them as inconspicuously as possible. After surgery, you should avoid strenuous activity and overhead lifting for several weeks.

Surgery for reducing the size of breasts or uplifting sagging breasts also usually involves general anesthesia and a short hospital stay, although some uplift surgeries can be done in a surgeon's office or outpatient surgical facility under local anesthesia. Both procedures use incisions on the lower part of the breast and around the nipple through which fat and excess tissue are removed and the nipple is repositioned on the new breast shape. Scars in both cases remain highly visible for up to a year after surgery, but are placed so they cannot be seen in low-cut clothing or bathing suits. Surgical fees for operations like enlarging, reducing, or uplifting range from one thousand to five thousand dollars. Additional expenses vary with the type of anesthesia used and where the surgery is performed.

Risks associated with these kinds of breast surgery are:

• Implants that leak silicone gel. They must be removed and replaced.

• Implants that move slightly and make the breasts appear asymmetrical.

• Implants that harden. Some hardening during the first few weeks and sometimes months after surgery is normal, and self-massage can help alleviate it. But some implants remain hard, and removal and replacement with a new implant is the only way to restore softness.

• Infection and localized collection of blood. Both are treatable with medication.

• Loss of nipple sensitivity. The loss is greatest right after the surgery, and some sensitivity may return eventually. With surgery to reduce or uplift the breasts, there is some loss of feeling to both the nipple and the breast skin, which improves with time.

• Asymmetry of the breasts. May result from a difference in the healing process on each side.

• Scars may prove unacceptable. The only solution is further surgery to remove scar tissue.

• Scar tissue within the breast, called capsular contracture, may cause breasts to become too firm. Self-massage done twice a day during the first year after surgery can help avoid formation of scar tissue. Further surgery to remove this scar tissue can soften breasts.

• Implants can make interpretation of mammograms to detect breast cancer difficult.

• Implants can produce sagging breasts and become prominent if you breastfeed after implantation.

• Use of general anesthesia always involves certain risks.

For any of these surgical solutions you should:

• Realize that board-certified plastic surgeons; general surgeons; ear, nose, and throat specialists; dermatologists; and thoracic (chest) surgeons all do cosmetic procedures to some degree. To find a doctor experienced in the kind of operation you want, you can contact the American Society of Plastic and Reconstructive Surgeons (233 N. Michigan Ave., Suite 1900, Chicago, Illinois 60601) for the names of board-certified plastic surgeons in your area. Your county medical society or your family physician may also be able to refer you to someone.

• Shop around for the doctor who is best for you. You need to find the doctor who has performed the most surgeries like the one you want. There is no better teacher than experience. For example, a surgeon skilled in abdominoplasty may know how to hide the long scar from the surgery better than someone who is more used to altering the shape of people's noses. Try to find former patients of doctors you are considering and talk to them.

• Check with your insurance company to be sure under which conditions they will and will not pay all, part, or any of the bill. Most will not pay any costs unless the surgery is medically necessary.

• Listen carefully to what the surgeon you choose says about the projected outcome of the surgery. Cosmetic surgery can accomplish a lot, but it's not magic. Be realistic about what you expect, the risks involved, and the differences this surgery will—and will not—make in your life.

• Before you opt for surgery, be certain you are through having babies, and that you have achieved the weight you can live with for the rest of your life. These kinds of surgery can solve some body problems, but if you get pregnant again or if you significantly change your body shape by gaining or losing a large amount of weight, you may find the good results of the surgery have disappeared. If you got stretch marks once, you can certainly get them again.

• Consider carefully your reasons for opting for surgery in the first place. Sometimes a life-style change (healthy eating and more exercise) can take care of body problems. But body changes won't necessarily take care of life-style problems—like a sagging marriage or low self-esteem. Talk it over with a close friend or even a professional therapist or counselor, and give yourself lots of time to make a decision.

Besides changes in body size, your abdomen, and your skin that tend to be greater for mothers of multiples and take longer to right themselves, you may also see other changes mothers of single babies see after pregnancy. Those things, like hair loss or subtle changes in shape or size of bone structure (slightly wider hips, somewhat larger feet for some people), don't seem to be much different for mothers of twins.

LET EXERCISE SHAPE YOUR BODY AND YOUR LIFE

While you are learning to cope with so many changes after the birth of twins, you might want to be extra sure that you include exercise in your plan for taking care of yourself. And if your twins are far from being newborns, it's not too late to start either, if you haven't already. In fact, you might want to make exercise the basis for your whole self-care plan. A 1986 Gallup survey conducted in conjunction with *American Health* magazine showed that people who exercise were more likely to change their diets and improve their health habits. A commitment to exercise wasn't just a benefit in itself, but an impetus to make changes in other aspects of a person's life.

If you're already thinking that you hate running and you'll never be able to make the time for three or four thirty-minute workouts a week, and the nearest aerobics class doesn't offer baby-sitting, stop and consider these ideas:

• Shorter workouts adding up to the thirty-minute/three times a week minimum may be better for you if you're not in great shape already. For example, if you entertain your babies by energetically dancing to the music on the radio for ten-minute bursts, three times in a day, you've done a thirty-minute workout. As your body—and your mind—adjust to the activity, you may be willing after a few months to tackle a more formal sort of exercise.

• Workouts don't have to be work. In fact, they should be play or at least fun. If you don't like jogging, don't do it. If you do it even though you hate it, you'll never develop the commitment it takes to keep it up anyway. Find something you like. Many women swim instead. Some aerobics centers do offer baby-sitting along with alternatives to hard-hitting aerobics like low-impact, muscle-shaping, or postpartum classes. Consider riding a bicycle, playing touch football, or playing soccer with your older children. Find a partner and play tennis at a facility where baby-sitting is offered. (Try a city recreation center, or trade baby-sitting with other mothers for workout time. You'll all get going on your exercise program then, and you can compare notes and provide support and encouragement for each other.) Join a city-sponsored softball, volleyball, or bowling league.

• Do what you can; don't dwell on what isn't possible for you. With the beginning of a very real fitness boom in the U.S. during the 1970s and 1980s, the emphasis has often been on sports like running, tennis, and aerobics. But it you don't want to run because it's boring, and you don't want to play tennis because chasing after a little ball is too trivial, and you don't want to do aerobics because you'd rather die than be seen in a leotard jumping around to rock music—don't give up. There is always another option.

Walk

Walking for fitness is becoming one of the more popular options for many people who want to exercise but shy away from organized classes and find jogging too jarring. Walking as workout—known as striding—is more than the kind of strolling you do with the children in the evening, but less than the athletic racewalking you see on "Wide World of Sports." With striding (as in strolling and racewalking), one foot is always on the ground so the maximum impact per step is about half that of running. In fact, racewalking has the lowerst injury rate of any sport.

Racewalking also burns more calories per hour than jogging—530 for racewalkers compared to 480 for joggers. That's at least partly because of the torso motion required when you are keeping one foot on the ground instead of leaping from foot to foot. And whether you are moving fast enough to become a racewalker, or simply getting a good workout as a strider, you also get the plus of tightening your abdominal muscles as you walk. This type of walking specifically reaches stomach muscles that other types of exercise—like jogging—miss. Striding also offers the same type of cardiovascular fitness that any aerobic sport does, because you can get your heart rate high enough to condition that system.

If you think striding might be your kind of workout, the Walkers Club of America can tell you where to learn about the techniques and meet other walkers in your area. They are at 445 E. 86th St., New York, New York 10128. Or check at your local recreation center or health club for walking or striding clinics that teach the simple technique. Some companies that make sports shoes (like Reebok and Nike) sponsor clinics around the country in striding too, and advertise them in local newspapers ahead of time.

Swim

This is an option many women favor, because it can be a gentler approach to fitness, and because swimming laps doesn't require you to show up on time for a class. You might like to know that if you are trying for cardiovascular fitness through swimming, you don't have to reach a heart rate as high as you would if you were jogging, in order to get the same effect. One reason is that the horizontal position of swimming means that since your heart doesn't have to pump the blood uphill as it does when you are vertical, it doesn't have to beat as many times to move as much blood. And your heart's ability to move blood around is what fitness is about, not just the number of times it beats. Another reason your heart rate won't be as high when you swim is that, although no one knows why, your heart slows down in cold water, even if you only splash your face with it.

Experts have found that with swimming too, shorter but more frequent workouts are better than long, infrequent ones. That's what Dr. David Costill, director of the Human Performance Lab at Ball State University, found when he had the swim team do shorter but daily training. The team members set better records and recovered energy faster. So you don't need to knock yourself out each time you swim to be getting a good workout. You just need to be consistent.

Ride a Bike

Here's another one you can do on your own, or you can form an informal group and ride together. Generally speaking you have to ride more miles on a bicycle to get the same conditioning you would if you were jogging or walking. For example, during one week, nine miles of running gives you the same conditioning results as twelve miles of walking, or nine hundred yards of swimming, or twenty-four miles of cycling. But the good news is, as with the other activities listed here, harder is not necessarily better. One orthopedic surgeon said the best cycling workouts result from using a lower, easier gear in which you will pedal more revolutions per minute, instead of straining in a higher, slower gear.

Jump Rope

You probably did it when you were a child, so you know how. Just get a piece of rope (regular clothesline rope will do, although sporting-goods stores have special jump ropes too) that's long enough to reach your armpits when you step on it and pull it taut. Then jump. You can do it indoors if the weather is bad—even in the kitchen if the ceiling is high enough—or outdoors when it's nice. Start out by jumping only long enough to become out of breath, then walk around a bit until your breathing is normal. Then jump again. You might count your jumps and try increasing them from day to day. After a few weeks of this, you'll probably see a real difference in how long it takes you to get out of breath—that's conditioning. If you get a jump rope at a sporting-goods store, it often comes with an instruction book that can give you details on workout programs centered on jumping rope.

Some seasonal workouts you might try are hiking or skiing. Working in the garden is another. Energetically digging weeds burns more calories per minute (5.75 calories per minute for a person weighing 127–137 pounds) than does an equal amount of time spent doing calisthenics (4.50 calories per minute for a person of the same weight). It doesn't matter what you do, so long as you like it and so long as it gets you moving.

These are just a few of many options you have to begin exercising on your own. No matter which you choose (except swimming), be sure you have two vital pieces of equipment—a good, supportive exercise bra and the correct shoes. The bra will make you more comfortable, particularly if you are still nursing, and the shoes will help avoid foot and leg injuries. They are both worth the investment.

When *American Health* magazine and Gallup researchers asked committed exercisers what kept them on their exercise programs once they got started, they said there were five keys to their success:

1. *They made their exercise goals realistic.* Don't think you're going to swim twenty or thirty laps a day when you haven't worked out since before your babies were born. Just making a commitment to be at the pool for a certain number of days a week may be enough for you to begin with. Build the time you spend on your activity slowly. It's the time you spend doing the activity that's more important for fitness than the intensity with which you do it.

2. *They found the right time to exercise.* For some people, morning is the perfect high-energy time to work out. But for mothers with small children, it may be the busiest time of day, and they will have to look elsewhere for a good workout time. Others find that working out at high-stress times of the day is best. For mothers, that may be late afternoon. You could trade baby-sitting with another harried mother and take turns working out.

3. *They varied their exercise routines.* Just because you like walking for exercise doesn't mean you can't swim sometimes too. You'll avoid boredom that may come with the routine, and you'll balance your body development as well.

4. *They kept track of their progress.* You don't have to keep a whole diary, but it will help you to jot down on a calendar how long you exercised, what you did, and a word or two about how you felt. You'll be pleased and maybe amazed after a few months at how hard your workouts may have felt at the beginning, and how much stronger you became.

5. *They kept it fun.* By keeping their focus on how pleasant it is to jog around the neighborhood alone, or how good the breeze feels when they're on their bicycles, committed exercisers find it easier to continue. Focusing on a "No pain, no gain" philosophy is a sure way to drop out, as is boring repetition.

No matter what kind of exercise you choose, you are bound to reap benefits that are not only physical, but mental and emotional as well. The principles of biofeedback have shown that the three are closely linked—change one, and you always affect the others. Biofeedback researchers know that you can learn to control your physiological state through your mind and emotions. And researchers who study stress know that the reverse happens when you exercise consistently. For example, experts who study stress and the immune system at Loma

Linda University Medical Center in California have seen that consistent exercise stimulates the pituitary gland in the brain to produce endorphins, a natural traquilizer that helps the body deal with physical and psychological stress. Regular exercise not only tunes up your body, but your endorphin-release system, too. The more you use it, the better it works.

People who exercise regularly also report that they feel less tired. If your babies are small, fatigue may be part of the picture until they have somewhat regular sleep patterns. But when your sleep/wake routine is relatively civilized, and you are able to fit in a regular schedule of working out, you may find, as many regular exercisers do, that the workouts add energy rather than subtract it.

Perhaps the biggest plus of all to making time for exercise in your life is that it is one way you can regain some control over what you do and how you feel. Psychologists know that a feeling of control over your fate makes a difference in your overall well-being as well as in your heath and your resistance to stress. And the *American Health*/Gallup survey showed that people who exercised regularly tended not only to feel in control of their health, but to feel better about themselves in general. They felt that taking charge of their health by exercising produced that sense of well-being more directly than any other aspect of their lives—including their salaries.

FOOD AS FUEL

Food is many things to each of us, but you may find yourself feeling best when you treat food as what it is in its most basic sense—fuel. In fact, as a mother of multiples who may have other children too, what you eat and what you don't eat have everything to do with how much energy you have, how much patience you have, and with how resistant you are to depression and illness. Instead of grabbing the crust left from someone's peanut-butter-and-jelly sandwich and calling it lunch, you could be devising your own best plan for getting the equivalent of high-test fuel into your body. That doesn't mean that you have to plan and cook elaborate meals for yourself. And it doesn't necessarily mean that you must keep extra, unwanted pounds around, just because you are eating a healthy diet.

What it does mean is that you need to understand which foods will give you the most nutrients and energy for the least number of calories. Luckily, nature has arranged things pretty well for you—the most nutrient-dense foods are usually not the most calorie-dense. Devising your own high-energy diet also means understanding which vitamins and minerals have been targeted by nutritionists as having the most effect on things that may be important to you, like having enough energy to get through the day and being even-tempered with your children.

Of course the cardinal rule for good nutrition is to eat a variety of foods from those four food groups you learned about back in eighth-grade home economics classes. But some nutrition experts have narrowed it down a bit, by listing what they consider to be nutritional superfoods. For example, health writer Jean Carper bases her list on the United States Department of Agriculture analysis of nutrients in over twenty-five hundred foods. Here are the foods she considers the best nutritional bargains—the most nutrients for the least calories:

almonds	apricots (dried)	beans (dried)
broccoli	cabbage	cantaloupe
carrots	collard greens	liver
milk (skim)	oat cereals	olive oil
oysters	potatoes (esp. sweet)	salmon
sunflower seeds	tofu	tuna
yogurt (nonfat)	wheat bran and wheat germ	

Probably no one eats *all* of those, but you may be able to find several foods you like from this list that you can include in your diet. Betty Kamen, who specializes in nutrition education, offers another, slightly more general list, of what she considers to be the top ten foods for best nutrition:

—fresh vegetables, including leafy greens
—whole grains
—liver and other organ meats
—fertile eggs
—deep ocean fish or fish with high fat content (cod, salmon, snapper, mackerel)
—nuts and seeds (especially sprouted)
—legumes (peas, beans, and lentils, especially sprouted)
—brewer's yeast
—fruit
—fermented dairy products (yogurt, kefir, etc.)

It's easy to see similarities between the two lists. They both emphasize fresh, whole foods (no potato chips or cookies on either list), and they both offer a wide range of choices. What they also offer are foods rich in nutrients that have been associated with increased stamina and their abilities to combat the effects of stress. While you're eating a well-balanced diet, you also might want to be especially sure you are getting enough of those super stress- and fatigue-fighting nutrients: iron, folic acid, vitamin C, vitamin E, and all the B vitamins.

If you've already had your multiples, you probably know about the contribution iron can make to your energy level. Many mothers of multiples require an iron supplement during pregnancy, and if your twins are newborns, you might consider continuing your iron supplement. If you're not taking an iron supplement, you might want to consider eating liver regularly. One 3½-ounce serving of calf's liver gives you 14 milligrams of iron, and a nonpregnant woman needs 10–18 milligrams a day. If you want to start taking an iron supplement, your physician may have samples of various brands you can try, to find one that works best for you. Some brands may be constipating to some people and not to others.

Deficiencies in folic acid are associated with anemia and irritability. You might have taken extra folic acid during your pregnancy, because it is vital to the manufacture of genetic material and red blood cells. As a nonpregnant woman, you need 500 micrograms a day, and the best sources are dark green leafy vegetables like spinach (110 micrograms in ½ cup), and wheat bran (100 micrograms in ½ cup).

Besides helping increase your resistance to infection, vitamin C has also been called a stress-fighter. You can get the 50–60 milligrams you need each day by eating one orange. You can get half again that much by munching six or seven brussels sprouts.

The other high-energy nutrients, vitamin E and all the B vitamins, can also help fight stress while they help increase stamina. No one knows what effect a vitamin-E deficiency might have in humans, but B-vitamin deficiencies have been known to cause anxiety, depression, and mental confusion, among other things. Wheat germ is a good source of vitamin E and some of the B vitamins. Liver, several kinds of meat and fish, and many whole grains are also good sources of B vitamins. But perhaps one of the best and easiest ways to be sure you are getting a good supply of all the B vitamins is to use brewer's yeast, also known as nutritional yeast.

Any health-food store will have at least one brand of nutritional yeast. It comes in powder form and can be mixed with beverages or sprinkled on some foods. You might want to try different brands until you find one you like, because the taste does vary somewhat between brands.

One tried-and-true way to take nutritional yeast is in a milkshake devised by nutritionist Adelle Davis. In the thirty years since she first wrote about her Pep-Up milkshakes, thousands of mothers have sworn by Ms. Davis's concoction as a dependable pick-me-up during pregnancy, and as a sure cure for waning milk supplies during breastfeeding. In fact, mothers of children of any age find that even a small glass of

Ms. Davis's Pep-Up is made from milk fortified with non-fat dry milk, fruit, nutritional yeast, and mineral supplements like calcium and magnesium. You can find her recipe in her book, Let's Have Healthy Children. Or you can try this simplified version:

1 cup skim milk
1–2 tablespoons nutritional yeast
1 teaspoon vanilla
1 tablespoon undiluted frozen orange juice concentrate (or other fruit juice)

Mix in blender or shake in a jar.

Pep-Up in the afternoon makes that notorious time of day noticeably smoother.

Start with just ¼ cup of the milkshake sipped between meals or at meals, until you are used to the yeast. If you haven't had it before, or if you have been deficient in B vitamins, too much nutritional yeast at one time can cause intestinal gas. Some people don't like the taste of the yeast. Experiment until you find a fruit and a brand of yeast that taste good to you.

Many books on nutrition will have variations on this milkshake theme. Find the one that is the tastiest to you, and that provides the highest nutrition, and keep a bit mixed in the refrigerator. Sip it in an almost-quiet moment before the kids get home from school. Or substitute it for a doughnut and cup of coffee midmorning. Either way, you'll be doing yourself a favor.

Another, even quicker energy boost is to drink a big glass of carbonated water and eat a high-potassium fruit, like a banana, orange, raisins, cantaloupe, or strawberries. The carbonated beverage helps your body to absorb the potassium quicker, because the pressure created by the gas that forms the carbonation (bubbles) forces open the valve between the stomach and the small intestine, where food is absorbed into your body. Carbonated beverages get to where they can be absorbed quicker. (That's why some people get tipsy on champagne faster than they do on plain wine.) The fruit provides complex carbo-

hydrates that your body will covert to glucose to make your brain more alert and give your body more energy. If you don't have any of these fruits around, mix orange juice with the carbonated water.

BUT NOBODY'S PERFECT: TAKING THE BITE OUT OF BAD HABITS

Supplementing your diet with high-energy high-nutrient foods can have a positive effect on your energy level and your outlook. But most of us have some habits that can undermine even the best efforts at good nutrition. Any habit dies hard, and sometimes it's just too much to think of giving up caffeine, for example, when you feel you really depend on that morning cup to get started. Instead of adding stress to stress by changing habits now, you might consider trying to fill in the nutritional blanks some of your habits might create.

Caffeine. It seems to be all around us. Most people know there is caffeine in coffee, black teas, and cola drinks, but it's also found in chocolate (both eating and baking forms and cocoa) and many over-the-counter pain relievers and cold remedies. It's also in some diuretics and medications for menstrual discomforts, and in weight-loss drugs. And while that first cup of coffee (or chocolate bar) might produce the familiar surge of energy, the caffeine effect is gone in two hours. With it have gone plenty of B and C vitamins. Caffeine depletes potassium, calcium, zinc, magnesium, and vitamins A, B (especially B_6, B_1, and B_2), and C. It also reduces the iron you absorb from foods, which in turn produces fatigue. To combat the ultimate caffeine effect, eat foods high in those nutrients, or take a multivitamin that will cover your losses.

If you want to reduce your caffeine consumption, try mixing regular coffee with decaffeinated coffee and gradually increasing the decaf. Or try substituting one of the many flavors of herb tea on the market now.

Smoking. Vitamin deficiencies pale in the face of the real damage smoking can do (increased risks of heart disease, cancer, emphysema, and a host of other diseases for the smoker and those around her, including children). But if you choose to smoke, you might want to know that thirty-one cigarettes, the daily average for American smokers, destroys 775 milligrams of vitamin C in the smoker's body. For some people, that's enough to bring on a cold. Just one cigarette uses up a day's worth of vitamin C, or 60–80 milligrams. While smoking doesn't directly destroy B vitamins, extra B's might help counteract some of smoking's effects, like raised cholesterol and other blood fat levels, and skin wrinkling. You might also consider supplementing these vitamins for those who are around you when you smoke.

Sugar. If you're trying to devise a high-energy diet that will help keep your feelings on an even keel, sugar may be your biggest enemy. For example, it's that sugar-plus-caffeine coffee-and-doughnut break-fast or break that virtually all nutritionists now recognize can produce fatigue, nervousness, mental confusion, and indecisiveness in many people. The reason is, your body uses up a lot of vitamin B_1 (thiamine) as it metabolizes sugar. As more and more thiamine is used, more symptoms of its deficiency appear for many people—like intolerance of noise, inability to concentrate, irritability, depression, and memory de-fects. To combat the effects of sugar, don't eat it (or at least cut down), or increase your B vitamins. Sugar also interferes with protein use in your body, so you might want to increase that a little too. Some nutri-

	has/have a negative effect on
alcohol	*water-soluble vitamins, especially B_1, also magnesium, potassium, zinc
antacids	*water-soluble vitamins, calcium, iron, phosphorus
antibiotics	vitamins A, B, K, **inositol
aspirin	vitamins B, C, and K, folic acid
black tea	iron
caffeine	vitamins A, B, C, iron, potassium, calcium, zinc, magnesium
codeine	vitamin B_{12}
laxatives	calcium, potassium
marijuana	vitamin B_6
nicotine	vitamin C
oral contraceptives	vitamins B and C, copper, folic acid, iron, zinc
sedatives	folic acid
tetracycline	vitamin C, calcium, magnesium
thyroid hormones	vitamin E

* Water-soluble vitamins are B and C vitamins. They are not stored in the body and must be consumed daily. Fat-soluble vitamins are vitamins A, D, E, and K. They can be stored in the body and need not be consumed daily.

** Inositol is one of the B vitamins.

tionists suggest sugar should be no more than 5 percent of your daily calorie intake. For most Americans, sugar makes up 20 percent of our daily calorie total.

Nonprescription Drugs. These are just a few of the many available. If you must take them, be sure to make it up to your body to keep your energy level up.

How can you fit all of this into your already crowded life? Here are a few guidelines that may help.

1. Shop the perimeter of the grocery store more heavily than the interior. Most of the nonprocessed (and therefore higher nutrient) foods are around the outside of the store (like produce, for example).

2. Concentrate on whole grains, fresh vegetables, and fruits, fish, and poultry.

3. Stay away from prepared, processed, canned, and packaged foods. They often have lost nutrients in processing, and may have more sugar, salt, preservatives (known to be mood-altering in some people), and other additives that won't contribute to your health and energy.

4. Consider supplementing your diet with high-energy, high-health drinks like the Pep-Up milkshake, or with a multivitamin complex intended for people under stress (they usually have higher levels of iron, and B and C vitamins).

5. If you are going to eat sweets, make them yourself and cut the amount of sugar called for in the recipe. Add wheat germ to replace B vitamins.

> "My husband thought I'd really lost it when I told him I was using the breathing techniques I'd learned in our childbirth classes to help me get through the day with our two-year-old twins. It first happened almost by accident. I found myself taking deep breaths one day to control my temper, and that calm way of breathing I'd learned for labor just came back to me. Now I use it on purpose to head off problems."

LEARN TO RELAX

Just as you will never find time for yourself lying around waiting to be filled, you will also never find hours for personal relaxation, particularly when your multiples are very young. Leisure hours are a dim memory for most mothers of young twins. But with all that's going on in your life with these children (and possibly with your career, your friends, your husband), you *need* time to unwind. Where will it come from?

The answer is that you won't magically produce extra hours in the day, but you can learn to unwind in short "time-outs," whether you are at the office all day, or in the kitchen.

Besides the obvious feeling of calm that deep relaxation can bring, there are other benefits associated with learning to relax well. Researchers have found that people who learn to relax their minds and bodies can control physiological effects of stress, like tense muscles (you may be able to feel your neck muscles tensing just before a headache, for example) and raised blood pressure. Many people who have been taught relaxation techniques have been able to control effects of diabetes, heart disease, and asthma, and have increased the effectiveness of their own immune systems.

A quick survey of some relaxation methods in use today show that many of them concentrate on one of two techniques: controlled breathing, or relaxed breathing combined with focusing the mind.

Breathing. The most basic form of relaxation involves learning to wash away tension through deep breathing. The opposite of deep breathing is shallow breathing, and, carried to extremes, shallow breathing is hyperventilating. When you have just blown your top at your children, if you could stop and notice, you might see that your breathing is quick and shallow. A prolonged harangue might even produce hyperventilation. And hyperventilation can put you the rest of the way over the edge into tears. In fact, an actress once described to me in one word how she got herself to cry on stage: Hyperventilate.

In order to slow down the rush of emotions you may feel when you are tense or upset, slow down your breathing. You probably already know how to do that effectively if you attended childbirth education classes. The deep, slow abdominal breathing you learned then can help you through tough days now. When your twins are at each others' throats for the fifteenth time that day, maybe you are the one who needs the time out. Make sure they are safe, then leave the room, find a comfortable place to sit (preferably out of hearing of the squabbling), and practice your deep abdominal breathing for a minute or two. You might feel refreshed and calm enough to handle the situation without an explosion.

Here are some other breathing techniques that only take a few seconds each:

1. *The Quick Release* (Developed by Robert H. Phillips, Ph.D., director of the Center for Coping with Chronic Conditions, Garden City, New York):

- Get into a comfortable position and close your eyes.
- Inhale, and hold a single breath for approximately six seconds while tensing muscles.
- Exhale, and let your body go limp. Continue to breathe rhythmically for approximately twenty seconds.

- Repeat the six-second/twenty-second cycle two or more times.
- Continue the cycles for about one minute.

2. *The Quick Relax* (Developed by Antoinette Saunders, Ph.D., for her work with stressed children):

- Become aware that you are upset. Feel your fast heartbeat, headache, sweaty palms, etc.
- Smile inwardly and tell yourself that you can calm yourself down. Instead of feeling like a victim, you can help yourself know you can be in control.
- Breathe slowly and easily through imaginary holes in the bottoms of your feet. Feel cool air flowing up through these imaginary holes, through your legs, up into your stomach. Hold the air in for a few seconds, then push the "stressful air" down your body, down your legs, and out through the holes in your feet.
- Go in your mind to that place where you are fully relaxed and happy. Breathe normally and imagine your own special place. It could be your mother's lap, a pristine beach, or a favorite easy chair; it will be different for everyone. Picture how you look, what you are wearing, what you see around you, how the place smells, and how you feel inside. Conjure as many details as you can. Then relax and enjoy yourself there for a few seconds.
- Take a few deep, cleansing breaths as you come back to your present world, and stretch for a moment.

3. *Breathing for Mental and Emotional Balance.* Have you ever exhaled through your nose near a mirror or a window? Did you notice the pools of condensation from your two nostrils were different sizes? That's because while we see with both eyes, and hear with both ears, we each breathe primarily through one nostril at a time in cycles lasting from one to three hours. Some researchers believe there is a relationship between the nasal cycle and which side of the brain is dominant at the moment—the intuitive right or the analytical left side. Some also believe that this breathing exercise can balance these two sides, producing a relaxed, calm, and broad mental view. They also believe you shouldn't do this if you are an epileptic, or when you are driving a car or under the influence of drugs or alcohol.

- Sit with your spine straight, close your eyes and focus them on the point where your nose and eyebrows meet.
- Use your right thumb to cover the end of your right nostril, rest your left hand in your lap, and inhale *slowly* through your left nostril.

"I'd always been suspicious about meditation as a cure-all. But since I've learned how to use this relaxation technique through an adult education class at our community hospital, I've found it's not weird at all. It's just a great way to for me to relax without taking up a lot of time or having to find a baby-sitter."

- Remove your thumb, place your right little finger over the end of your left nostril, and exhale *slowly* through your right nostril.
- Then inhale through right and exhale through the left.
- Repeat this alternating pattern. Do not hold your breath in once you've inhaled; begin to exhale immediately. Also, when you're done exhaling, inhale immediately.
- The more powerful the breath, the more powerful the effect, so start moderately at first. Continue for a maximum of ten minutes, less at first.

Breathing and Mind Focus. One of the first people to popularize this technique was Dr. Herbert Benson in his book *The Relaxation Response,* published in 1975. There are many variations on this technique, but the basic principles remain the same: To achieve deep relaxation you breathe normally following your natural rhythm, and focus your attention on a specific word, sound, or phrase.

1. *Mind-Focus Relaxation.*

- Get into a comfortable sitting position in a quiet room. Close your eyes.
- Become aware of your breathing.
- Focus on a word, sound, or phrase that means something to you. You could say the word *relax,* or repeat a phrase that fits with your religious beliefs like *peace, shalom,* or *Jesus.* Then with each exhale, mentally repeat that word.
- Let thoughts or mental images that come up float easily into your mind and out again. It's normal for these to appear—just don't let your mind grab on to them, or feel that you must push them out of your mind. Just let them wander through and observe them as they go by. Keep breathing calmly and regularly, repeating your word focus.
- Allow yourself to relax in this calm place for several minutes.
- When you are ready to finish, take a few deep cleansing breaths, stretch, and slowly open your eyes.

Benson notes that his technique can take on new meaning if you do use, as a focus, a phrase or word associated with your faith or your belief in a higher power. He also suggests using the technique when you exercise, with the rhythm of your breathing as you jog, for example, as your focus.

2. *Progressive Relaxation.* This is similar to the relaxation response technique, but it adds muscle relaxation.

- Go to a quiet room and get into a comfortable sitting position, feet flat on the floor, eyes closed.

- Become aware of your breathing.
- Take in a few deep breaths. As you let them out, mentally say the word *relax,* or use a focus word or phrase meaningful to you.
- Concentrate on your face and feel any tension in your face and eyes. Make a mental picture of what this tension looks like to you. Then mentally picture it relaxing and becoming comfortable.
- Feel a wave of relaxation spreading through your body as you feel your face and eyes relax.
- Tense your eyes and face, squeezing tightly, then relax them, and feel the relaxation spreading throughout your body.
- Use this method for each part of your body—jaw, neck, shoulders, back, upper and lower arms, hands, chest, abdomen, thighs, calves, ankles, feet, toes.
- When you have relaxed each part of your body, rest quietly in this state for two to five minutes.
- Let the muscles in your eyelids lighten up, become ready to open your eyes, and become aware of the room.
- Then let your eyes be open. Take a few deep cleansing breaths, stretch, and you are ready to resume your other activities.

RECHARGE IN WAYS YOU MIGHT NOT HAVE CONSIDERED

If you sat down and counted them up, there are probably more ways than you have fingers and toes that you can recharge your spirit and your body. You can do things like indulge in a bubble bath, take a nap, read a favorite book. The list can be a long one, and it will be different for everyone. But most of those favors we can do ourselves take time —a precious and scarce commodity for many mothers of multiples. If you have the time or can make the time, terrific—indulge. But if you don't have the time and can't rearrange one more minute's worth of activities in your day to make it, you can still recharge. You might want to try one of these ways:

1. *Music:* There's a whole new way of thinking about music and its value that goes far beyond entertainment. For example, soothing music is being used in some hospitals to replace some sedatives and calm patients before and during surgery under regional anesthesia. Anesthetists and a music therapist in one study found that soothing music reduces heart rate and blood pressure. They also found the need for sedatives to help patients remain calm was reduced by half, a figure

also found by research in a second study done in another country. One nurse anesthetist in the first study even said that soothing music is equal to about 2½ milligrams of Valium. That study used classical selections and popular music from the forties and fifties—all with an emphasis on even tempos and rhythms.

While you may not be contemplating surgery, you might think about how sound—music and background noise—in your home can promote a calm atmosphere rather than a frantic one. Composer and recording artist Steven Halpern, author of *Sound Health: The Music and Sounds That Make Us Whole,* suggests first that you do an inventory of the sounds you commonly hear at home. That background noise, like the refrigerator motor, dishwasher, washing machine, a constantly running radio or television, can be stress producing. Even though you may not be conscious of it, Halpern believes that constant, even low-level, sound can bombard your senses, making some people feel the way they do after listening to an hour or so of children fighting. He suggests you control the background noise that you can—when you buy appliances look for quieter-running models (some are advertised as "silent partners" these days); place sound-absorbent material (thick carpet, rubber, or soundboard) under and around noisemakers like dishwashers, refrigerators, blenders, and typewriters; and try lowering the volume of the television, radio, and stereo.

For a musical lift, listen to what Halpern calls "anti-frantic" relaxation music. Some suggestions: Try classical selections. Listen to them at a record or tape store with facilities to sample the sounds if you don't know what you like. Find something that appeals to you. The slow movements of the pieces might be best (the "largo" or "adagio" sections). Or try "new age" music. It's designed to assist the listener in attaining a peaceful, relaxed state of being, with rhythms that are gentle or barely present. You can sample these, too, at record stores and some health-food stores. You might try *Starborn,* by Steve Halpern (Halpern Sounds label), or *Autumn* by George Winston (Windham Hill).

If you can reduce bothersome background noise, and use "anti-frantic" music, you might be rewarded with calmer babies and children too.

2. *Visual Imagery.* This is a natural extension of the relaxation techniques using mind focus. If those techniques seem to work well for you, you might want to go a step further and use a special kind of visual imagery developed by Dr. Carl Simonton and Stephanie Matthews-Simonton for their work with cancer patients. It's part of a program of positive visual imagery that helps people see their bodies as strong and capable. The Simontons call the process "finding your inner guide to

health," but they describe the inner guide as simply the "intuitive, wise, responsive part of your personality with which you are generally out of touch." They believe if you can develop a strong relationship with your inner guide (the symbol you choose for your deepest self), you can receive an extraordinary amount of information and advice about your feelings, motivations, and behavior. Here are the steps they offer to finding your inner guide:

- Sit in a comfortable chair, feet flat on the floor, and use the progressive relaxation process on page 172 to become very relaxed.
- In your mind's eye, see yourself in a natural setting that gives you a feeling of warmth, comfort, peace, and serenity. Select a spot from your memory or your fantasies. Concentrate on the details of the scene. Try to experience it with all your senses— as if you were really there.
- Notice a path emerging near you that winds toward the horizon. Sense yourself walking along this path. It is pleasant and light. Notice that in the distance there is a radiant blue-white glow that is moving slowly toward you. There is nothing threatening about the experience.
- As the glow comes closer, you realize it is a living creature— a person (whom you do not know) or a friendly animal.
- As the person or creature comes closer, be aware of the details of its appearance. Is the creature masculine or feminine? See its shape and form as clearly as you can. If your guide is a person, notice details of face, hair, eyes, bone structure, build.
- If this person or creature makes you feel warm, comfortable, and safe, you know it is an Inner Guide.
- Ask the guide's name, and then ask for help with your problems.
- Engage the person or creature in a conversation, get acquainted, discuss your problems as you would with a very close friend.
- Pay careful attention to any information you receive from your guide. It may come in the form of conversation or through symbolic gestures, such as the guide's pointing toward something or producing an object that represents its advice.
- Establish an agreement with your guide about how to make contact for future discussions.
- Then when you are ready, let your consciousness come back slowly into the room where you are sitting and open your eyes.
- Take a few deep breaths and stretch for a moment.

3. *Write a Journal.* Although this will take a little time, it doesn't have to mean rearranging your schedule. Sociologists and psychologists have long recognized how important it is for all of us that we tell our stories. One of the frustrations of motherhood, for many women, is that they often feel they listen to everyone else, and no one listens to them. If you have someone who really listens to you, you may know how therapeutic it is to pour out all your feelings to a trusted friend. With journal writing, you can still pour out all your feelings, and you don't need a willing ear.

Besides the feeling of relief you may get from expressing what you feel, some researchers have found that people who bare all to their journals have better immune functions. The study, reported at the American Psychological Association meeting in Washington, D.C., in 1986, found that journal writers also made fewer doctor visits and enjoyed better overall health.

All you need to get started is something to write in like a spiral notebook, and a pen; and a few moments after you put the children to bed. Some adult education programs offer courses in journal writing, and many libraries have books with suggested writing exercises and questions to prime your thoughts. But if you don't feel you need those, just write about what happened to you that day and how you feel about it. Try to stay away from a grocery list of daily events, unless listing all that happened acts as a lead-in for you to more fertile ground. The real value of journal writing comes not in producing a simple record, but in providing an outlet for feelings you might not express to anyone else.

4. *Smell Therapy.* You don't need researchers to tell you that different smells produce different effects in people. That's the whole principle behind that expensive perfume you buy (or wish you could). But what we know about smell is being carried into the medical field now, and certain scents (plum and peach) are being used to help alleviate pain. Researchers at Yale University have found that the smell of spiced apple lowers blood pressure in some people. You might consider visiting a gourmet foods store or gift shop where they have herb and flower-petal potpourris that can be simmered in water on the stove. The concoctions release the scent to spread throughout your house. It might provide a relaxing lift some afternoon.

THE BOTTOM LINE

There probably isn't anyone who has the luxury of taking really good care of herself *all* the time. And maybe all the suggestions in his chapter look like more work than reward. You don't have to make a project out of taking care of yourself. Pick and choose some—or even one—of these ideas and use it as it fits your life and your needs.

Still, there will be plenty of days when you just can't squeeze in *any* self-care, despite your best efforts. On those days, instead of lying in bed at the end of the day berating yourself for what you *didn't* do that day (for yourself or someone else), try to feel grateful to yourself that you made it through. Spend a moment appreciating how hard you work, and with what heart you try. Thank yourself for being who you are. The peace and acceptance that can come with that might help you to wake up with a smile tomorrow.

6 | Feeling the Changes: Fathers and Families

"I'm not sure exactly what I thought being a father of twins would be like, but I never thought it would be like this."

KEEPING EXPECTATIONS IN PERSPECTIVE

It is virtually impossible for any expectant parent to accurately predict what it will be like when the baby arrives. And when that baby turns out to be two or three babies, predictions may be that much further removed from reality. You might be able to keep your expectations in perspective if you can minimize them—realize you can't anticipate what life as a parent of multiples will be like, good or bad—and, if you can, see the expectations you do have as just that—things you *think* may happen, but not rules for behavior cast in concrete.

Many parents are aware of the kinds of expectations other people have of their multiples. I once heard an eight-year-old telling my identical girls that when one cut her knee the other would feel it because they were twins. Parents hear school principals tell them their twins would never do well in class together because twin relationships are always a problem. Mothers pregnant with multiples have often told me they hoped that at least they wouldn't have identical twins because identicals have so much trouble figuring out who they are.

What all those expectations and beliefs about twins have in common is that they are seldom true, and often irritating. Feeling each other's pain is a phenomenon that happens to some people, but there is no research that shows it happens with any more frequency to twins than to anyone else. Some siblings would indeed have a difficult time being in the same classroom, but it doesn't necessarily have anything to do with twinship. And mothers who have lived with identical twins can attest that their children know perfectly well who they are—it's everyone else's doubt about it that sometimes causes problems.

And so it is with parents of multiples. It seems the world has expectations of them, too, that have little root in fact. The parent myth is this: People outside of the family tend to see parents of multiples—mothers and fathers both—as Superparents. If those people are parents themselves, maybe it's because they know how hard it is sometimes for them with one child. But they often believe that these parents are able to quiet small babies with a single word; they are more adept, more energetic, and more efficient than other parents, simply because they have more children. For some parents, these beliefs or expectations are a plus.

But for others they are not. According to one study, those kinds of expectations were seen by many parents as robbing them of their individual identities. (Which is, incidentally, an interesting way for parents of multiples to get a little firsthand information about how their twins or triplets might feel when they are treated like oddities.)

Parents in that study reported that other adults treated them as "special" or "odd." Many added that at parties and other social occasions they were introduced as the "parents of twins," and in conversation that followed an introduction like that, people made vast assumptions about how tolerant and noble the parents of twins were. While all that respect and admiration can bolster a father's or mother's sagging attitude, some parents reported they felt pressured to live up to those expectations and become the Superparents who were always in control of themselves and their children—something they also felt was impossible. Some even found themselves not wanting to reveal what life was really like for them, or how they felt they were at their wits' end sometimes, because they would burst the bubble of belief others held about them.

Whether you are a father or a mother of multiples, it might be good to keep in mind that others may place you in a special category just as they may place your children in a special category. Having a positive attitude about your position as a father of multiples can be a big help to you, but there is a fine and vital line between that and trying to live up to someone else's myth.

"Fathers of twins never feel left out."

WHAT IS IT REALLY LIKE FOR FATHERS OF TWINS?

Perhaps the most often heard complaint from new fathers of single-born babies—particularly first-time fathers—is that they feel left out. They may feel they've slipped a rung or two in how important they are to their partners, falling from indispensable helpmate during pregnancy and birth to fifth wheel and uninvolved observer after the baby arrives.

The good news for fathers of twins and triplets is that they never have to feel left out. They continue to be the indispensable helpmate, and many fathers of multiples report that their vital position leads to stronger bonds with both their partners and their children. In fact, some studies of fathers of multiples have shown that in the midst of the chaos and difficulties of the first year or two with twins or triplets, most dads rise to the occasion admirably. Both mothers and fathers of multiples report that, compared to fathers of single-born babies, these dads help more with infant care, and they reap the benefits of closer families in later years.

Although there are distinct advantages to being a father of multiples, it may be difficult to discern what they are at 3 A.M. when dad is warming bottles, wondering how he will make it through the business meeting he knows he has in about five hours. It may be hard to remember that his help has strengthened his relationship with his entire family when he comes home from work to a house that's less than tidy, at least two fussy babies, an exhausted wife, and take-out pizza.

Fathers can fall prey to the same kinds of myths and expectations anyone can about their role in the family. They, too, face enormous changes at the birth of twins or triplets. How do fathers see those changes affecting themselves and their relationships with their wives and other children? Understanding their viewpoint can help both parents better understand what they can do to smooth the way for each other during the early years with multiples.

Fathers aren't the only ones who feel these changes. There probably isn't anyone in any family who remains untouched when a new being arrives. And when two or three arrive at once, the impact can be that much greater. Siblings and grandparents, other relatives and close friends, all can have an effect on the family with multiples. And if they haven't been around twins or triplets and their families before, they may find some ideas here for how to understand and how to help—and how not to.

While you can't predict exactly what it will be like for you and your family when your multiples arrive, you can get some idea of how it will be by hearing from other fathers. And if your multiples are already here, it might be helpful to know what most concerns other fathers of multiples, and how they handle those concerns.

The most complete survey to date of fathers of twins and triplets was done in 1981 by the Parents of Multiple Birth Association of Canada. They asked 348 fathers about their lives with multiples. And the fathers confirmed that indeed, they were not left out. Nearly half (42 percent) said they were more physically and emotionally involved with

their multiples than with single-born children because of the increased workload, and because many of the infants were ill at birth, which involved more anxiety for the fathers as well as the mothers. And 52 percent felt their role in the family had become more important with the arrival of their multiples. More than half (60 percent) reported that they helped with feeding the babies, and 45 percent said they got up at nignt to feed them. About 30–40 percent of the fathers said they helped at least part of the time with bathing (27 percent helped daily), housework and cooking (30 percent daily, 40 percent occasionally), and other children (37 percent daily). For some reason (which they didn't examine), first-time fathers were more helpful than fathers who had been through it all before. Another study, this one concerning twins and their mothers, found that fathers of identical twins were more likely to help out than the fathers of fraternal twins. (Again, no reasons were offered.)

Probably because most of these fathers were the breadwinners in their families, almost one-third of them worried about finances, with most of those saying that they wished some form of assistance would have been available—like discounts (which many manufacturers of diapers and baby food, for example, no longer give because of the increase in multiple births in recent years), or a tax benefit of some sort.

It's not surprising that nearly three-quarters of first-time fathers reported that their lives changed dramatically with the birth of multiples, compared to less than half (40 percent) of experienced fathers who felt a dramatic change. Those first-time fathers also felt the changes in their relationships with their spouses more dramatically, with nearly half feeling that they deteriorated because their wives were either too absorbed in infant care or too tired for social activities or for sex. The other half—fathers who saw an improvement in their relationships with their wives—said it was because they enjoyed being part of a "team" in caring for the babies, and they admired their wives' ability to cope.

SHOOTING DOWN THE MYTHS

In a perfect world, a father of newborns might be seen as the strong center of a family picture: a protector confidently encircling the mother and babies with his arms. It is a lovely picture, and one that many fathers may feel comfortable with. But it is a good bet that just as many fathers—at least part of the time—may feel more like jamming their hands in their pockets and walking away. The responsibility for creating a calm, supportive environment in a situation you didn't choose—having multiples—may seem to be just too much at times for some men.

Others may feel fine creating that environment, but they are just as concerned with the babies in the center of the circle as the mom is. Still other men might feel comfortable being the protector when that is needed, but they just wish the mom would look away from the center of the circle sometimes and smile at *them.*

And we thought only women were stereotyped in their roles.

Maybe the easiest way to begin sorting out what role the father of twins or triplets plays—or needs to play—is to look first at what that role isn't. Perhaps by discarding the myths, the facts will become clearer.

Father Myth 1: "Everyone knows men aren't good with babies. I would probably just make things worse if I tried to help."

Fact: No one becomes adept at anything without practice. Few women feel themselves to be mothers the instant their first baby is born. The first time many women hold their tiny babies, they are apt to feel as clumsy and incompetent as any man. The difference is that our culture tells them they're not supposed to feel that way. Our culture assumes that they will quickly learn how to be a mother, and that assumption rubs off on most women—so they learn.

Until about twenty years ago, our culture also assumed that a father would not learn how to be a parent, *really,* until the kid was old enough to play catch. The loosening, for some people, of rigid role definitions for men and women has shown that dads can be great at calming babies —if they take the time and make the effort to learn how. It's that time and effort that not only teaches the dad how to calm the babies, but also turns him into a parent, just as the time and effort the mother puts into the babies turns her into a parent.

Father Myth 2: "What's the difference if it's me (the dad) or her (the mom) who holds and plays with the babies? It's the same stuff being done by a person of a different gender. There isn't anything special about *my help.*"

Fact: The same actions (say, playing with a baby) done by persons of different genders are *not* the same actions. Anyone who has watched a dad play with a baby, and then watched a mom play with the same baby, knows that men and women play differently. Now studies on fathers' and mothers' interactions with babies have lent a little extra credence to what many people have seen. More than one study has shown that dads play games more often with babies and poke and tickle them more than moms do. Their style is so different that by the time babies in this study were six weeks old, they behaved differently toward each parent, acting like they expected play and excitement when dad approached, and behaving a little more soberly with mom—who means business with feeding and diapering. Pediatrician T. Berry Brazelton has noted that these differences exist for single parents too. He reports that a single father in his practice admitted that when his small daughter wanted to play, she called him "Daddy," but when she needed something, she called him "Mommy."

That playfulness is not just the optional icing on the cake. Recent studies have shown that it's the substance of certain kinds of development. Researchers at Loyola University found that toddlers with an active, playful father learned how to interact with others earlier and more smoothly than those with no father around or a noninvolved father. Brazelton, too, believes that children with participating fathers grow up to be more successful at school, to have a better sense of humor, and to get along better with other children. He also sees that these children have greater self-esteem and are better motivated to learn. By the time the child with an active father is six or seven years old, Brazelton says she will have a higher IQ than her peers who haven't had the advantage of a participating father.

Other studies cited by researchers at the National Institutes of Health confirm Brazelton's belief in the value of fathers. They, too, show that an active father produces significant differences for children in sex-role identification, thinking style, and intellectual level.

Father Myth 3: "Even if my husband could learn to be good with babies, I know he's just not interested in infants."

Fact: If you are pregnant with multiples and they are your first babies, you can't judge your reaction or your husband's reaction to babies by what's happened between either of you and other people's babies. Just because you never wanted to baby-sit when you were in junior high school doesn't mean you'll be a terrible mother. And just because your husband can't stand that screaming, drooling six-month-old niece of yours doesn't mean he'll be a terrible father. It's just not the same.

If you or your spouse wonders how he will get interested in your babies, you might like to know what a study from the Center for Research on Birth and Human Development at Berkeley showed. Researchers there found that fathers who participated in the birth of their babies were more interested in them later. Attending childbirth classes, taking part in selecting equipment for the babies, and being a needed person at the birth all contributed to fathers feeling they had a place in the process. Being there when the babies are born is not a fail-safe route to happy fatherhood, but it makes sense that if fathers are shut

out of the fun stuff—like making preparations for the babies—they probably won't be too interested in helping with the not-so-fun stuff—like changing diapers and burping fussy infants.

Whether or not a father is at the birth of his babies, he can still develop what psychologists call "engrossment"—that keen interest and compelling bond—with his babies, particularly if he can be with them and hold them in the first hours after the birth. Researchers have found parallels between mothers of premature babies and fathers of term babies who were encouraged to hold and touch their babies soon after the birth. Traditionally, each of these had been excluded from their babies' early care. But when these parents are included, and they do hold their newborns, researchers found that both the mothers and the fathers develop a closer attachment to their babies sooner than those who didn't have the chance to hold them.

In another study, first-time fathers who did hold their babies soon after birth, whether they were at the birth or not, were often overwhelmed and extremely surprised at the extent of their feelings for their newborn. During the first three days after the birth, these fathers all developed that bond called engrossment with their babies. In interviews with the fathers, researchers saw that for them, engrossment meant:

• They thought their own baby was beautiful. ("The other babies [in the nursery] all looked a bit ugly, rubbery. Then when she came out, she looked so beautiful, really, a little gem, so beautiful.")

• They loved to touch and hold their baby. ("I feel great, just great. I can't stop picking her up. It's really a strong feeling of pleasure.")

• They were acutely aware of characteristics of *their* baby. ("I would definitely be able to recognize him by his face . . . I think I could pick him out of a crowd.")

• They saw the infant as perfect. ("Everything [about the baby] seems to be going into action and everything seems to be just right, just right.")

• They felt a strong attraction to the baby that focused their attention on the baby. ("I keep going back to the kid. It's like a magnet. That's what I can't get over, the fact that I feel like that.")

• They felt extreme elation often described as a high. ("I took a look at [the baby] and I took a look at the face and I left the ground—just left the ground.")

• They felt an increased sense of self-esteem. ("I'm delighted when other people look at [the baby] . . . I have a great deal of satisfaction from their reaction.")

Of course not everyone feels the same way about their newborns, but it is interesting to see that in this study, even fathers who weren't at the birth, and who were by their definition uninvolved during the pregnancy, were swept away by their feelings for their firstborn when given the chance to get to know the baby soon after birth.

Father Myth 4: "I know everyone thinks Jones, down the street, is a great dad. But I'm just not like him. If he's a great dad, maybe I'm just not cut out for this job."

Fact: Just as every mother finds her own way to be a mother to her own children, so every father finds his way that is just right for his family. What works in one family (vigorous roughhousing, sarcastic humor, family camping trips) may spell disaster in another. There is no cookie-cutter mold for the Good Father any more than there is one for the Good Mother. Two researchers at the National Institutes of Health found that out when they tried to define normal father-infant relationships. The result of their study was that they couldn't come up with a definition—there was no single consistent factor that defined all the fathers.

Father Myth 5: "We did all the prenatal classes, and I was there at the birth of our twins. I wanted to do everything I could to be a good father. But it's been so crazy since the babies came home that I don't want to spend all my time there. Then I feel like a louse for ducking out at night to have a beer with the guys, because I know my wife is home alone with the kids. I guess all the preparation didn't work because I'm not turning out to be the kind of father I thought I'd be."

Fact: Having your life turned upside down by a situation beyond your—or anyone's—control is a good reason to feel like you want to run away sometimes. That feeling hits mothers, *and* it hits fathers. And it doesn't mean that either of them are bad parents when they feel that way. It just means that both parents need a break. The best way to have that break without hurting someone else in the process is to acknowledge that you need it, then arrange for it. Having a beer with the guys isn't a cardinal sin. But if both parents can acknowledge that dad needs that time and that contact as much as mom needs to go out to lunch with her friends, maybe they can each be patient and prepared about spending some time alone. Or maybe they can arrange for someone—either friends or paid baby-sitters—to come spend that time helping the parent at home. Another way to handle individual time away is to plan it for a time that is the least stressful for the parent at home. For example, if dad helps get the babies bathed and in bed before he leaves, his time away might give mom time to put her feet up and read for a while without interruption.

"Up to now, I didn't really feel all that involved, I suppose. I didn't really have much strong feeling one way or another. But the little something was born, and—I did a complete switch, just a complete switch. I thought I wouldn't take too much interest in it until it was old enough to be a small human being. But it already is a human being."

Keeping these five myths in mind, fathers can know that:

• Being a parent is a learned ability.
• They have something unique and valuable to offer their children.
• Given the chance, fathers can be just as attached to their babies as mothers.
• There is no one way to be a dad.
• Everyone has ups and downs as a parent. One difficult period doesn't necessarily mean you've blown your chance to be a good one.

What all of this means to you, as a father, is that you can trust your best instincts—by listening to your family and listening to yourself—to find your way to be the father you are and the father your children need.

That's what defining your role as a father is all about—throwing away the myths, listening carefully, staying involved, and then coming up with your own definition.

COPING STRATEGIES FOR FATHERS

There are a few things you, as a father, can do to prepare for the birth of your multiples. If you are already a father of multiples, you might check this list to see if you've left some of these out.

• Learn how to look after yourself. If you do the grocery shopping, some of the cooking, and you throw in a load of laundry once in a while, you are a step ahead of all the guys who have those things done for them. If you haven't set foot in the kitchen for ages—except to eat something someone else cooked—and you don't know where the laundry room is, you might want to use the months of your partner's pregnancy to reacquaint yourself with (or learn for the first time) where the pots and pans are. If you want to help after the babies arrive, you are more likely to be a pain in the neck than helpful if you have to ask for detailed instructions every time you make a sandwich.

• Believe that your life may change dramatically. Expected change may be easier to deal with than unexpected change. Simply ignoring the fact of impending multiples, or thinking you'll handle it when the time comes, might mean you are setting up yourself—and your family—for a rockier adjustment than you need to have. The more you can plan ahead for financial needs (Will you be losing an income from your partner? For how long?), for household help (Who will help? How much will it cost?), or for changes in your work schedule (If you'd like to take some time off right after the birth, will you be paid? What is your

company's stand on paternity leave?), the smoother the transition might be for you and your family.

• Tune into your partner. A sense of humor can be a great asset when the going gets tough, but it is a rare woman who likes to be reminded of how huge she has become, or who likes to be compared to animals like cows and cats, who produce gallons of milk and large litters. Most women, whether they are still pregnant or have already had their multiples, like to feel that some part of them, somehow, has remained attractive to their partners. It may be hard for your partner to believe she is still appealing to you if she doesn't find her body size appealing to herself, but regular doses of sincere attention, affection, and admiration might help convince her.

• Try to stabilize your life. Changing jobs, moving from one house to another, or planning your yearly hunting trip close to the birth of your multiples are not conducive to making a smooth entry into life with twins. Sometimes these kinds of changes cannot be planned for, and then you must simply do the best you can. But if you can plan the timing for big changes or your long absences, plan for them to happen after the babies are a year old. There may be enough turmoil in your household for a while without piling on things like moves and job changes.

• Find other fathers of twins or triplets, and talk to them. Sharing child-care tips is not a strong topic of conversation with most fathers, and if you do get together with other fathers of multiples, you don't *have* to talk about diaper rash. For most people in the midst of major life changes, whether the change stems from the birth of multiples or the loss of a job, for example, it helps to know you are not alone. One father of twins told me he always liked to talk to dads of twins older than his, because he liked to see someone who had already done what he was doing, and by that, to be reassured that life does go on. Even if they only exchanged two sentences about how great their kids were before they moved on to football, this dad felt he had made contact. You might find other fathers of twins at some twins club functions, or through prenatal classes for parents expecting a multiple birth. You also might be surprised at how many parents of twins you meet when your children enter preschool, kindergarten, or Little League, and they are more visible to the world. It's not uncommon for parents of twins to discover each other through their children's activities and compare notes because of their common experiences.

• Remember to give yourself a break. You may become a more vital and needed part of the family when your multiples arrive, and you may become your partner's right hand in helping around the house. But you and your partner need to remember that dads need breaks too. They may feel the changes that multiples bring as acutely as do moms. And they, too, need to feel they haven't left their old friends and activities irrevocably behind. Try for balance in time off for moms *and* dads.

HOW MOMS CAN HELP DADS HELP THEM

If you've ever watched an aquarium show with trained seals and dolphins, you have seen positive reinforcement in action. Dolphin trainers know how to get dolphins to do what they want them to do and keep the dolphins happy in the process. If the dolphins weren't happy and willing to work for the trainers, they would just swim away, and the dolphin trainers would be out of a job. You might be wondering what dolphins and their trainers have to do with you, with the father of your twins, and with how much he helps you after their birth. Well, at least one dolphin trainer, Karen Pryor, believes that what she knows about dolphins has everything to do with you getting what you need from your partner—and both of you being happy about it.

In her book *Don't Shoot the Dog,* Pryor has shown how principles of positive reinforcement that are used by animal trainers can be more helpful to people than are the negative reinforcers so many of us use. For example, if your dog barks all night and disturbs the neighbors, you could use the ultimate negative reinforcer and shoot it. That may be extremely negative, but it will stop the unwanted behavior. But instead you might use a variety of positive reinforcers, like rewarding the dog for periods when he *doesn't* bark, putting the emphasis on the wanted behavior to get rid of the unwanted behavior.

It's not too hard to see the parallel with people's behavior. If your partner doesn't help with the babies, you could use a strong negative approach and leave him. Or you could use another negative approach and make life unpleasant for him by threatening, cajoling, and criticizing him into helping you with the babies. But then he might also react negatively and just walk away. On the other hand, you might get what you want *and* keep the peace by using positive reinforcement when he does do even a little bit of what you want. Sincere and glowing praise for the help he *does* provide could motivate him to help more, in exchange for the praise (or for his favorite brownies you bake as a thank-you for a day of baby-sitting, or for a special European beer you buy for him for being such a good dad, or for a love note you leave in his lunch box, etc.). Some other ways to use positive reinforcement and avoid negative reactions:

• He may feel as awkward holding those little babies as you may have the first time you held them. You probably have had plenty of opportunities for practice since then, so let him catch up. Your praise and approval of his efforts might build his confidence as a competent handler of babies. Besides, who would want to do much of something they don't believe they're good at?

• Focus on the things he does well with the babies (like taking them to the park), instead of those that need some work (like feeding them breakfast). Everyone has strong points and weak points. Praising the strong points may take the pressure off the weak points—and give the dad a chance to work on the latter without being under fire.

• Try not to redo chores he's done for you because they aren't quite "right." What's the point of putting out the effort to help if the reward is criticism and constant correction? Don't sabotage your best helper!

TOO TIRED TO HAVE FUN?

Fathers of multiples may never need to feel left out of family life. But after the initial crunch of adjusting to new twins or triplets is over, some do feel left out of their partner's life, because the two of them have never resumed their sexual relationship in a satisfying way. Many couples of single-born babies find that it takes two or more months to begin the road back to what, for them, is a normal sex life. But parents of multiples report that, just as the mother's return to her previous body size might take longer, the couple's return to their previous sexual relationship may take longer too.

The details will be different for everyone, but there are some basic reasons for a lagging or absent sex life for a time after the birth of multiples.

1. The mother may have had a complicated birth or a cesarean, which may mean more healing time after the birth. Most fathers, especially those who have been educated about the healing process, are understanding about the lack of sex during the first weeks after birth, or infrequent sex during the following months. But some fathers find it much harder to understand when those weeks stretch into *many* months.

2. Body changes for the mother of multiples may take longer to be resolved. Chapter 5, Mothercare, explained that a mother of twins may have more weight she wants to lose after the birth, and she may have more stretch marks and loose skin. In many ways, she may be getting used to living in a body that feels totally different to her. Those things may not be a big deal to her partner, but for some women, those changes may make it difficult to feel comfortable enough with themselves to make resuming sexual relations a pleasant thought.

3. For some women, childbirth and breastfeeding put the emphasis on the functional (child-care) aspects of their bodies rather than the recreational (sexual) aspects. For them, the intensity of the change in how they see their own bodies—particularly when they have had twins or triplets—may require more practice in making the transition from maternal function to recreation.

4. Because of hormonal changes following birth, a new mother may find intercourse uncomfortable or even painful because her body might not produce vaginal lubrication in the same quantities it used to. It is normal for estrogen levels to be lower than usual in new mothers, which is what produces vaginal dryness for a few months. You might consider using extra lubrication when you do have intercourse. Some women

also report vaginal dryness whether they have recently given birth or not, if they are having intercourse less often than what is normal for them.

5. Mothers *and* fathers of young twins or triplets are tired. Many of them report being tired to some degree—from mildly pooped to all-out exhausted—most of the time during the first year with their multiples. And people who are constantly less than well rested don't usually have sex on their minds. In fact, to a mother of four-month-old twins, the idea of even the most romantic evening may be enough to send her straight to the couch for a nap—if only she could get the babies to go to sleep, too.

Sleep-deprivation studies have shown that even when people have been deprived of sleep for one hundred hours, they don't become incapable of functioning, but they lose their willingness and motivation to perform the most routine tasks. For example, soldiers participating in war games shoot just as straight when they are sleep-deprived. But Israeli soldiers in one study forgot to fill their water canteens—a vital chore for dessert troops. And British soldiers in another study didn't bother to change cold, wet socks to avoid frostbite. For these soldiers and for people in other sleep-deprivation studies, the major tasks get done no matter what. But those tasks perceived as routine, or low demand, or self-motivated are the ones that fall by the wayside.

Parents of multiples know that. No matter how tired they are, the major things get done: The babies get fed, changed, and probably bathed (though not as often as the single-born baby, experienced parents note). The parents get fed. Laundry gets done. But sex may slide to the bottom of the list, or simply get crossed off the list altogether.

6. By the end of a long day with infant twins, some mothers of multiples feel "touched out." Not that holding and cuddling infants is, in itself, a chore. But after all that physical contact, some moms just want everyone to go away and leave them alone. For those moms, the feel of yet another person touching them—no matter how lovingly—is the last thing they want.

Sometimes it seems that for parents, there are hundreds of reasons *not* to have sex—all of them legitimate at one time or another. And then, even when both partners are willing, there never seems to be enough time, energy, or privacy to get together. But you might like to know that statistical evidence shows parents who have only one child have sex less frequently than parents with two, three, or more children. Perhaps parents just have to be patient and give themselves time to get the hang of having sex once children are around.

For most people, the way to maintain the closeness of their early

"My husband and I make a point of it to talk on the telephone every day. He tries to call at the time he's pretty sure won't be chaotic for me, so we can chat a little bit. It's only a few minutes, but it means a lot. I know that no matter what, he will call me and at least tell me he loves me."

attraction is through the intimate sharing and emotional bond that grows out of a sexual relationship. That's probably the biggest reason to take a look at your sex life and decide what it means to you and your partner.

But studies show that the childbearing years are the years of least sexual activity for most couples. Does that mean that you can't be sexually content—much less feel happy and close to your partner—during those years, and particularly during the early months of multiples? Not necessarily. You may not be having intercourse five times a week, but you might be able to retain a physical and emotional closeness during times when one or both of you aren't very interested in sex. Here are some ideas you might try:

• Try taking the emphasis off intercourse, and placing it on affection and sexual playfulness for a while. Some couples find that when sex is boiled down to whether they have intercourse or not, a lot of the fun—and some of the attraction—goes out of it.

• Continue to court each other. Remember how you felt near the beginning of your relationship when *this* relationship was the most important thing in your lives? For many couples, most of what they did then was focused on letting their loved one know how much they cared, and how valuable and special each was. Fathers who feel they are a low priority for their partners, and mothers who feel they only get attention when someone wants something from them, may not have had much courting lately. Anything you can do to let your partner know you've been thinking of him or her—a note, a kiss at a nonsexual time, a word of appreciation—helps you both keep the courtship going.

• Continue to find ways to make contact. If sex isn't a big part of your relationship right now, that may be a stage that fits the times. But if you also let your closeness fade away now, it may be that much harder to revive your sex life later. One way to maintain an emotional closeness is by writing letters or journals to each other. A love letter that tells how you feel about your day, your life, or the last five minutes may tell your partner more about you than you might be able to express verbally. Exchanging love letters a couple of times a week might keep you in touch with your partner's feelings in a way conversation often cannot. Be sure your letters aren't used to criticize or "unload" unfairly; and they will be best received if you write them in a spirit of love, whether what you have to say is negative or positive.

• Communicating regularly and consistently through short letters, or by telephone, or in other ways you find meaningful may help you both avoid burying feelings of being left out or being misunderstood during a chaotic time. Those kinds of feelings, left alone to fester, can become resentment and anger later, if not sooner.

• Make the time to be together. Here is yet another item you need to fit into your schedule. Whether you are having an active sexual relationship now or not, you still need to create time to be alone with your partner. Trade baby-sitting time with another couple, or hire a baby-sitter and go out for a walk, get a bite to eat, do anything you enjoy together.

If making time to be together becomes a habit when your children are small, you may find you have built-in time to resume your sexual relationship more actively later. And if centering your lives on your children seems more important than going for a walk with your mate, remember that your children will likely have a smoother life with two happy parents. The relationship between you and your partner is the foundation on which your family lives.

The bottom line for most fathers—and most mothers—is that nothing replaces a good sexual relationship. But there are times—because of fatigue, stress, and physical changes—when an active sex life just doesn't happen. Those times might be more acceptable if both of you know that this hiatus doesn't have to last forever. But a few months can *feel* like forever if either partner believes there is no end in sight.

"Ever since the babies arrived, Shelley and I have agreed that when we get to go out alone, we either limit how much we talk about the babies, or agree to not talk about them at all. Our lives revolve around them so much, it's nice when we do get away to think about something else."

EVERYONE FEELS THE CHANGES

When mom goes to the hospital and comes back with a baby, the three-year-old at home who seemed so ready for a new brother or sister may surprise everyone by throwing tantrums, forgetting where the potty chair is, and demanding to nurse or be given a bottle.

But when mom goes to the hospital and comes home with two or three babies, the whole family may brace themselves for the worst the three-year-old has to offer. It may seem logical to think that if one new baby can be upsetting to the child who was there first, then more than one new baby can send that child into fits of regression and generally antisocial behavior. And that does happen with some children. But others don't experience any more trauma after the birth of multiples than do siblings of a single newborn, and some may even enjoy their status as "owners" of the neighborhood's favorite topic of conversation.

Perhaps more than at any other time, parents of multiples need to be sure their concern for the siblings of twins or triplets doesn't become a self-fulfilling prophecy of doom for those children. At the same time, they need to be sure they balance their expectations with the understanding that an older child, even if she isn't insanely jealous, probably won't be thrilled at the prospect (or the reality) of losing her place as Queen of the Castle. One mother likened a child's feelings upon meeting the newborn "intruder" as similar to the feelings of a wife, to whom her husband has just explained, "Honey, I love you so much, I decided to get another woman to keep you company. Won't we all have fun together?"

Any parent of a newborn and even one two-year-old will tell you life isn't always smooth when a new being joins the family. Learning to balance all those needs isn't easy. But people have been having more than one baby for a long time, and having children close together, whether that means ten minutes apart or fifteen months apart, does not automatically mean these children and these families will have problems.

Before considering specific ways to help siblings make the adjustment to newborn multiples, you might like to know what some child-development experts say who have studied the emotional development of preschool children. They found that while it is true many parents may see their preschooler becoming more fussy or demanding at the birth of multiples, it is difficult to discern how much of that behavior

would occur anyway at that age, and how much was intensified by the arrival of siblings. Judy Dunn, an expert on sibling relationships, noted in her book *Siblings: Love, Envy and Understanding* that "We cannot come to any real conclusions about how much the birth of a sibling has contributed to the changes in the children we have studied," because so little solid information exists about the emotional development of children during their second, third, and fourth years of life.

So while you don't have to assume that the birth of multiples will destroy your older child, you will nevertheless want to be sure the arrival of two or three babies at once doesn't accidentally eclipse that child either. One way to do that is to provide special attention for the sibling of multiples. Mom may have too many other things to do, but dad and/or grandparents can step in and provide even a half hour of one-on-one time on a regualr basis in an activity the child chooses. Mom might also be able to do that by establishing little rituals, like a bedtime story or song that she provides while dad takes care of the babies. It's only a few minutes, but if it is a dependable few minutes, owned *only* by that child, those minutes can mean a lot.

Studies have shown that siblings of twins may take it on themselves to find ways to fit in with the group. Siblings do this all the time whether there are twins or triplets in the family or not. Everyone has to figure out where his niche in the family is, and how he will relate to each sibling. Siblings of twins:

- may try to become one of "triplets" and emphasize how much like their multiple siblings they are, or they
- may try to separate the multiples to minimize the closeness of the multiple relationship, or they
- may appropriate one of the multiples as their favorite, and try to exclude the others.

None of these is necessarily bad—shifting loyalties and grouping and regrouping are facts of life to many siblings. What's usually the issue for the brother or sister of twins or triplets is that he or she does find a place for him- or herself in relation to the multiples, and that he or she feels comfortable in it, whatever that particular place may be. It's also important to remember that, as with most observations of relationships, few of these descriptions of behavior ever exist alone, nor do they necessarily exist in one way forever—relationships between siblings are as fluid as the relationship between any two people.

It's not hard to see that how twins or triplets are perceived by other family members may have a bearing on how their brother or sister sees them and reacts to them. For example, parents who dress identical twins alike may be subtly telling the sibling that there is real value in

"My three children have always slept in the same bed—they like having each other to cuddle with. At first, the younger sister of my identical twins always slept on the end, because she was more likely to get up at night. But when she turned four, she suddenly insisted that she sleep between her older sisters. I guess she just wants to be sure that she is indeed part of the group and not left out."

"Before my twins were born, my fifteen-month-old loved to be off on her own playing. She'd like to be in the same room with me, but she could get interested in her toys without my constant help. But after their birth, she was right on my lap all the time for the first few months. It seemed like she had to be touching me all the time."

being part of a "unit," which is a status that the single-born sibling can never achieve. These parents could also be subtly encouraging the sibling to see her situation as two or three against one: the "unit" against the individual. On the other hand, twins or triplets who are regarded (and dressed and treated) as separate children the same as their siblings may be less formidable to those siblings, and it may be easier for each sibling to be flexible enough to find her own niche, instead of fulfilling someone else's view of twinship, or of the sibling of twins.

Both parents, then, can set an example for how siblings may regard their twin sisters or brothers. Of course experienced parents know that children don't always do exactly what we believe we are showing them, but actions generally do speak very loudly to most children.

You might be able to go a long way toward silently reassuring the sibling of twins or triplets that she is just as precious to you as she ever was by refraining from making little "stars" of your twins however you can. Nonfamily members will probably not be as sensitive to this issue as you, and it wouldn't hurt for you to gently explain to relatives and visitors (out of earshot of the sibling in question) to reserve some of their attention for her. You might also explain that the sister or brother of twins is not always interested in being the sister or brother of twins. Reflected glory might be better than none, but everyone also likes to be valued for himself, not for what he is in relation to someone else.

Whether you are looking at how siblings relate to twins, or how they relate to their parents after the birth of twins, the common denominator seems to be that the sibling wants to be extra sure that there is a place for him in the family.

And that may be the source of a lot of the stress mothers of multiples report when they bring two or three babies to a home where a toddler used to reign supreme. Meeting the needs of more than one infant at a time is hard enough—but adding a demanding toddler to the picture puts some mothers over the top. That's where the father and grandparents come in. Pediatrician T. Berry Brazelton believes that "fathers are crucial to helping older kids accept a new sibling." Many fathers of multiples find that as their relationship with their other children develops—while mom is busy taking care of the babies—they begin to see more clearly how their role differs from that of the mother and to appreciate the contribution they can make to the family. For some fathers, their most valuable contribution early after the birth of multiples may be in spending time with other siblings when their mother is too tired or too preoccupied to give them the attention they need.

This is also where grandparents can be a priceless aid. During the last decade or two, the role that grandparents play in most American families has changed from authoritative head of the family to a relative who is just about on the same level as anyone else in the family. That's how hundreds of grandparents defined their role when they were interviewed for a book by A. Kornhaber and K. L. Woodward called *Grandparents/Grandchildren: The Vital Connection*. What that often meant to the grandparents and their families was that the grandparents tended to shy away from involving themselves with their grandchildren for fear it would appear they were intruding. So if your family is anything like these, you may have to specifically invite your children's grandparents to help, either by asking them to be special friends to older children or by directly requesting their help in other ways. If you are afraid they will in fact intrude, it might help to know they are often afraid of the same thing.

Some grandparents, while they might be willing to help, may feel apprehensive about jumping in for other reasons. For some, the thought of being responsible for two babies at once (even if the babies are asleep) while you run to the grocery store is intimidating. If you want

"My mother-in-law just seemed nervous at the prospect of staying with nursing babies, even if I left a bottle for them. But once they were weaned, she jumped in with both feet. My boys spend two or three weekends a month at grandma's now —and we all love it."

them to help in this way, break them in easy—try taking one baby with you and leaving just one with grandma or grandpa. One baby for half an hour sounds a lot easier than two babies for the same amount of time. You might also be careful to ask their help in small doses at first. Coming over to lend a hand once or twice a week is much more palatable than being expected to show up every day.

Chapter 2, Transitions, offered some ideas on defining the kind and amount of help you need, so those who want to help will know what to do. You might want to be particularly sure you define what you want where grandparents are concerned, for your benefit and theirs. No one wants to feel taken advantage of, and few grandparents relish the thought of being harnessed with a second family to raise. You can banish the child-care fears many grandparents harbor ("Give them an inch, they'll take a mile") by being specific about the amount of help you want, then sticking to a mutually agreeable plan.

Even though grandparents have all taken care of children before, for most of them it has been a very long time since they've held a baby, much less tried to comfort a crying one. Keep in mind that, like the new father (or mother), grandparents could use some reinforcement and encouragement where their baby-handling skills are concerned. A grandfather who hears over and over how great he looks holding that baby, how much the baby must like him because the little one seems so content, and how good he is at playing with that baby—will start to believe it. And for most people, the more they believe it, the more those skills become fact. Many grandparents (and their families) are somewhat uncertain about just what their role should be now that they are no longer usually considered the indisputable head of the family. Your reassurance that they have a place with you and your children will help you all define what that role should be for you.

Few grandmothers breastfed their babies, so if you are breastfeeding your multiples, that may require a little extra sensitivity on your part to grandma's concerns. If you are breastfeeding, you may have already done enough homework and have enough confidence to assuage what doubts she may have about your ability to produce enough milk, etc., etc. If you don't feel sure about these things, you might want to be aware of what you might hear: "Won't breastfeeding tie you down too much, make your breasts sag, tie your children to your apron strings?" Then you can decide ahead of time what you might say: "I'm tied down anyway right now. I don't know if my breasts will sag, but good nutrition is more important than the shape of my breasts. It's okay for babies to be attached to their mothers." A calm and reassuring attitude on your part (along with healthy, happy babies) can help grandparents feel comfortable with whatever feeding method you choose. If you are not supplementing with formula, or offering bottles of your breast milk to your babies, you might have to wait a while before grandma and grandpa feel comfortable staying alone with your children.

Maybe you are uncertain about whether you want grandparents to have this kind of role at all. Maybe you've never gotten along with your father, and you're not close to your mother. For many parents of single-born babies, grandparents' help is truly optional, and many opt not to try it because of previous conflicts with their parents. But parents of multiples are in a different situation. For them, help is not optional. And for many of them, help from grandparents or other relatives may be the least painful way to get what they need. Many parents of multiples find that once the news spreads of their two or three babies, people come out of the woodwork offering help. Sometimes they are surprised by how well it works to have grandparents lend a hand, even those with whom they'd previously been at odds.

Here are some things to keep in mind if you do want grandparents to become more involved with your children:

1. If there are child-care issues that are particularly important to you—like holding down the amount of sugar your children consume, even at grandma's, or adhering to a certain bedtime—be sure you let the grandparents know what they are, just as you would anyone with whom you would entrust the care of your children. For example, you might say, "I don't mind if the children have an occasional oatmeal cookie or a non-sugar-coated granola bar, but I really don't want them to have chocolate, as in brownies or chocolate-chip cookies."

2. Most grandparents will try to respect parents' wishes, but slip-ups seem to be inevitable. Try to keep them in perspective. Your children's lives will probably not be ruined by the occasional candy bar you don't like them to have, but they'll definitely notice the sudden halt in their visits to grandma's. If slipups seem to be the rule rather than the exception, you might consider ways to keep temptation at a minimum. If the issue is food, for example, you might:

- send foods or treats with your children that are acceptable to you
- limit visits to times when children are least likely to eat a meal there
- have a heart-to-heart talk, alone, with the grandparent(s) involved, and explain your feelings
- consider limiting the visits if it really bothers you

3. Grandparents provide a built-in way to offer separate time for twins or other siblings. A weekend or an afternoon alone with grandma

"My children used to visit a particular aunt and uncle during the summers when they were small. They always went alone and always enjoyed their visits. It wasn't until recently (and my children are all adults now) that I found out that each of them threw up at least once during those visits because of all the cookies and junk food they weren't used to having at home. They never mentioned that when they reported how much fun they'd had."

"I wasn't thrilled at the idea of having my mother come help with my twins. But there really wasn't anyone else who could, and I was too scared to face staying home alone all day with two babies. I was pleasantly surprised to find how wonderful those times were. We hadn't gotten along very well in years, but those months that she helped me were some of the best we've ever had. She visited me two mornings a week, and all we really did was drink tea, talk, and play with the babies. Sometimes I'd go out for a few minutes, but that was it. Most of that closeness we shared during those months seems to have faded now, but I'll never forget those times. That was quite a gift she gave me."

and grandpa—as the sole focus of all their time and affection—can work wonders for children who must always share their parents.

4. Try to let the relationship between grandchildren and grandparents develop in its own way. Your children will gain a wealth of knowledge by relating to another adult without the protective insulation that a hovering parent can provide.

5. Perhaps the most important thing to remember is that if it doesn't work for you to involve your childrens' grandparents in this way, you don't have to.

Some parents of multiples find that after they have thought about it, defined what they want their children's grandparents to do, and feel certain about including them, lo and behold, they get turned down flat. Not all grandparents want to be that involved with their grandchildren, and that is, of course, their choice. Some grandparents are feeling (and enjoying) some degree of freedom for the first time in their lives and are reluctant to give that up. Some really don't like the noise and mayhem that is inevitably involved with having children around. Some just can't overcome their apprehension about being saddled with another family to raise. If your best efforts to include them are all for naught, leave them alone. And then you might consider adopting a grandparent.

Some senior-citizen centers or other community or church organizations have programs that match families with "grandparents" who either don't have grandchildren or whose families live far away. These are not free baby-sitters, but rather companions from another generation who can offer friendship, a different view of life, and the precious gift of time to you and your children.

All this family and extended family involvement can add up to stronger ties for many familes who have twins or triplets. One study, which polled over six hundred families of members of the National Mothers of Twins Clubs and compared their responses to those from families without twins, showed that families of twins were emotionally closer within their families, and they saw themselves as working exceptionally well together. Another study, this one of eleven families with quadruplets or quintuplets who had participated in the study from the birth of their multiples for the next five years, showed that all of the familes (including siblings) believed themselves to be stronger and happier as a result of their experience with multiples.

Brothers and sisters of multiples have an excellent chance to learn things about life that many people wait a long time to realize. They can understand at an early age that their parents are human beings with finite resources, that they can turn to another caring adult besides their parents to fill in the blanks their very human mom and dad may leave, that no one—including mom and dad—is perfect, and that people just get tired and that is not a reflection on their children. Your job as the parent will be to broaden the base of support your children can get, letting fathers as well as mothers, and grandparents, other relatives, and friends, all enrich your children's experience.

7 | Going Back to Work

"People ask me how I can work part time and be a mother of toddler twins. I tell them the time I spend at my office is the easiest part of my day."

"I tried working for a year when my boys were about eighteen months old. I nearly went nuts trying to keep the household running, the kids in decent daycare, and myself pulled together enough to think. After a while it just wasn't worth the hassle —emotionally or financially."

Dressing up and going to the office can be a lifesaver for a mother of twins or triplets who feels like she's drowning in strained peaches and disposable diapers. A part-time waitressing job where the tips are big and the hours are short can be just what another mother needs to add a little padding to the family budget. Whether they are continuing a career, providing sole or partial support for the family, or just earning their own money, working outside the home can be a bright spot in the lives of many mothers of multiples. And their earnings, in somes cases, can bridge the financial gap that may have been created by the birth of their multiples.

But there are also plenty of mothers of multiples for whom the idea, much less the reality, of arranging for employment for herself, and

"I have a part-time job now, which I love because I get to use my training in counseling, but I'm worried about the amount of time I spend away from my two-year-old twins. My boss wants me to increase my hours to thirty a week in a few months, and I don't want to because I think that's too much time to be away from my children at this age."

arranging and paying for care for her children, is much more hassle than it's worth.

Mothers of twins and triplets have many of the same kinds of decisions to make as mothers of single-born babies must when they consider going back to work after their babies arrive—plus a few more. A clear and current look at who works outside the home and why, and what effect experts say those employed moms have on their children, might help pave the way for your decision. If you do decide to become employed, you might like to know when, in your children's lives, is the best time to make your break. And if the nine-to-five grind doesn't look attractive, but a paycheck does, there are some options you can consider to help you create the job—and the hours—to suit you.

Once you have those details in hand, you can begin looking at who will care for your children and how you and your family can make the job-and-home juggling act work for you.

WHO IS EMPLOYED AND WHY?

According to the U.S. Department of Labor Statistics, half of all women with children under the age of six are employed outside the home. That is more than three times the number of mothers of young children who were employed in 1950. The 1940s and 1950s saw increases in the number of employed mothers of school-age children, and in the 1960s, the biggest surge was in the number of employed mothers of preschool-age (under age six) children.

Why are all these mothers of preschoolers heading off to work each day instead of staying home? Most people agree that part of the reason is economic. A private institution called 9 to 5, the National Association of Working Women, says that 41 percent of all married working women have husbands who earn less than fifteen thousand dollars a year. And government figures show that while women don't earn as much money as men for the same time spent at work (it's actually gone down—from an overall average of sixty-three cents for every dollar earned by a man in 1956 to an overall average of fifty-nine cents for every dollar earned by a man in 1981), an employed married woman typically contributes between 25 and 38 percent of the family's income, depending on whether she works year-round full time, or part time.

For some women, the reasons are more personal than economic. For the relatively small group of women with professions or highly technical careers (18 percent of all employed women), going back to work after having twins may be more of a career decision than a financial necessity.

Another reason why so many mothers of preschoolers are working outside the home now may be that most mothers have fewer preschoolers at one time to deal with. In the 1950s, three or four children per woman were standard, and it was likely that those children would be born within eighteen to thirty months of each other. Just one or two children are the norm now, as half of those mothers of preschoolers leave home to work. It may be that arranging work schedules, daycare, and the rest of your life around a career seems a bit more possible when you have fewer preschoolers at home.

IS IT GOOD OR BAD FOR MOMS TO WORK OUTSIDE THE HOME?

That question can only be answered by the families who have an employed mom, and the answer will be different for everyone. But if you're trying to decide whether to get a job or not—here are some issues to consider:

1. *Consider the costs—in dollars and time.* The median weekly earnings for a woman employed full time in 1982 were $240. If you don't have a job yet, and if you are one of the majority of women who will seek employment in clerical jobs (like secretarial or other office work), or service jobs (like domestic work or waitressing), this may be a realistic figure for you. Of course if you are debating about returning to a higher-paying job, the figure may not be right, but you, too, will have to consider the cost of daycare. A fact of life quickly learned by parents of multiples is that children are not necessarily cheaper by the dozen— or by twos and threes. And the cost of daycare and the ease with which you arrange for it with more than one child are not exceptions. Parents of multiples looking for daycare typically run into one or more of these situations:

- You have two or three children to place in a daycare center or home. They have one or two slots. You must decide if it is worth it to you to beat the bushes until you find a place that can take all of your children at once, or if your schedule can accommodate the extra time of dropping children off at more than one location every work day.
- Daycare centers, homes, and, to some degree, individuals who come to your home usually charge by the child. Occasionally, a center or home will offer some discount (say, 80 percent of full price) for the second or third child, but not always. Daycare centers, nursery schools, or preschools often have their

"My work outside the home is what makes me a decent mother. When I didn't have the creative outlet and contact with adults that my job allows, I was grouchy all the time. My children see a happier mother now. I think it's good for them that I feel fulfilled."

own problems making ends meet, and the fact that you have more than one child to place is not really their problem. Certainly ask about discounts, but expect to pay double or triple what your neighbor with one baby pays.

• Many preschools won't accept twins or triplets for enrollment in the same class. If you are combining daycare with preschool, you must decide if your schedule (or that of your baby-sitter) can accommodate taking one child to the Tuesday-Thursday session and the other to the Monday-Wednesday session, for example. Or you could try to talk the preschool of your choice into making an exception for your children. (Which is unlikely if separating twins is their policy. Right or wrong, a private institution is entitled to its opinion.) Or, once again, you could beat the bushes until you find the combination of preschool and daycare that fits your needs.

The price of daycare varies widely depending on where you live and on what kind of care you choose, but if you have twins or triplets, you need to look carefully at those costs when you consider working outside your home. Add to those costs the price of transportation, clothing you'll need for your work, and incidentals you know will be involved even occasionally, like going out to lunch, before you count on how much money you'll be taking home.

2. *Consider the housework.* While some things have changed for women during the last twenty years, for most women, being responsible for most of the housework hasn't. So maybe your partner empties the trash or gives the babies a bath, but if he does much more than that in the nitty-gritty grind of keeping the house livable and food available, he is part of a tiny minority. Most women employed outside the home, no matter how many children they have or how many hours they spend at their job, report that they still do 80–90 percent of the housework. If they make enough money, they may hire someone to do some of it for them, but the responsibility is still theirs. You may be able to work out with your partner an equitable arrangement for taking care of those menial chores, and it may be worth trying. But history isn't with you.

On the other hand, studies done by University of Illinois sociologists showed that married couples with the lowest rates of depression were those in which both parties worked outside the home by choice, and in which domestic chores were fairly equally shared. They also found that the higher the education level of the man and the higher the income level of the woman, the more likely the man was to help with housework. In the same study, the most often depressed women were those who were employed only because of monetary reasons, although neither they nor their partners wanted them to work outside the home, and who still did most of the household chores. In these marriages, not only were the women more depressed than any of the other women, but the men were generally even more depressed than their wives.

3. *Consider your mental health.* Sometimes just getting out and being with adults for a few hours a day is worth whatever hassle and expense it takes to arrange it. Most child-care experts recognize that a happy mother is more likely to have happy children—your sense of self-esteem can spill over to enhance their sense of self-esteem. If having a job has this kind of meaning for you, by all means find a way to make it happen. Work part time and find a friend to trade baby-sitting with. Work during a few of the hours your husband is home so he can take care of the children. Or enlist a grandma to fill in so you can get out.

If you're worried that working outside the home will add to the stress in your life rather than relieve it, that is a legitimate concern that only you can evaluate. But you might like to know about one survey of over two thousand women aged twenty-five to sixty-four. It showed that employed women had an improved level of "general well-being," fewer personal and mental problems, and less need to seek "professional assistance" than nonemployed women. It also noted that although an equal proportion of employed and unemployed women felt at times they were going to have a nervous breakdown, a larger proportion of the nonemployed women actually did.

Another study carried out by a team from the University of Texas Health Science Center at San Antonio found that working outside the home may lower a woman's risk of coronary heart disease. They found that levels of high-density lipoprotein cholesterol (HDL)—the "good" cholesterol that has been identified as a major protective factor against coronary heart disease—are significantly higher in currently employed women than in housewives. This was true for employed women whether or not they smoked, consumed alcohol, used estrogen or oral contraceptives, or were overweight. The higher levels also occurred in employed women no matter what their age or socioeconomic status. Although the researchers speculated that "women's associations at work" with one another might be responsible, they admitted that the reason for the healthy HDL levels remained a mystery.

4. *Consider your children's mental health.* If you were old enough to be reading magazine articles written for mothers in the 1950s, every one of them would have struck fear into your heart about leaving your children for the workplace. Experts now believe that the fear that employed mothers will raise warped children isn't warranted. They cite the healthy attitude of children on the kibbutzim in Israel, who are

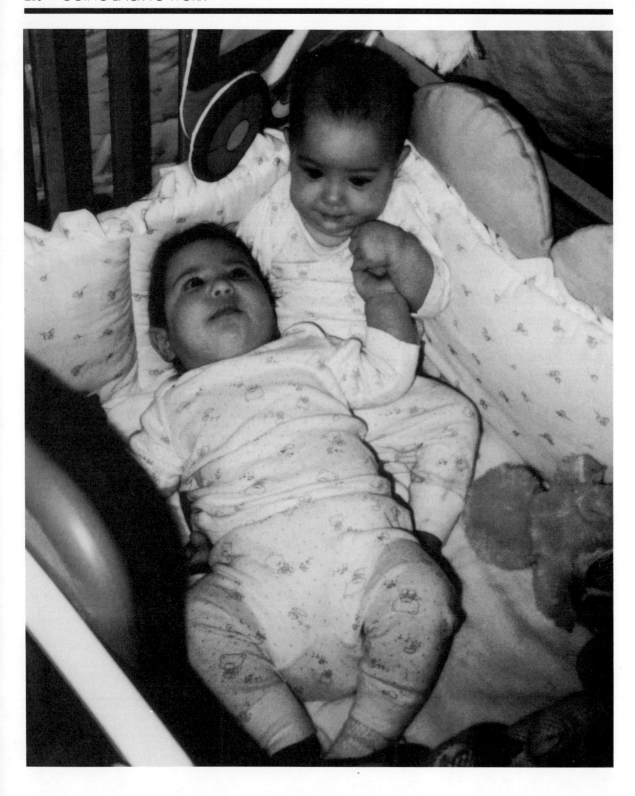

typically in daycare from the time they are six weeks old. Those children forge the same strong bonds with their parents we traditionally value, but also have the ability to be close to other caregiving adults. The conclusion has been that children with loving adult caregivers can operate from a broader base of love and security, rather than a narrower one.

No one has found children who really don't know their mother and father because both parents are employed. That bond is too deeply rooted to be seriously disturbed by hours in the care of others. What researchers *have* found is that the parents can model an attitude for their children about parental work. Parents who don't want the mother to work outside the home, but feel she must because of economic necessity, may present to their children a whole different feeling about her absence than would parents who both support and find value in the mother's work. Those attitudes and beliefs are bound to have some effect on the children.

5. *Consider your family and your marriage.* According to the results of scores of research projects examined by pediatrician Mary C. Howell, employed mothers offer many advantages to family relations and the lives of their children, and they have no uniformly harmful effect on family life, nor on the growth and development of children.

But, Howell found the reverse is true when the mother's conditions of employment are demeaning to her self-esteem, when other family members are strongly disapproving of her work away from home, or when mutually agreeable arrangements for children and housework cannot be made. Without support and approval from her family, the employed mother's energy levels and self-esteem both suffered—which didn't exactly contribute to a satisfying family life.

What this all means to you is that there is no single path to follow in making your decision about working outside the home with young (or even with older) multiples. You can consider how you believe each of your children will react, how you feel about your working, how your husband feels about your working, what your psychological and financial needs are—and then make the decision that fits your life.

Another issue for some families is what happens when father returns to work. While paid paternity leave is hardly the norm in this country, some families arrange to have dad work part time or take a leave of absence around the time of the birth of their multiples. In families where the mother makes more money or holds a more fulfilling career position than the father, it is she who returns to work relatively quickly, and the father who stays home. And some families have dreamed up job-sharing arrangements. (The mother and father might

The experts say simply that working outside the home is terrific for some mothers and their families, and it is a disaster for others. The difference seems to lie in whether you make the decision according to the rules and needs that fit you and your family, or whether you make it according to someone else's (like your relatives, your friends, your colleagues, or just "other people"). No one knows what will be right for you and your family but you.

share a teaching position, for example, and earn one-and-a-half times a single salary.) If a job-sharing schedule can be worked out, the parents may simply take turns caring for children and working, and avoid day-care costs altogether.

No matter who stays home and who goes off to the office, the issue for the children seems to be consistent, familiar, loving care—which, in most cases, either parent or a sensitive caregiver is perfectly capable of providing.

WHEN TO GO

If you talked to a dozen employed mothers about when, from the baby's point of view, was the least traumatic time for mom to return to work, you might get a dozen different answers. For some, it probably was "the earlier the better," and for others, a year or so at home was heaven. You, as a mother of multiples, might want to take a few things into consideration as you decide when to go back that a mother of a single-born baby might not.

No one has to tell you, whether you are currently pregnant with twins or triplets, or you've already given birth, that a multiple pregnancy can be pretty hard on your body. Certainly there are mothers of multiples who sail through their pregnancies, but there are probably more who feel acutely the extra weight, the extra size, and the extra energy it takes to produce more than one baby at a time. Many mothers have learned from experience that giving themselves a month to six weeks to really rest after the birth of one baby pays dividends later in their health and energy. Conversely, talk to mothers who "felt fine" and plunged right back into the demanding home or office routine soon after their births, and you are likely to hear stories of exhaustion, vulnerability to illness, and for breastfeeding mothers, breast infections and lagging milk supplies.

If you have just given birth to two or three babies, it makes sense that you might feel better six months from now if you allow your body time to recharge. You may feel great three weeks after the birth, but experienced mothers know it's worth the effort to resist the temptation to carry on as if nothing had happened. So if you can arrange it, you might consider waiting significantly longer to return to work than would a mother with a single-born baby.

If you are ready to return to work, and are deciding about daycare for your babies or young twins, you might want to review chapter 9, Halves of a Whole or Complete in Themselves?, on individuality. While your babies most likely coo and giggle at each other, and while your toddlers may love having their built-in playmate/sparring partner, try not to make unfounded assumptions about their relationship that may affect the kind of daycare you choose. For example, it is important to understand that while these young twins and triplets may enjoy each other and provide some emotional sustenance for each other, their relationship does not eclipse their need for consistent, loving adult care. The fact that they have each other certainly may shield them from some degree of loneliness or isolation a single child in daycare may feel, but in an overcrowded daycare center, it won't take the place of a caring adult.

When you get down to choosing a day to go, you might like to know that most dates that are traditionally used to determine when mom goes back to work have nothing to do with how most babies will adjust at that time. For example, six weeks to recuperate and then get to work may be too little for a new mother of multiples. She may feel that staying home for a whole year after the birth will get her adjusted to being a mom, and will give her babies the start she feels is best for them. But when she finally heads out the door to work one day, she's devastated to find her babies are inconsolable. And they continue to be inconsolable every time she goes to work, and often when she just leaves the room. The screaming and clinging leave her wondering— "Didn't that year do these babies any good? How could they be so insecure after all that?"

Her year at home probably did a lot of good, but it's important to understand that one-year-old babies who panic at the sight of their mother walking out the door don't care if she's going into the bathroom or she's off to work. Developmentally, it's normal for most one-year-olds to want to keep their prime loved one in sight at nearly all times. In fact, the period between ten months and fifteen months may be the worst time for you to begin leaving your babies. That is just when most babies are learning to take a few steps away from mom, and they are most comfortable if they can do it in little doses and at their own pace. They are often most upset if those periods of separation are foisted on them. It's also normal for babies, at around eight months for some, to develop a healthy fear of strangers. That's why the same babies who at six months of age smiled and goo-gooed for a visiting grandma may at eight months cry and refuse to be held by her. They are beginning to understand that there are people they see all the time whom they know, and there are people whom they either have never seen before or whom they don't remember, and those are strangers.

Many child-development experts say that the easiest time to return to work, from the child's point of view, is when the child starts pre-school or kindergarten. That's when children begin to develop their own lives separate from yours, and the fact that you are also gone while they are gone is less likely to be disruptive then. The next easiest time, many experts agree, is before your babies are six months old, and preferably before they are three months old. There are typically strong ties that develop between babies and their primary caregivers between three and six months. If you go back to work at this time, your babies can develop that bond not only with you, but also with the person you choose to care for them. If you wait until after six months, when, developmentally, your babies are more likely to see only you as the appropriate caregiver, they may have a more difficult time accepting someone else, too.

BREASTFEEDING AND WORKING

If you are breastfeeding and you decide to become employed while your babies are still young enough to be dependent partially or completely on your milk for nourishment, the good news is you don't have to stop nursing to go back to work if you don't want to. Many employed mothers know that you can nurse only once or twice a day without risk of losing your milk supply altogether.

Once your milk supply is well established at around two or three months (and as a breastfeeding mother of twins or triplets, you are likely to be producing abundant milk by that time) you can gradually reduce the number of feedings, either supplementing with bottles of formula or bottles of your expressed milk. Some employed mothers breastfeed their babies in the morning before work, return at noon to relax, eat lunch, and nurse, and then nurse again in the evening. Others nurse only morning and evening; and still others may choose to alter their work schedule, working part time for example, in order to miss only one feeding. It is possible to work out the schedule that fits your life best. There are some excellent books available that describe in detail what employed women who want to continue breastfeeding need to know about scheduling, pumping their milk, and safely storing it. One of those is *Breastfeeding Guide for the Working Woman,* by Anne Price and Nancy Bamford.

NEW APPROACHES

When all is said and done, spending a full day at work knowing that twins or triplets (and their accompanying empty stomachs and dirty laundry) are waiting for you at home just may not seem too enticing. If that is the case for you, it doesn't necessarily mean you have to give up hope of ever bringing home a paycheck. According to the Bureau of Labor Statistics, there has been some increase since 1970 in the number of women voluntarily working part time, mostly among those who are married to a full-time worker, who have children, and who have at least a high-school education. They are most likely to be employed in white-collar positions, probably performing clerical duties or selling.

But there's more to it than that. Employed women have come up with a range of alternatives that allow them to work fewer than forty hours a week. Here are some of them:

1. *Part-time work.* Many women with a long-term commitment to their jobs choose part-time work, at least for a time after their babies are born. Government figures show that in 1983, 14 percent of the country's professional and managerial workers voluntarily chose to work part time, and 22 percent of all female employees opted for part-time work. Try these sources if you're looking for part-time work:

> • *The federal government* employs thousands of part-time workers, many of whose jobs have been mandated by legislation passed in 1978 and reauthorized in 1979. The Comprehensive Employment and Training Act directs that special efforts be made to provide for alternative working arrangements such as flexible hours, work sharing, and part-time jobs especially for parents of young children.
> • *State governments.* Many states have passed legislation similar to federal legislation to provide for part-time jobs.
> • *The U.S. Postal Service.* Thousands of workers have part-time jobs here, and they receive the kinds of medical and insurance benefits normally associated with full-time work.
> • *Private industry.* A 1979 survey for the U.S. Department of Health, Education, and Welfare showed that 17 percent of the responding firms, which employed over two hundred thousand workers, had adopted part-time options policies. A 1977 American Management Association survey estimated that 12.8 percent of all private-sector organizations nationwide use flexitime or flexible work schedules.
> • *Specific occupations* may be more likely to offer part-time work. Some of those are: health-care occupations (and their administrative support), education (especially as teachers of things like special education or art, for example), daycare, home services (like household maintenance, home repair, painting, decorating, and lawn care), social services (counseling and therapy), business support (clerical and administrative), leisure ser-

vices (travel and recreation fields), and personal services (beauty, auto maintenance, care of clothing and personal belongings, and others related to personal needs).

2. *Job sharing.* This is a voluntary arrangement in which two people hold responsibility for what was formerly one full-time position. The job may be shared equally, or in a one-third/two-thirds manner, or any other way the sharers choose to divide the time, and the employer accepts. Some jobs that could be good bets for a sharing agreement include: teacher, administrator, program developer, secretary, receptionist, clerical worker, counselor, social worker, psychologist, researcher, or technician.

3. *Self-employment/working at home.* One of the newest solutions to the working-mother dilemma is for mothers to work from home. They can more easily trade baby-sitting or work during their children's naptime, thereby avoiding high daycare costs, and they may find setting their own hours and their own goals more satisfying than punching someone else's time clock. Two national organizations that are acting as links in the network of home-working mothers are:

The National Alliance of Homebased Businesswomen
P.O. Box 306
Midland Park, New Jersey 07432

Mother's Home Business Network
P.O. Box 423
East Meadow, New York 11554

Both organizations offer a national newsletter with business guidance and information for mothers who want to pursue their careers (from public relations and writing, to selling copier supplies and quilting) at home. They also offer mothers a chance to get in touch with other mothers in similar fields, peruse classified ads of others soliciting work or looking for workers, and find where they can get assistance to help their businesses grow.

DAYCARE ISSUES

If you do choose to work outside the home, who takes care of your children and how well they do it will be a major issue for you. Your children are not the only consumers of daycare services—you are, too. One survey released by *Fortune* magazine showed that child care has as much impact on an employee's productivity as her relationship with a supervisor, or even job security. The survey, for which four hundred working women and men with children under twelve were polled, showed that problems with child care are the most significant predictors of absenteeism and unproductive time at work for both mothers and fathers. So the happier you are with the child-care choices you make, the better your whole employment picture may seem. The better child care you have, the more likely your children are to feel well-adjusted and happy, too.

No matter what form of daycare you decide on, you can make life simpler for the new caregiver by writing down each child's schedule for the hours you will be gone. This is especially important for twins and triplets, since there will no doubt be a period of adjustment for the caregiver, as she or he figures out who each child is. You might make up a sheet with the following information on it for each child:

• Identifying characteristics (like birthmarks, hair growth patterns, freckles—any physical differences that will help a new person keep the right child attached to the right name until personality differences become clear)
  • Special likes and dislikes
  • Medical information (allergies, etc.)
  • Favorite toys and books

You can add other information that will help the caregiver distinguish one child from the other.

In addition, if the caregiver will be in your home, the information sheet should of course have both parents' names, places of business, relevant telephone numbers, and emergency information (like the Poison Control Center nearest you, physician's office, etc.). If your children will be in a daycare home or at a center, that information is usually requested on the registration form. You should also record a sample schedule for the day (for each child if they tend to differ), including mealtimes, snack times (and foods you do and do not want them to eat), and nap- or bedtimes.

You will also probably want to ask caregivers you interview about their attitudes toward multiples. Whether your children are in a daycare center or at home with a sitter, the adults who spend time with them during your working hours will become very important to your children, and some of their attitudes and beliefs are bound to have an effect on your little ones, no matter how young. If you want to avoid some confusion and working at cross-purposes, you might want to find a caregiver whose beliefs about multiples mirror your own. For example, if you want to emphasize your children's individuality, and the daycare-center worker who will spend the most time with your identical twins thinks twins are cuter when they are dressed alike, you might want to consider another center.

You might also want to ask caregivers, particularly if you are considering having someone come into your home, how they see needs of your twins or triplets. If it's difficult for the caregiver to see that each baby or child will have her own special set of needs (one demands warmed bottles, the other couldn't care less), whether they are identical or fraternal twins, you might want to keep looking. It might also be good to ask how, specifically, the caregiver who would be alone with two or three babies plans to meet those varying needs. Many people who have not been around babies much tend to underestimate the job.

And of course, getting and checking references is always necessary, and it provides insight into these and other issues you couldn't get any other way.

One of the surest ways to tell whether a caregiver will be right for your children is to have that person spend some time with you and them. You can see how your children act with the caregiver, they can check her out, and you can leave the room and listen for a while to get an idea of her style. If you are considering having someone come to your home to care for your children, certainly have that person in for a half hour once or twice before you make a final decision. To keep your interviewing on a professional level, you might also consider paying the person for the time she spends with you, at the rate you plan to pay, especially if you do want her to spend very much time in these tryouts.

If you are considering using a daycare home or center, you might want to choose one that will allow not just you, but also your children, to observe. Not only will you all be able to see what life would be like there, but your children might feel just a bit more secure if you are there, watching them play for a morning or two before they are there on their own. Some preschools welcome this kind of participation from parents, and observation by both parents and children—others won't even consider it. If it's important to you that both you and your children check out the preschool before you make commitments, keep looking until you find one that fits your needs.

There are some standard child-care arrangements to choose from, and numerous books and magazine articles focusing on this area give plenty of detail to help you make your choice. (One good one is *Mother Care/Other Care,* by Sandra Scarr.) Census Bureau reports show that about one-third of employed women with children under the age of five have their children cared for in another's home, one-third have their children cared for in their home, and the other third primarily have their children cared for at an organized child-care facilty, with a small number (8 percent) caring for their children themselves at their workplace.

If you are looking for care for preschool-age or infant twins or triplets, here or some arrangements you might want to consider:

1. *Care by a close relative or friend.* If you have a grandparent, aunt, or best friend close by who would be willing to take care of your young twins while you are at work, by all means try to work out a mutually agreeable arrangement. For many families, there is nothing like the spontaneous love and caring that comes from blood ties. And for some close friends, the bond is just as strong. These are all people with a vested interest in your children. As with all forms of child care you may investigate, be sure that your two or three children don't make the situation intolerable for the caregiver, or make the adult-child ratio less

than optimum. The Federal Interagency Group, a group of child-development experts who advise the government on standards for daycare, recommends that for child care in homes, there be no fewer than one adult for every five children between birth and age two. So if your willing and patient sister-in-law has two or three preschool-age children of her own, you might think twice about taking her up on her offer to baby-sit for your two six-month-olds. You, as their mother, know better than anyone that while infant twins can be disarmingly charming, they can also be incredibly demanding.

If your schedule permits, you might have your sister-in-law or a grandma take care of your babies on a trial basis for a week or so before you actually begin your job, just to see how it really works out. Some people are perfectly capable of single-handedly dealing with groups of small children, and a short trial period may prove it to you—and to them. The number of hours of care required and where those hours fall in the day make a difference, too.

If you are planning to work part time, you might be able to work out a trade with a friend, or form a co-op with a few friends. This can be an ideal arrangement if the children are of ages and inclinations to get along well, and if work schedules can be set up to complement each other.

> *PRO:*
> • Can be relatively inexpensive.
> • Children may get more loving, individualized, and/or familiar care.

> *CON:*
> • Can provoke family disagreements over care. Might be more difficult for some people to stand up to family members if they disagree about child-rearing practices.
> • Might strain a friendship when the duties are underestimated or the services are underpaid.

2. *Care by an unrelated person who comes to your home.* For parents of young twins or triplets, this may be much simpler than wrapping up two or three babies and carting them and all their paraphernalia off to a center or daycare home every day. You can find quality caregivers by placing an ad in your community newspaper or in other appropriate publications or on bulletin boards. Check church newsletters, high-school or college newspapers, community parenting center bulletin boards or publications. To find the perfect person for you and your children, you can talk to applicants on the telephone, choose the ones who seem most likely to meet your needs, and make an appointment to interview those in your home. Try to narrow the field significantly over the phone to save time and hassle for everyone.

PRO:
• Could be the simplest arrangement of all, in terms of logistics. *You* are the only person you have to get ready in the morning; you walk out the door alone when the baby-sitter comes.
• Very young children don't have the additional trauma of being taken out of their homes when their mother is gone. Familiar surroundings may ease separation pangs for some children.
• The motherlike care a single caregiver can offer when she only has your children to care for may be the best alternative for some children.

CON:
• You must feel very certain of the trustworthiness of a person who will be alone in your home with your children while you are gone. A careful check of references is a must.
• One person alone with twins or triplets has no one to spell her during rough days. Again, a careful check of references may help you to see how the person you are considering handles difficult days. If your schedule permits, you could also drop in unexpectedly a few times at first, if you want to see how things are going. And you can observe how your children react to the caregiver after a while, when she arrives and when she leaves, to get an idea of how her relationship with your children is developing. You can also gain insight into her relationship with your children by listening to your children. Preschoolers aren't known for being accurate reporters, but if you have questions about whatever they tell you about their caregiver, it's legitimate—and necessary—that you discuss those question (positive or negative) with the caregiver.
• Older children at home with a sitter may miss the contact with other children that is part of a daycare or preschool setting.

3. *Care in a daycare home.* Most states have licensing programs for daycare homes, which set standards for care and cleanliness, and prescribe limits on the number of children an individual can care for. While licensing is not a guarantee that your children will receive the kind of care you want them to, it does set a standard. But there are, no doubt, also unlicensed homes in every community that are some parents' idea of heaven for their children. It's up to you to check out each situation thoroughly.

In some communities there are networks or associations of daycare homes through which daycare providers can get ideas for activities for children in different age groups, collect materials for preschool learning programs, and learn about how to handle special situations like chronically difficult children. You might be able to contact this kind of association or individual home daycare providers through a community parenting center, through a health-care provider like your pediatrician or family doctor, or through the classified ads in your local newspaper.

PRO:
• May be the least expensive alternative in some regions.
• A sensitive, loving caregiver in a daycare home may be the most likely (after your own family) to provide individualized attention for infants and children under three. This may be a special consideration for parents of multiples.
• You may be more likely to find exactly the atmosphere (kinds of toys, activities, foods) you want for your children in a small daycare home than in a larger daycare center.

CON:
• May be too restricted a setting for older toddlers and preschoolers who might profit from more contact with peers or slightly more structured activities.
• You will have to get everyone—yourself and your babies—ready to go at one time before you leave for work.
• Many daycare home caregivers are not trained in child development or education. Their experience with their own children and with caring for those of others may well be enough, but that is for you to judge in your interviews with them.
• You may be limited in finding a daycare home because your multiples can put the number of children over the licensed limit.

4. *Care in a daycare center.* Depending on your childrens' age and how closely a center's policies match your beliefs, this could be a good choice. Many daycare centers provide special accommodations and adult-child ratios for infants, and most group children by age, within roughly a two-year span. For young toddlers of two or three, this can be a drawback, because many children of this age are easily intimidated by four- or five-year-olds. Larger groups, even of their peers, can also be uncomfortable for some two- or three-year-olds. You should pay particular attention to group size, age grouping, and the mix of structured and free play time when you are considering a daycare center.

You should also scrutinize the staff's attitudes toward twins and triplets. In a larger setting like a daycare center, your children may gain their first notoriety as multiples among the children as well as the staff. The way in which the caregivers understand issues that apply to multiples, how they think they will treat multiples as individuals, and how they will handle the other children and their beliefs about multiples are all important issues for you to discuss with the staff before you make a commitment.

PRO:
• For three- and four-year-olds, a high-quality daycare center may provide beneficial contact with other children their age, and exposure to the kind of structure they will find in preschool.
• Many caregivers at high-quality daycare centers are well trained in child development and early education.
• Play facilities and materials may be more extensive and of higher quality at some daycare centers.

CON:
• May be too large and lack individual attention needed by two- or three-year-olds, particularly if they are multiples.
• May have institutionalized policies about twins or triplets that don't fit with your ideas.
• May offer more exposure to a wide range of diseases than you would like, especially for young children.

BACKUPS

Almost every mother who has ever worked outside the home knows that no matter how well you think you have planned your daycare arrangements to cover every contingency, something eventually pops up that catches you unaware—and you miss work because there is no one else to care for your children.

Here are some backup ideas that may help you fill in the blanks:

• Discuss the possibilities of daycare disasters ahead of time with your employer and/or coworkers, and come up with an acceptable plan. Everyone knows you sometimes have to be with your children when you are scheduled to be at work, and if you acknowledge those times in advance and find out what solutions are acceptable in your company, it might not be so traumatic when the time comes.
• Arrange ahead of time with another parent who is at home in your neighborhood, or with a stay-at-home relative, to fill in during an emergency.
• Arrange with other parents who also work outside the home to allow your children to join their children and their sitter, or to have them pick up your children from daycare in an emergency.
• Check out community backup resources for daycare ahead of

time. Some city-run centers (and some private centers) will take children occasionally on a drop-in basis.

• Be sure you offer—and make good on your offer—to return the favor if another parent takes up the slack for you in an emergency.

MAKING IT ALL WORK

It isn't surprising that juggling the paid work of your job with the unpaid work you do at home is no easy task. But for some mothers, it just never seems to work; for others, being employed not only works well, but it's the only way to go. If you are one of the former, here are some ideas that may help you pull it all together and make it work for you:

1. *Be clear* about your decision to work outside the home. You can create the life-style you want for yourself and your family, but no life-style will work well if you are ambivalent about it.

2. *Be flexible.* Your career or job needs will change. And the kind of daycare your children need will change, too. What works well for three-month-old babies will never do for three-year-old toddlers. Every employed mother would like to hire Mary Poppins to come stay forever with her children. But even Mary Poppins doesn't stay forever. You may be able to avoid wasting energy resisting change if you know ahead of time it's an inevitable part of the picture.

3. *Be in charge.* If you feel that you are in charge of your fate—even if only of small parts of it—it's within your power to make some kind of change. If you are unhappy at home—look for a job. If your job is driving you crazy—find ways to change your family's life-style enough so that you can afford to quit. If you can't get all the housework done and get to the office, too—split up the chores or forget about what's not absolutely necessary. Take charge of your life and mold it the way you want it.

4. *Be simple.* Dinner doesn't need to be any more than some kind of protein, vegetables, and fresh fruit. Your whole family will be healthier for eating lighter in the evening, and you'll be less frazzled. You might also be less frazzled if you keep weekend and evening plans to a minimum, and then make them simple as can be.

5. *Be kind to yourself.* In your heart of hearts, especially if you are a mother of multiples, you know that as a human being, you can't do absolutely everything. And you may also have learned that there is a

price to be paid when you go overboard trying. Knowing those two things, it might be useful for you to recognize a few realities about working outside the home. For example, unless you have a house-keeper who picks up after everyone, by the end of your work week your house will probably look like Attila the Hun just cruised through. You could spend the weekend knocking yourself out to put it right. Or you could enlist some help from older children or your partner to do what's necessary, and learn to ignore the rest. Your children probably never noticed the dust on the piano and the crumbs under the couch anyway. Give yourself a break.

8 | Language Ability and Brains: Is There Enough to Go Around?

"When I was pregnant with my twins, one of my biggest concerns about them was that they would have all kinds of problems just because they were twins. Everyone I talked to took it for granted that they would have a secret language, and one person even told me twins are never very bright because they have to split the intelligence of one person."

A good part of the concern many parents of multiples have about their twins and triplets has to do with development—with how their children will acquire skills like walking and talking, and with how their children will do in school socially and academically. Much of what they hear as expectant or new parents about these issues is negative—everyone "knows" that multiples are slow to walk and talk, that they do poorly in school and, because of that, they are socially maladjusted. And it's all supposedly because more than one baby occupied the same womb at the same time.

What many parents don't know is that plenty of those beliefs are based on a kind of mythology about twins that parents of multiples and their children may encounter all their lives. Seeing through the myths, and then putting solid information about twin development in context, can help parents of multiples gain confidence in their childrens' competence. That kind of understanding can also make clear how parents can help their multiples over rough spots.

Major Myth 1: The whole pattern of development for twins and triplets is different from that of other children, simply because they are multiples.

Fact: Studies have shown that while some twins and triplets may have a different timetable for development of some skills like language, they don't actually acquire the skills in a pattern any different from that of everyone else. In other words, some multiples may take a little longer to learn to speak with as large a vocabulary as some single-born children of the same age. But researchers have seen that twins and triplets acquire language in the same way single-born children do— there is no difference in *how* they learn to speak. And there is no biological difference between twins as a class and single-born children. Other factors, like heredity, family environment, and birth complications may affect any child's development, just as they may affect twins' development.

Major Myth 2: Twins and triplets are less intelligent than single-born children.

Fact: In some studies twins average two to five points lower on intelligence tests than single-born children. Many experts would agree that for anyone but a person doing research, two to five points on an IQ test means nothing in terms of how a person gets along in the world.

Other studies show that when verbal testing is not used, twins score the same as single-born children, which researchers interpret to mean that language difficulties may be at the root of these IQ score differences, rather than some innate deficiency in twins. Some researchers even speculate that since verbal and nonverbal scores are typically averaged to reach a total IQ score, the nonverbal abilities of twins have been underestimated. Another study, this one on 148 four-year-old twins whose co-twin had died in infancy, showed that IQ differences between twins and single-born children are more environmental than biological. The twins whose co-twin had died early on had the same average IQ score at age four as single-born children, even though they had experienced the same rate and kinds of prenatal, birth, and postnatal difficulties as other multiples. The only difference for them was that they were not raised with a twin.

The conclusion is inevitable—where IQ scores are lower for some twins, it is usually not the physical fact of their twinship, but how they are treated *as twins* that is at the root of it. Twins and triplets are not intrinsically dumb, they just get treated differently from other children.

Researchers have found that the same kind of thing happens to some children of large families (with more than four children) and some siblings who are close in age. Such children sometimes have IQ scores slightly lower than those of only children, or of children who are born more than three years apart. Some researchers interpret the lower IQ scores to mean that children of large families get less attention, which produces a less enriching environment, which produces lower IQs in the children. Others say their studies show parents with large families generally have lower IQs themselves, so they reason from a genetics viewpoint that their children would, too. (Although it is hard to believe that the majority of the people in the U.S. had lower IQs as recently as the 1950s and 1960s, when large familes were the norm.)

These two interpretations reflect one of the most intense controversies in the field of behavioral genetics. That controversy revolves around intelligence and how people acquire it. One camp believes that genetics are responsible for 40–60 percent of an individual's intelligence (with some reporting study results showing genetics account for 100 percent of intelligence—meaning family environment has *nothing* to do with how smart a kid turns out to be). The other camp believes that environment makes a significant difference in a child's intelligence— that genetics can provide potential (contributing as little as 10 percent to a child's intelligence, some say), but the potential won't be realized in an unstimulating environment.

Neither side has proved its case conclusively. And neither side has been able to come up with a reliable ratio illustrating exactly how big a role genetics plays compared to environment in how intelligent a child will be. While behavioral geneticists continue to conduct studies using twins to try to prove their genetics/environment points about intelligence (or any other aspect of human development or behavior for that matter), it may be interesting to the parent of twins that few of these studies ever focus on twins themselves.

As one prominent researcher in twin studies said, "Twins have often served science, but science has rarely served twins." Consequently, little is know about intelligence differences between twins and single-born children. Although some researchers have noticed differences under certain circumstances in certain tests, few have really examined why those differences exist.

While the behavioral scientists are sorting out the genetics/environment controversy, here are some things you can know about your twins and triplets and their intelligence:

• There is no reason to believe that twins or triplets are biologically different from anyone else. There is no reason to believe their level of intelligence will be significantly different than that of single-born children. In fact, believing your twins or triplets are, by virtue of being multiples, operating with a mental handicap can be a self-fulfilling prophecy: They may live down to your expectations.

• Intelligence test scores are not guarantees of success or failure. These tests (specifically the Stanford-Binet) were originally intended to pick out children who were significantly behind their peers in order to give them help they needed to catch up. They were not designed as predictors of academic achievement. Some newer tests attempt to predict academic ability rather than identify deficiencies, but most educators would agree that while there is some correlation between test scores and achievement, they are never a guarantee of performance.

• Intelligence test scores usually represent the average of verbal and nonverbal abilities. Without breaking it down, and without some knowledgeable interpretation, the raw score means little in terms of representation of overall ability. In the case of twins who, on the average, score the same as single-born children in nonverbal tests, the overall score can be particularly misleading.

• Contrary to what a quick review of much of the research on twins and intelligence would have you believe, there are gifted twins, too. Just as single-born children range from low to high on the IQ scale—so do twins and triplets.

• You can use your common sense about how you deal with your own twins and triplets. It never hurts to provide a stimulating environment for your children, but remember that even the best environments are not guarantees of success. Most people have heard about those cases in which environment turned out to have little to do with a child's achievement—like the teacher's son who flunked out of high school, the ditchdigger's daughter who won a Fulbright scholarship. Those cases are reminders that you can't *make* your children be what they aren't. But you can provide opportunities for learning, and an atmosphere in which it's easy to take advantage of them.

Those who study twins have seen this perhaps more clearly than some. Ronald S. Wilson, former director of the Louisville Twin Study, said that twin studies can offer "a great appreciation for the range of individual differences, a moving away from the notion that we can control the way things happen. We can focus, direct, and support children, but only within reasonable limits."

Major Myth 3: Twins and triplets are bound to have language problems.

Fact: There is no denying that some twins and triplets have language problems. So do some single-born children. But the mythology has grown to the point that one of the first questions many parents of multiples encounter from strangers in the shopping mall is whether their children have a secret language.

To put the study of language in twins and triplets into some context, it is interesting to note that much of what researchers know of language acquisition in multiples comes from studies done more than fifty years ago, and from studies done on French, Russian, and Yugoslavian twins. What they don't know is how many of the issues that apply to twins learning Serbo-Croatian (or French, or Russian) apply with equal validity to twins learning English. And no one has measured how cultural factors (for example, whether being twins is generally considered good

From a nontwin mother: "Although my brothers and I weren't even very close in age, we had our own language for as long as I can remember. In fact, we still, as adults, sometimes call meetings of our secret club and use our language!"

or bad) in these countries affect how twins learn the language. Researchers at La Trobe University in Australia are looking at language acquisition in multiples, and they may produce useful answers to these and other questions, since their research is based on children learning English in a culture similar to that of the U.S.

According to the Australian researchers and to others in the U.S., twins between the ages of three and five, on the average, are about six months behind single-born children in language development. That doesn't mean that *every* twin pair is six months behind, or that just because your children are twins they *must* be six months behind their peers. Studies have shown that the lag, where it occurs, is not because

twins acquire language any differently than anyone else; some twins are just on a different timetable, probably for environmental reasons. They also have found that twins, on the average, are about a month later than single-born children in uttering their first word other than *mama* or *dada*. But the studies show that after the age of five, twins differ little from single-born children in their language ability, sometimes showing a slightly smaller vocabulary at age six.

These findings cover the areas that most people identify as "language problems" in twins:

• Some twins tend to begin speaking later on the average than single-borns.

• Some twins use fewer words to express themselves than single-borns.

• Some twins use shorter sentences than single-borns.

(Some multiples may have to relearn pronunciation of certain sounds too—possibly because they've copied each other's incorrect sounds as they learned to talk—but that is not seen by most people as a major problem.)

The other speech issue for twins that is identified by some people as a problem is that of twins inventing a secret language for use only with their co-twin.

A look at these language issues, what they really mean, and what the repercussions of problems with any of them are, might dispel some fears for parents of twins and triplets.

1. Secret languages (called cryptophasia or idioglossia by those who study them) are actually rare. Most researchers estimate that only 1–4 percent of twins invent a language—and those estimates are based on parents' reports or treated cases. (One researcher claims all identical twins invent their own language, and more than 50 percent of fraternal twins do. According to what most parents report, though, these figures are hard to believe.) What many people forget in talking about invented languages is that they aren't something only twins use. Plenty of single-born adults can remember secret clubs with code languages or fantasy games with their own special words.

The freakish aspect of secret languages among multiples is an easy one to play up, but when stories of twins who don't speak an identifiable language show up on the evening news or in your favorite magazine, it might be interesting for you to look carefully at the enviroment in which those children lived. One story publicized in the late 1970s focused on identical girls in San Diego who were sent to school at age six and were found to be speaking a made-up language. When social workers looked more closely at the girls' lives, they found that the girls' parents spoke German at home, but that they both worked outside the home and the girls were cared for by a grandmother who spoke Yiddish. The grandmother didn't encourage the girls to find playmates in the neighborhood (which would be difficult anyway, since she herself didn't speak English), and she accepted signals and nonverbal grunts in lieu of words from the girls as communication.

You wouldn't have to be a twin to invent your own language with your best friend in such a situation.

While some people make a big fuss over invented words among twins, some researchers put the whole issue in a different light. They claim that invented words are simply normal baby talk that hangs on, particularly during play, for some children.

"My brother and I had special names for each other, and that evolved into our own language. I still remember some of the words. And no, we are not twins."

Perhaps more important than who invents words, and even why they do it, is the effect on later speech for children who do. Except in extremely rare cases like that of the San Diego girls, in which children are allowed to substitute their own language for understandable words with people other than their twin, researchers have not been able to tie made-up language to any later speech problems in twins or single-born children.

2. During their early years, many twins use fewer words, shorter sentences, and smaller vocabularies. Instead of being a deficiency, at least one researcher has called these efficient adaptations to a particular circumstance. For many twins, particularly when there are other children in the family, if they want to be heard, they had better say what they want to say quickly and succinctly, or they won't be heard at all. One study has even found that twins tend to respond more quickly to speech than single-born children, but that their responses aren't as long.

These adaptations tend to disappear by age six. Researchers aren't sure why there is such a developmental leap between age five and six for most children. Studies are currently being done in Australia to determine if the surge is because of increased contact with other children at this age or because of other developmental factors.

Some researchers believe that these speech differences are more pronounced in twins or triplets who have older siblings than in those who are firstborn, simply because firstborn twins may have less competition. Others believe that identical twins have more of these kinds of speech problems than do fraternal twins, but results of a variety of studies addressing this question aren't consistent. However, many researchers would agree that male twins are more likley to have language problems than female or female-male twins, just as single-born males are more likely to have language problems.

Only one thing is clear from the research: that there are a lot of variables at work in how multiples (or single-born children) acquire language. But a profile does emerge of those multiples who *may* be more likely to have a language problem than others.

Your twins *may* be more likely to (but won't necessarily) have a language problem if they:

- spoke their first words (other than *mama* and *dada*) later than eighteen months of age
- were born at less than thirty-six weeks gestation
- are boys (regardless of whether they are fraternal or identical boys or the boy in boy-girl twins)
- come from a large family

  - are the youngest, or nearly the youngest, in a large family (more than four children) where the children were born two years or less apart
  - are identical twins

Obviously, your children are at lower risk for language problems if they have characteristics opposite to these, like being fraternal girls born at term, for example.

Some characteristics were found to have no significant effect on language problems one way or the other. It doesn't seem to matter if either of your twins:

  - sat up or walked later than the developmental norm
  - are left-handed
  - are first- or second-born
  - had a difficult birth
  - have a mother who was over age thirty when they were born
  - are short or tall, heavy or light, for their age

Major Myth 4: Twins and triplets usually have problems in school, including reading disabilities.

Fact: If twins are believed to be less intelligent as a class than single-born children, it is not surprising that many times they are also seen as ripe for social and academic problems in school. No one knows the extent to which these kinds of attitudes affect the behavior of multiples in school, and virtually nothing is known from a research point of view about social behavior of twins over the age of six or seven, because that hasn't been studied either.

One area in which the Australian studies have shown a difference between single-born children and twins is in reading disabilities. In 1982, one study found a surprisingly high correlation between twin boys whose parents had reported some kind of language delay or problem at preschool age (which had subsequently disappeared by age five or six) and those whose parents reported a reading disability when the boys were from nine to thirteen years old. (A reading disability is usually defined as reading eighteen to twenty-four months below the norm for the child's age level.) In this study, it seemed that the early language difficulties may have laid the ground work for a faulty understanding of the structure of the language that resurfaced in reading problems later.

Single-born boys are typically behind girls in literacy at age ten, but they catch up almost completely by about age fourteen. The Australian study found that some twin boys were not catching up by this age, and most of those who didn't were indeed those whose parents said they had some language difficulties in preschool. This seemed to be true for some male twins whether they were fraternal or identical, or whether they came from a large family or a small one.

What this means for parents is simply that if one or both of your twins seems to be at risk for language problems, you may want to pay attention, even if the problems seem to go away by themselves. While these kinds of problems are not necessarily crises that require professional intervention, they nevertheless demand your attention. There are some suggestions at the end of this chapter for simple things you can do to help.

WHAT ABOUT TWINS' SOCIAL ISSUES?

Some studies of young children say that female twins are less social with other children than single-borns, and more exclusive to one another. Some take the opposite view and say that preschool girls are more social because of the confidence they gain from having a constant buddy. Other studies show that male twins are maladjusted because they are more likely to have reading problems, and then they are more likely to repeat a grade than single-born boys. It's clear that the behavioral sciences have hardly reached a consensus about twin sociability, but, in general, it doesn't sound good.

But if you talk to adult twins, or read studies in which adult twins are interviewed, you get a completely different picture of twin sociability in school. Adult twins in these studies report they felt they were sought after as friends, that people saw them as intrinsically trustworthy because of their loyalty to their twin. These adult twins, for the most part, look back on their childhoods as times of positive social attention. Obviously their perception of themselves doesn't match with the perception some researchers have of young twins. The difference may lie in the individual's view of herself as valuable, useful, and lovable. The fact that the majority of twins grow up to feel this way about themselves may say more to parents than the few studies that have been done on twin sociability in school.

WHAT DOES ALL THIS MEAN?

Given the lack of research about twin development, and the variety of results in studies that have been done, you might still be asking what all of this means to your children. That's a legitimate question. Knowing what little we do, you might also ask:

• Will a six-month language delay at age four ruin my child's life?

• Will five points on an IQ test keep him from getting a job when he's twenty?

• Will inventing secret words at age three mean she's socially maladjusted?

And knowing what we do, the answer to all those questions is NO.

At the same time, parents of twins and triplets need to acknowledge that while not all multiples are full of problems, some do have problems with early language, which can lead to problems in school, and later, with reading. If you would like to head off problems before they start, here are some things you can do:

1. Forget about what kind of mobile you hang over their cribs and simply TALK to your babies individually. Play peek-a-boo when you change their diapers. Tell them each what the weather's like when you get them dressed. Studies show that mothers of twins talk to their children as much as do mothers of single-born children, but they talk to both children at the same time, so the amount of individual conversation each child gets is likely to be less. And with children who are old enough to talk back, parents of multiples are often likely to get some kind of combined answer—both children talking at once, one child speaking for the other, or half an answer from one child and half from the other. None of these examples is the same as one parent speaking to one child and getting one clear response—which is what researchers say parents of multiples should shoot for.

2. Forget about the housework and PLAY affectionately with each of your children. Studies show smoother development patterns and sometimes higher IQ among children who consistently enjoy a lot of affectionate, touching play at home.

3. Get a baby-sitter for one—or have one visit a friend or grandma —and BE ALONE with the other. Multiples can be very good at one-on-one relationships, and it never hurts to practice those skills with someone other than the co-twin. It's a great opportunity for more talking, too.

4. Require that children old enough to speak ANSWER YOU INDIVIDUALLY in words or sentences. Siblings close in age, as well as twins, will sometimes tacitly agree that one child will be the "spokesperson" for the others. If this is happening with your children and you are concerned about it, you might require that the silent one make requests in his own words instead of letting his twin speak for him.

5. Require that each child GIVE THE OTHER TIME TO FINISH what she's saying. The quick, short bursts of speech found in some twins

may be born of necessity. Create the atmosphere as best you can that will let each of your children express herself.

6. APPRECIATE YOUR CHILDREN'S FLEXIBILITY and adaptability as they learn to do exactly what the situation requires of them. You can make the situation require that they scream to be heard, or you can set the scene for them to know that their words are valued and will be listened to.

7. MAKE YOUR TALKING WITH THEM AN OUTLET FOR YOU, TOO. Try to tell them how you feel as often as you give them instructions. Words can become to them more than just a vehicle for orders and demands. Your children can learn by your example that words are also tools of the heart and of the mind.

HOW DOES ALL THIS AFFECT THE SCHOOL ISSUE: TO SEPARATE OR NOT?

If the school your children attend has a policy concerning twins, it probably is that they should be separated. This seems to be the traditional viewpoint of many school administrators, and it certainly works for some twins; but it certainly doesn't work for all of them. While most researchers who study twins and their development find little to agree on, they do agree on this: There is absolutely no evidence—developmental or otherwise—to support separating twins in school as a general policy.

In fact, some researchers say that the only twins who complain about what happened to them at school are some of those who were separated.

The best policy seems to be no policy at all, which means that each year, you and your children need to decide what will work best for you. Many parents find that most preschool- and kindergarten-age twins are best left together until they are used to a classroom situation. When your children are about to enter first grade, you might ask them separately what their preferences are, and discuss with them the pros and cons of being together or apart. Before you discuss it with them, you would want to think through whether you are willing to respect their wishes (even though they may not be the same as yours), and be sure that there is indeed a choice to be made. Know the school's policy and how far you may be willing to go to change it before you talk with your children about being together or apart in school.

You can read more about individuality and separation in school in chapter 9, Halves of a Whole or Complete in Themselves?

If you agree with your school's policy concerning twin placement, you don't have a problem. But if you don't agree with it, you might want to work with the school administration to change the policy for your children. Many parents have done this, and if you want to do the same, you might fare better if you understand beforehand that changing policy can mean a long, hard battle, or it can mean a single conference with the principal. Understandably, not everyone feels compelled to fight the long battle. And in most cases children are more resilient than we give them credit for: Many children can adjust to, and even learn from, a less-than-ideal situation.

But if you are convinced that this is not the case for your children, here are some ideas on how you might be able to make changes:

1. *Think before you speak.* Clarify the issue for yourself, and be extremely specific about what you want and why. If you are crystal clear about why you want your twins to be in the same class, for

example, you can keep the discussion (when you get to that) with school administrators from lapping over into irrelevant areas, like relative merits of teachers, what your other children have or haven't done, etc. At all costs, don't let yourself get mired in "how all twins behave," because you don't know that. You *do* know about your own twins; limit your discussion to that.

You might be able to better clarify the issue for yourself by writing down what it is you want in one sentence. Then write down the reasons why you want it.

2. *Do your homework.* This might mean just being clear about what you want and why you want it. Or it might mean remembering (and writing down, for your reference) good examples of your children's behavior that illustrate why what you want is necessary, and why it would work. It might mean checking facts (like last year's report cards) or even finding evidence to back your opinions in books like this one.

If what you want (putting your twins in the same class, for example) involves someone besides you and your children (like their prospective teacher, or their current teachers, if you want to move your children into one class from separate classes), part of your homework might be to talk to him or her before you present your case to the administration. If you don't, you may win on the higher level, but lose because the teacher was not consulted. She of course has her own feelings about having twins together in her class. Maybe she doesn't like the idea of putting twins together, which may mean you need to start with her, not the principal, in making a change. If you do gain her support and understanding first, you may have a stronger case—and a united front—to present to the administration.

3. *Meet only with those who have the authority to do what you want.* Once you have gained the support and understanding of others involved, you don't need to waste time meeting with second-in-command administrators if they do not have the power to override the policy. Be persistent about setting up a meeting with the person who counts. In most cases, that means the principal. When you do have an appointment set:

- Treat it as a business meeting; dress appropriately.
- Write down the points you want to make—bring all the notes you need. Borrow someone else's briefcase if you don't have one so you're not shuffling disorganized bits of paper.
- Consider bringing someone with you, like your spouse or your partner, who is prepared to speak on your behalf, even though that other person may end up not saying a word. Having someone beside you who is on your side will give you moral support,

and may even the numbers if the administrator happens to invite a counselor or someone else to sit in on the meeting.

• Remain calm and businesslike during the meeting. Avoid emotional accusations. You can help set the tone for the meeting.

• Listen and respond. Understand where they are coming from, but be persistent in repeating your position if you think it is not clearly heard and understood.

4. *Follow up.* Once you've had your meeting, follow up with a short note or a phone call in which you can summarize the points you believe were covered.

5. *If no decision was reached, keep following up.* Don't let the issue die from neglect if it is important to you, but do decide how long you are willing to wait, and be sure the administrators understand your position.

6. *If you have not gotten the results you wanted,* you can review your options:

• Accept the results you did get.

• Change schools.

• Restate to administrators your position and why you hold it, and inform them that if an agreement cannot be reached, you will . . .

• Go over their heads to the district or state level, where you repeat the process listed in numbers 1–5.

7. *When you do get what you want,* follow up with all involved to reassure them (and maybe yourself) that you are all really on the same side—that of your children. Thank them for their time and consideration.

If this sounds like a lengthy process, it can be. But in some cases, you may feel strongly enough to go through it all step by step. But it would also be normal and understandable if you found that by the time you got halfway through the process, the issue you were fighting for just didn't seem that important anymore, and you felt like giving up. That may be appropriate. Not every issue concerning your children is worth investing this much time. Only you can decide.

But if you do go through the entire process, you might like to have an idea of what you might encounter. Here's what some school administrators have been known to say to parents who attempted to change a policy, and what you might be able to do about it:

1. "You are a hysterical mother." (—Or panicky, overprotective, etc.)

> • You can show them clearly and calmly how businesslike you are at your meeting. That doesn't mean they won't still label you a hysterical mother who is overattached to her children, but if you don't rise to the bait you will at least be able to keep the tone of the meeting on a business level instead of a personal one.
> • You can have a colleague with you to back you up at the meeting and provide moral support just by being there.

2. "But our past experience with twins shows that . . ."

> • Counter with an example illustrating the opposite situation. You know you can't pigeonhole twin behavior any more than you can pigeonhole the behavior of any child.
> • Keep the discussion centered on *your* children, not last year's children.
> • Repeat why (from your homework) you know what you do about your children. Be ready with examples.

3. "Which twin is dominant?"

> • It is easy to attribute rafts of "problems" or "potential problems" to theories about dominance/submissiveness. But most parents know that dominance usually switches between twins,

so for many people this is a nonissue. If it is a nonissue for you, be clear about explaining why, and give examples.

4. "We'd like time to consider your request."

- Set specific limits on the amount of time until the final decision.
- Make specific plans about what happens next in the process—don't leave the meeting without a clear picture of the next step.
- If there is no decision by the agreed upon time, decide what action you will take next (see number 6 above).

While you need to be well prepared if you expect to change a policy in which administrators believe, remember that the point in all of this is to make *allies* of school officials, not *enemies*. They do want what is best for your children, but they don't know what you know. You will be much more effective (and your children may be happier at school) if your information and viewpoint can gather everyone happily to the same side.

PUTTING IT ALL INTO PRACTICE

As your twins or triplets enter school, you can be confident in their abilities to adjust to their lives away from you; and you can be confident in your own ability to continue to affect their environment—in school as well as at home—in ways you may think are necessary. You may find yourself seeing through the mythology that surrounds multiples more clearly, particularly as your children grow and you begin to see them as children first, and multiples second.

None of the developmental issues discussed in this chapter, in themselves, constitute a major crisis. And one of your biggest jobs as a parent of multiples is no bigger than simply talking to your children individually and requiring that they respond to you individually as well. The benefits of this kind of communication can be enormous, in terms of the relationship you develop with each child, in terms of their language development, and eventually in terms of their sense of individuality, too.

9 Halves of a Whole or Complete in Themselves? How Multiples Realize Individuality

One identical preschool-aged twin said to his brother as they splashed in the bath, "Am I just like you?" His brother answered, "No, I have a boat."

SEPARATION—THE SURFACE ISSUE

Your mother-in-law has probably asked you what you plan to do about *it*. Your friends may have already told you how to handle *it*. And you may still be wondering how you *are* going to deal with *it*.

The big *it* here is the issue of separating multiples. Separation—if, when, and how—seems to be one of the first and most serious questions for parents of multiples. Everyone has an opinion on it, and most will gladly offer it or even impose it.

The rule in many public-school systems used to be—and still is in some places—that all multiples are separated, period. Others will allow twins to be in the same class up to a certain age, but then require their separation. Some do leave it up to the parents, but most urge them to at least consider separation.

"I can remember being so angry in high school. My sister and I each wanted to take physics, but there was only one class offered in our small high school. We fought and fought over who should get to take it, and she won. I was really furious that the school's policy of separating twins no matter what kept me from taking a class I really wanted. It didn't help our competitive relationship much either."

Why this emphasis on separation of multiples? Some think that it is because in our culture, where great value is placed on individualism, the assumption is that any two or three people who have been together since before they were born will end up being pathologically dependent on one another if they aren't forced to strike out on their own while they're still young.

Another reason offered by those who favor separation early and often is the fear that others' comparisons of every aspect of twins will hurt them and get in the way of their ability to develop separate identities.

There are certainly times when separation can be the right thing to do, especially when twins or triplets themselves request it. But before you jump off the deep end and decide how much your multiples will be together and how much apart for the rest of their young days, it could be helpful to look at what exactly is the role of separation in the development of identity in multiples.

THE TWIN BOND: WHAT IS IT?

When we talk about needing to separate twins, or helping them develop their own identities, we're really talking about how we see the twins' relationship with each other. It's how we think of that bond between them that makes us want to separate them or allow them to be together. If we think the bond is a healthy one, no problem. If we see it as an interdependent one, then we begin to worry.

Traditionally, many people have assumed multiples have a mysterious bond that will keep them from developing as two distinct individuals unless they get a hearty shove in the "right" direction from their teachers. Twins and triplets have so often been looked upon as extraordinary beings that what started as an accident of birth has become a personality trait.

Anyone who has read what little popular literature there is on twins would agree that the traditional view of the twin bond is more bad than good, particularly in our culture, which prizes individuality sometimes to the point of isolation. Oh, most people recognize that it would be great to have that one lifelong best friend (an idealized view of twinship, most twins would say), but beyond that hangs the fear that the friendship will become too exclusive to be healthy.

What do the experts say? Behavioral scientists have just begun to study the relationship between twins, so there isn't much hard evidence yet. But some of their results have shed new light on many of the *myths* about the twin bond:

Myth 1: There is a definable "twin relationship."

Truth: Just as singleton relationships are each unique, so relationships between twins and triplets vary almost infinitely. Multiples and the ways they relate to each other can't be squeezed into pigeonholes any more comfortably than can singletons and their relationships.

Myth 2: Twins establish a certain way of relating as children and maintain that pattern all their lives.

Truth: The twin relationship changes over time—the same as relationships between singletons do. We tend to assume the twinship *is* a certain way—we say "twins are best friends," or "twins always compete fiercely," based sometimes on experience, sometimes on stories from friends. But do you know of a single long-term relationship of any kind (between siblings, spouses, or anyone else) that has stayed exactly

"When my young twins and I started looking for a preschool, we were surprised to find that all but one we were interested in wouldn't allow the girls to be in the same class. How could those administrators think they knew what my children's relationship as twins was? And how could they *not* trust my judgment, as a mother, as to whether my girls should be together or not?"

So the real issue underlying separation is fear. Fear that separate identities won't develop, fear that comparisons will hurt, and fear that the way multiples relate to each other is basically not good, if not downright bad.

the same over the years? For example, do you and your spouse have precisely the same relationship you did during your courtship? All relationships change—sometimes for the better, sometimes not—and so do relationships between twins. That includes who is dominant in a twin relationship.

According to researchers at the University of Louisville, who are conducting the largest and longest-running twin study in the world, individual twins may alternate as the more dominant or assertive of the pair. And the dominance doesn't necessarily follow a clear-cut line. One twin may be dominant in one respect, while the other is stronger in a different aspect of the relationship. For example, when my identical girls were three years old, they agreed that when I left them at pre-school, one would cry and the other would take care of her. Since then, the one who cries and the one who comforts have flip-flopped several times, but it seems that the important thing is that each gets to take turns being the "comforter" and the "comfortee," something singletons without close siblings may not have a chance to do. Researchers have also found that just as the relationship changes, so does the amount of involvement with or commitment to the twinship change. Psychologist Ricardo Ainslie found in his extensive twin studies that, particularly during the development that takes place in adolescence, many twins choose to concentrate on themselves rather than on the twinship.

Myth 3: The twin bond is different from any other kind of bond.

Truth: More and more researchers are finding the relationship between twins is like that between siblings close in age—roughly less than two years apart. Ronald S. Wilson, Ph.D., who was in charge of the Louisville study, says, "The facts are that twins have much the same kind of relationship as brothers and sisters who are close in age." And Ricardo Ainslie adds, "Twins are not fundamentally different from nontwins." He believes "nontwins raised under similar circumstances, for example siblings who are quite close in age, may very closely resemble twins psychologically." One internationally known twin researcher also sees similarities between twins' relationships and those of couples who have been married a long time. Fifteen-year-old twins, as well as spouses approaching their fortieth anniversary, each know their partners' likes, dislikes, habits, and idiosyncracies as well as they know their own.

Myth 4: The twin bond is based on ESP or some extraordinary kind of supernatural link.

Truth: Some twins probably have experienced ESP, but so have siblings close in age, couples who have been married a long time, friends who know each other well, and perfect strangers. The most recent effort to discern the incidence of ESP among twins drew thirty-two responses from eight thousand mothers of twins, indicating either little interest in the phenomenon (which is unlikely, since ESP is one of the most asked about topics both *by* mothers of twins and *of* mothers of twins), or a very low incidence of ESP. In this study, extrasensory perception was defined as "perceptions outside the known sensory process," including telepathy or thought transmission, clairvoyance or su-

pernormal awareness of objects or events not known to others, and precognition or knowledge of the future. Mothers who reported experiences of what they thought was ESP saw them in children ranging from newborns to young adults. But the actions they reported included things like babies yawning in unison, sleeping in similar positions, and coughing at the same time in different rooms; and older twins completing sentences for one another, experiencing pain or illness simultaneously, and sharing conversations that sparked similar memories.

Psychologist Herbert Collier, who administered the questionnaire

to eight thousand members of the National Organization of Mothers of Twins, concluded that most likely none of the experiences reported in his study was actually an example of ESP. They could all be explained as the result of identical genetics, similar genetically determined immune systems, and learned patterns of movement acquired by newborns while they still shared a womb. Sympathetic pains and illnesses —the phenomenon that occurs when one twin gets a stomachache while the other has abdominal surgery—Collier said are attributable to having been together since before birth, and having shared so much that one literally "feels for" the other. It's like what happens between couples who have been married for a long time. They commonly finish each other's sentences and often know when the other is disturbed or in pain, even though the other is far away.

If all this is myth, then what is true about the twin bond? The conclusion researchers have reached is that *the twin bond is the direct result of what happens between the twins themselves, between the twins and their parents, and between the twins and other adults.*

Myth 5: Twins experience their relationship as exceptionally close and satisfying.

Truth: Just as any brothers and sisters do, twins experience their relationship in a number of ways. Often it is close and satisfying, but twins fall prey to cultural myths about their relationship as much as the rest of us. In one study, twenty-six adult twins each said in separate interviews that while they liked being a twin, they felt disappointed that they weren't a "good" twin, the way "real" twins were supposed to be. A majority of the twins in this study were identical, but identical or fraternal, same sex or opposite, they all said they "did things more like normal brothers and sisters," and somehow missed the pinnacle of harmony and intimacy they and many others expect them to reach. In addition, these twins also reported the same difficulties in their twinships that most of the rest of us encounter at some time in almost any important relationship: They had trouble communicating to their twin what was *really* important. For example, identical teenage girls could talk about hairstyles, clothes, and school, but they couldn't tell each other what their first menstrual periods meant to them. The fact that everyone, including many twins, *expects* twinships to be different from any other human relationship leads to disappointment and, in some cases, disillusionment about the twinship.

Myth 6: Because of their unique bond, twins have a unique psychological development.

Truth: This piece of twin mythology would have us believe that twins develop in a fundamentally different way from singletons. According to the most current research, some aspects of psychological development are specific to twins, but overall the development process is

"After that first year with my twins I was exhausted. My husband helped, my mother helped, and we hired help, but I was still exhausted from the constant demands of caring for two babies. Around the time they turned one, I could see a difference in their behavior. They actually were more interested in 'playing' with each other for short periods than they were in me. What a relief to have a few minutes now and then when I could read the newspaper or write a quick note in peace!"

the same for twins, triplets, and quadruplets as it is for singletons. In fact, many psychologists and psychiatrists studying twins increasingly compare twin development to that of siblings who are close in age.

Myth 7: Twins, particularly identical twins, have a tight bond because they are so much alike in every way.

Truth: Identical twins are genetically the same, but they are not carbon copies, whether their friends and relatives can tell them apart or not. That goes for physical as well as psychological characteristics. For example, identical twins do not necessarily have identical teeth, bitemarks, handprints, footprints, or birthmarks when examined microscopically. In the course of forming their personalities, both identical and fraternal twins often develop different relationships to people important to them. These different ways of relating to those around them create different "mini-environments" within the family for each twin, allowing them to continue to develop along different lines. What strikes many twin researchers now is not how much identical twins are *alike,* but rather how *different* they are, given the same genetic makeup. Except in a few sad, isolated, but highly publicized cases, multiples don't walk around in lockstep, talking in unison, thinking identical thoughts. The bond for normal twins, whether they are identical or fraternal, is based on how they, as individuals who are keenly aware of the differences between them, *learn* to relate to one another.

SURE, THEY HAVE EACH OTHER, BUT THEY STILL NEED YOU

A tiny light does appear at the end of the tunnel for parents of young twins and triplets every time they see those little ones paying attention to one another. You begin to see how, someday, they will indeed look more to each other and to their peers for their social needs than they will to you.

Multiples can learn about relating to others sooner than their singleton counterparts. In fact, it's one of the good things about being a twin. Because they have always had a companion of the same age, twins get more practice at interacting with others. One study showed that not only do many preschool-age twins have less difficulty relating to other children their age, but they also have less difficulty separating from their mothers, presumably because having a twin gives many preschoolers the security with which to explore and play.

Part of twin mythology is a belief that twins and triplets share a

Parents need to recognize the fine line between allowing multiples to discover each other and develop their social abilities and isolating them from parents and peers because of beliefs about the twin bond.

special kind of communication from birth. Some multiples may, but child-development theory and research don't support this belief. Psychologist Sandra Scarr says that while arranging social time for babies to "play" together isn't bad, "Some parents have the idea that babies benefit from interaction with other babies. Peer play sounds like a good idea. Actually, other babies are quite irrelevant to infants' development." She points out that babies are not capable of playing *with* each other because their brain development hasn't reached the point where they can see each other as anything more than interesting objects, the same as a cuddly teddy or an attractive toy. Mutual play (you be the mommy and I'll be the daddy) doesn't happen, she says, until children are three or four years old. Before that, babies may "pat and make noises at each other" and young children may share a toy briefly. But there is no sustained play because they're just not capable of it yet.

What does this have to do with twins? A lot. If we believe that twins are indeed human children and not a breed apart, we can safely apply what we know about child development to them. What multiples always have is companions, and when they are developmentally ready to learn how to interact with others, they may do it earlier than their singleton peers because they have an earlier opportunity. Singletons don't necessarily have someone their age standing by at the moment the light

For every parent who has ever felt excluded from the twin or triplet relationship—even when those multiples were tiny babies—please know that although those babies are fascinated by each other, *you* are still the key to their development.

dawns about sharing toys, or using a helper in the sandbox or cooperatively building a snow fort in the yard. Multiples have an advantage here because the opportunity to practice getting along—and conversely, to practice fighting well—is usually there for them.

What multiples cannot do is develop an adultlike relationship with each other when they're six months old, or even when they're two years old. Many parents of multiples would respond, "Of course not!" to that statement. But we need to look carefully at what our expectations are of their twinship, and how the subtle assumptions we make about what goes on between them changes how we treat them.

Anyone who has watched four-month-old twins reach out their tiny hands to explore each other's face for the first time would agree it is a heart-warming sight. My own twins began holding hands when they were four weeks old each time I nursed them simultaneously. Mothers of six-month-old triplets know that soft toys are better than hard toys when the three babies are lying anywhere near each other on the living-room floor, because they're bound to bonk each other over the head with whatever is within reach. Examples of infant twins, triplets, and quadruplets being aware of each other abound. There's no doubt about that. But what do these actions mean? Did my girls think to themselves, "Oh there's my twin. I'm glad to see her. I think I'll hold hands with her."? Do the four-month-old babies note that the other baby has pretty eyes and it might be interesting to touch her? And do the six-month-old triplets really lie in wait for one another, planning each attack? From what we know of child development, the answer is no in each of these cases.

But what about the two- or three-year-olds who demand they share a bedroom, who know whose blankie is whose, and who understand why their twin is crying even when mommy doesn't? While they certainly have developed a relationship with each other, it is incomplete. Psychologist Scarr says, "Toddlers are incapable of giving meaning to their experiences without adult help." Familiar experiences don't need as much explanation from adults, so in most situations, toddler and preschool multiples go their merry way, chattering to themselves and each other, seemingly oblivious of mom. But that doesn't mean they don't need the direction and support adults can give.

Multiples have a wonderful opportunity to learn from each other how to relate to the rest of the world. But parents and other adults in their lives are the ones who give their worlds meaning. All babies and toddlers need adult love, approval, interaction, and interpretation of the world, whether they are twins, triplets, quadruplets, or singletons. Just because multiples can turn to each other for companionship, and at times for comfort, don't be fooled into thinking you're not still vital to them. Don't *let* or *make* multiples be parents as well as siblings to each other. You are their models for development as well as their primary caretakers, both emotionally and physically. As we saw in the previous chapter on development, parent interaction with infants and young children has everything to do with how those children develop on every level, including how they develop their identities.

Does all of this dash your hopes about a future full of leisure, because you hoped your twins or triplets would someday "entertain each other," just as all your friends and neighbors (who don't have multiples) have assured you? Don't get depressed yet. First, you should know that many multiples tend to fight with each other almost as much as they "entertain" each other. In fact, some mothers of multiples wonder if the fighting isn't what everyone means when they say the little ones will "entertain" each other! So you may feel more like a referee than a lady of leisure after the first year with your multiples. But on the other hand, you won't necessarily have to hover over them watching their every move to be sure they develop correctly—any more than you would with any normal singleton. To make matters a little clearer, here are four things parents of multiples can do to help set healthy patterns of behavior between themselves and their twins or triplets:

1. *Respond* to differences you see in your multiples rather than trying to *create* those differences. Studies show that twins and triplets will discern their differences. Follow their lead, and have confidence that they will act out those differences where it is most important to them. You most likely *will* naturally respond to rather than create those differences. Behavioral psychologists have found that a majority of parents of multiples do.

2. *Encourage* independent decision making by your multiples, even when they are very young. Taking control of the small things in their lives—like deciding what to wear to preschool or whether to sit next to each other at dinner—is good practice for taking control of larger things later—like deciding whether to be in the same class at school or whether they'll attend the same college. At first, it may be a good idea to approach each child separately about a particular issue to avoid "me too-itis."

3. *Allow* the way you see the bond between them to change. The bond will change constantly, and you will remove obstacles to your relationship with your multiples if you can remain flexible in how you see that bond. You'll also keep your expectations of—and conversely your disappointments in—their relationship at a minimum if you allow for the changes that are bound to happen.

4. *Discard* cultural stereotypes about multiples. You know they usually aren't true for anyone, and at best they are true for only a few.

In short, you, as parents, create the environment in which your multiples can develop their individual identities. They will do it if you give them room and allow them to tell you who they are and what their relationship with one another will be.

Cultural stereotypes, twin myths, and superstitions make your children (and *you*) into faceless objects, and contribute every day to misunderstandings about you and your children. You don't blindly believe them, because you have the truth (your children) in front of you. Help others to keep from blindly believing in those stereotypes by pointing out how your children, or how those you know, don't fit the mold.

HOW DO CHILDREN FORM IDENTITIES?

The good news is—your children *will* form identities, and unless they are seriously interrupted at the task, they will form clearly individual identities. According to behavior research done by psychologist Michael Lewis of Princeton, our brains may be "prewired" to develop the notion of self, of being different from all other things in the world. Lewis sees infants as actively taking part in influencing factors that help to determine their development. The infant who cries to be held or fed and coos when she is happy is hardly a passive blob waiting to be assigned an identity, Lewis believes. Seen this way, development of identity is a matter of course—we are built to do it. While infant multiples do have a different environment because they outnumber their mother, they still have the same brain as other human infants, and it's a brain that *seeks* to develop a sense of self.

From the moment of birth on, every infant chips away at the task of realizing his or her biological, and later, psychological self as separate and distinct from everyone and everything else. And everyone, multiple or single-born, goes through similar steps toward a separate identity during the first two years of life. Theories abound on exactly how identity comes about, but for the sake of simplicity, here are some early pivotal points in the process:

1. WE'RE A UNIT. At first, newborns seem to make little distinction between themselves and their mothers. For example, hunger pangs waken baby, baby cries in response, mother supplies food, pangs go away, and baby drifts back to sleep. The two have just acted as a unit in baby's best interests. And that's what they continue to do for the first couple of months. Baby's job at this early age is also to begin to figure out that her body is separate from mom's. She does that as she is held and as she discovers her own hands and, later, her feet.

2. WAA MEANS FEED ME. After that first couple of months, baby is beginning to get the picture that the person who meets her needs just might be someone outside herself. This is an in-between phase, but nonetheless an important one during which the stage is set for later

development. Psychologists believe that now baby begins to cry with some kind of expectation that help will arrive. When that help arrives pretty reliably, the need always to make sure help is going to be there diminishes, and baby can concentrate on other things. As one psychologist said somewhat poetically, mother's job now is to "light the infant's way to the small familiar world outside their commonly shared orbit." And that's what mom does when she makes life *within* the orbit comfortable and predictable enough that baby feels confident peeking outside.

3. HI, MOM! Voila! At five or six months, baby's got it down—the one who meets her needs is an entirely separate person. Being with her (it could be *him* if the primary caretaker is dad, and it could be the

baby-sitter if she's the primary caretaker) and somehow communicating with her is a major preoccupation. That's why all the wiggles, smiles, goos, and gaas for her and for other important adults. By eight months or so, unfamiliar substitutes will not do, as any mother knows who has tried to pry a screaming infant off her shoulder to hand her over to a new baby-sitter or to Aunt Gladys whom she's never met. Besides seeing that people are physically separate from herself, baby at this age continues work she started on Day One of her life: refining her ability to communicate with those who matter to her. As a newborn, she began by moving her body subtly and rhythmically in time to her mother's speech. Now baby and her mom, and baby and other important adults, continue to refine what psychologists believe is an innate push toward reciprocal relationships—by fitting more and more closely to each other's way of acting. "You soothe me when I cry. I play when you're quiet."

4. YES, I DO. WAIT, NO, I DON'T. The time between about fifteen months and two years of age might be described as ambivalent at best. Baby is secure and confident and ready to check out the rest of the world—but wait! Every time she moves away from mom, she runs right back and wraps herself around mom's knees. It's not usually an easy time for anyone—mom or baby—as baby graduates to toddlerhood. But the toddler figures out a way to weather the storm: the blankie, the teddy, the thumb, the finger! Psychologists call it the transitional object. Moms know it's something to hang on to when the going gets tough, or the toddler gets tired. And everyone knows it's good to have a friend of *some* sort to take along on the trek from infant-as-unit to toddler-as-individual.

HOW IS ALL THIS DIFFERENT FOR TWINS?

While twins go through the same stages single-born children do as they develop their identities, psychologist Ricardo Ainslie has identified some points at which twins and their parents may have some extra work to do.

1. WE'RE A UNIT. When babies are this young—two months and younger—life is still pretty straightforward. As long as basic needs are met—holding, diapering, feeding, burping, sleeping—everyone's happy. Or almost everyone. Some clever reasearchers have determined that mothers of very young twins spend 35–37 percent of their time on infant-related activities, while mothers of single-born babies spend 22–29 percent of their time on them. Any mother knows that

young babies—whether you have one or three—actually take 100 percent of your time. So mothers of multiples probably spend what feels like 135 percent of their time on baby matters. At any rate, infant twins are happy, and mothers of infant twins are *tired*-but-happy. Aside from the amount of time spent on babies, life at this point is similar for young infant twins and singles.

2. WAA MEANS FEED ME. Every infant, multiple or single-born, is introduced to frustration during this time. While babies may be crying with expectation now, they don't always get what they want as quickly as they want it. This could be one of the first and biggest frustrations for *parents* of multiples too—you just can't be there instantly for each baby every time. Sometimes it seems that there's always a baby crying —there's always a baby with unmet needs. And parents of multiples are always worrying that whichever baby is crying is being scarred for life. It might be refreshing to know that psychologist D. W. Winnicott, who studied infant behavior extensively, has noted that mothering at this point doesn't have to be perfect, it just has to be "good enough." In other words, no one is able to meet perfectly the needs of any infant *all* the time. Winnicott saw, through his research on single-born babies, that babies whose needs were met *much* of the time or *most* of the time turned out just fine—confident and secure enough to move on to the next step of development. So you can take some of the pressure off yourself, as you trust in the resiliency of your children.

But don't assume your children need each other more than they need you. The foundation for later identity formation is still being laid at this young age, and mom or the primary caretaker is the one stacking the bricks. Here is where the extra work for parents of multiples comes in. Just when you may be exhausted from two months of four feedings every night, your babies really need you to "light the way" for them to the world just outside the cozy orbit you've created. It's easy now to see more than actually exists in the simple exchanges between your infants—to believe they're satisfying each other's need for human interaction. Psychologists have seen in their research that when parents make this assumption, they tend to leave their infant multiples alone to "amuse" themselves much more than single-born infants. They've also seen that multiples and single-born children who, beginning at this age, have had less opportunity to talk and play with adults are the ones who have difficulty later with the development of language, identity, and intellect.

While it is good for you to be aware of this pitfall, remember that the quality of your care can still hover around the "good enough" rather than the "perfect" mark. Because you know how important your interaction is to your babies, you will probably want to make a point to join

their early "gooing" and touching of each other, just as you would with a single-born baby.

3. HI, MOM! Since you've been jabbering with your babies since they were a couple of months old, the three-way conversation should naturally expand into three-way play by five or six months. Now your babies can react more to you, and playtime is more fun for all of you. This, too, is the extra "work" parents of multiples have to do. Your fatigue probably hasn't lessened, so try to make playtime relaxing time for you, too. If you sit on the floor instead of the couch, you'll be accessible to the babies and they'll usually seek you out at first, then turn to each other, confident that you're there if needed. In this calm atmosphere, you can turn your attention from one to the other and back again to begin learning more about the individual style each has in playing with and relating to you and to each other.

As you spend time each day on the floor with your babies, you may think of it as just taking it easy. Psychologists would say you're building reciprocity and developing synchrony with each of your babies. Those are two important bricks in the foundation you've been building that will help your babies develop a strong identity later. Reciprocity helps your babies understand how to "fit" actions with others' in the give and take of a relationship, and synchrony refines the "fit" between mother and *each* child so each is in tune with the other's needs. Both of these are another way of saying that by playing with your babies, you'll see differences in them and build individual relationships with each of them.

4. YES, I DO. WAIT, NO, I DON'T. Language begins to emerge during this phase, and parents of multiples should still be right in there talking and talking to multiples. Conversation, no matter how primitive, with *each* of your multiples will not only sharpen the verbal skills of each, but will contribute to separate identity formation as differences in personality and habits become apparent. The main job at this phase for single-borns and multiples alike is to learn how to separate from mom, and your children can have the edge. You've been spending all these early months forming a secure base from which your multiples can grow, and research shows the more secure any child feels in his relationship to his parents, the easier it is to separate from them. That secure relationship you've developed will also balance how much your multiples look to each other for comfort during this time.

You have probably seen one-year-olds who can separate from mom, but who could never be without blanket, stuffed animal, thumb, or finger. As I mentioned before, psychologists call these transitional objects—they take the place of mom during what can be a stressful time as toddlers learn to separate from her. Twins can be a great support to each other during difficult times, and whether or not your twins use a blankie or thumb for comfort, they probably also use each other to some degree. Drawing confidence from having company in an unfamiliar situation is not necessarily a bad thing, but when twins do it, many parents and teachers are uncomfortable. Actually, moving between dependence and independence, between the role of "comforter" and "comfortee," is a part of any intimate relationship. We've each probably been a transitional object of sorts for someone, sometime, providing comfort when it was needed.

When twins use each other as a transitional object, a little is probably no big deal and a lot may be harmful. Just how much is okay for your children is something you must judge. But remember, adult twins in personality studies report that no matter what pattern of relating they established with their twin during their lives, the pattern always changed, as patterns change in any relationship. While your twins are very young you may want to pay attention to the kinds of patterns they have, and how often and under what circumstances those patterns change, before you make judgments about how your children may be using each other and what to do about it.

Besides noticing how much your twins use each other for comfort at this stage, you should also look at how much they're encouraged to do so. Does the daycare worker assume your twins will spend all their time together because they're so much alike anyway? Does grandma insist on taking them out for ice cream together for fear of appearing to favor one? Of course your twins will spend some time playing together at the daycare center, and they won't be emotionally crippled if they go out together with grandma. But be sure the daycare supervisors know that your children need *other* children too, and point out to grandma that separate-but-equal treat times may help get each child ready to stand alone when they need to.

WHAT ABOUT ADOLESCENCE?

Most psychologists agree that while the basis for identity formation occurs from birth to age two, the final throes of its formation occur during adolescence. Once again, all youngsters, including multiples, may face a tumultuous time in their teens, and once again, multiples may have a little extra work to do.

While most teens are struggling with how to separate from their families now, multiples are also working on separation from each other. Many twins find the first job so engrossing that the twinship takes a back seat for a while, which may make developing additional independence from a twin that much easier. It also may make the twin who is *not* struggling with independence from the family feel ignored by her co-twin. Many twins find themselves in a position similar to the one they were in when they were two years old. They want to separate from their family, and now from their twin, too, but they're afraid of losing both, particularly if one twin is more interested in independence than the other.

On the flip side, the good part about sharing adolescence with a twin is that twins have company at a time when many teenagers are feeling most isolated. Psychological studies are full of examples of adult twins who felt they "saved" each other or were "saved" during adolescence by having a twin who commiserated with them, listened to them, and provided them with a familiar secure base from which to operate.

At this stage, as with many other adolescent issues, parents can probably help most by doing the least. Adolescents who are multiples need practice at working out what their adult relationship with their twin will be, and your guidance should be available when it's asked for, but it might not be accepted if offered.

Many adult twins report that their biggest break with each other came during adolescence, either because they believed they couldn't establish independent lives without a complete break or because they simply found they had very different interests and values. In one study some recalled that the break lasted for several years while they established separate lives in different parts of the country. Many twins, as they felt more secure in their separate lives, then reestablished contact with each other. And as with some sibling relationships, some twins did not reestablish contact at all. Still others found a new way of getting along after their separation.

Pivotal Points for Identity Formation

In short, there are three times in the lives of multiples when their identity formation may require a little more attention than that of single-born children:

1. Around six months of age: Parents need to be sure that despite great fatigue and little time, they talk and play with their babies—together and individually.

2. Between fifteen months and two years of age: Parents need to continue to emphasize talking with multiples to discern differences and to enhance language development. They also need to observe the relationship between multiples as the children learn to separate from their parents.

3. During adolescence: Parents need to stand back and allow multiples the space they need to learn how to redefine their relationship with their twin as they become adults.

Everyone has his own environment to which he must adapt. The only child has a specific environment, and so does the middle child, the youngest, and the firstborn. The conditions within every family have an effect on the development of the children in that family, and no one can unilaterally say that one condition is better or worse than any other. Cases have been made on both sides of the question concerning the value of certain kinds of challenges (read stress) in a child's life. Stress strengthens some and weakens others, depending on the time, place, and person. Twins are no different. They have their own specific environment to which to adapt—that of having arrived together instead of singly. Despite the mythology and mistaken beliefs surrounding multiples, the vast majority make it to a happy, healthy adulthood. In fact, one study found that as adults, fewer multiples seek psychiatric care than do single-born people. Could it be that those who learn to develop and maintain their identities *within* the closest relationships have found what the rest of us always seek—a healthy balance between individuality and intimacy?

Perhaps the best part about understanding how all children form their own identities is that you won't have to worry about "giving" your multiples separate identities. They were born with separate identities.

> **The most important common denominator here is that children in each phase do best with an *accessible* central adult figure who can set the stage for the work that multiples must do for themselves as their identities emerge.**

WHAT DOES INDIVIDUALITY AND INDEPENDENCE LOOK LIKE IN MULTIPLES?

Multiples have the jump on single-born children in developing their identities, because they always have a point of comparison. It may take them years to find out who they *are* (as it does all of us), but at least they always know who they *aren't*. And they spend a lot of time as they grow up telling others who they aren't in many different ways. They might not have a word for those ways, but parents have several— sibling rivalry, competition, and comparison. And all of those have one trait in common: fighting.

Ask any parent of three- or four-year-old multiples what the biggest difficulty is with their children, and somewhere close to the top of the list will be fighting. That's what independence and individuality often look like with young twins and triplets.

Most experts on child behavior agree that fighting between brothers and sisters is universal, and a normal part of growing up. Unpleasant as

"My sister and I just never liked to compete head to head on anything. It always made one of us feel bad for the one who didn't do as well. Like once when we both took the college entrance exams, I did a lot better than she because I'm better at taking tests. When people asked how we did, we just avoided talking about it much because we didn't want people to think one was not as good as the other. We usually ended up doing our own things separately so we wouldn't have to compete."

it may be to listen to, sibling fighting can even contribute to a child's ability to be successful as an adult, according to child psychiatrist John F. McDermott, Jr. He believes that fighting that's been channeled by the sensitive parent into a healthy mix of competition and cooperation has a lot to teach youngsters about identity and getting along in the world as adults.

If that is true, considering how much most parents of multiples report that their twins fight, those twins should be great at getting along in the world when they become adults. That's exactly what one study of adult twins found: Twins who considered themselves healthy, well-adjusted adults also believed the competition they felt with their twin when they were children had helped them to develop successful careers and family relationships. Once again, twins have greater opportunity than singletons to practice social skills, including fighting, which with parental direction can turn into problem solving and collaboration.

Fighting, or as behavioral scientists say, competition, has another use for twins: It helps develop the differences between them. By more clearly defining who they *aren't,* they begin to show themselves, each other, and the world who they *are.* For some twins, competition leads to differentiation. For others, they manage to see the differences first, and avoid competition that they have found to be painful.

Siblings who are not twins often do the same thing, according to another study that looked at how brothers and sisters in families of more than two children perceive their differences. The study showed that the first two siblings had found the greatest number of differences between themselves, the first and third children found the fewest number of differences, and the "middle" group of the second and third children fell in between. The implication for multiples, of course, is that the closer siblings are in age and/or birth order—and multiples are the closest of all—the more differences between each other they seek, *and find.* Again, some find them relatively peacefully before they compete for them, and some find them after long, hard battles.

What makes some find the differences easily and others fight their way to them? No one knows exactly, but don't let anyone guilt-trip you into thinking *you* made your three-year-olds duke it out daily through some mysterious lack in your skill as a parent. Recent findings by psychologist Judy Dunn, an internationally known expert on sibling relationships, show that parents have less to do with it than do innate personalities of the children, twins or not. While the final word on battling brothers and sisters is far from in, these findings seem to say that, to a large degree, our children simply are what they are—they have their own personalities and their own ways of arriving at their identities. We need to acknowledge the personalities they were born with, along with the special role that fighting may have for multiples in forming their identities, and then move on.

A FEW MORE MYTHS ON TWIN IDENTITY

Just as there are myths about the twin bond, there are scores of myths about identity in twins. Here are clarifications of four myths that might explain a little further how twins develop individual identities.

Myth 1: Identity problems are more common with identical twins than with fraternal twins because identical twins look alike.

Truth: How twins look has little to do with whether they have identity problems. Psychologists have found that the *type* of twin one is, is less important than *how* an individual meets the specific developmental challenges multiples may have. Studies show that opposite-sex twins can have questions about identity, as well as same-sex fraternal twins and siblings who are close in age. The deciding factor in any of the cases was not whether the twins looked alike and were mistaken for one another by friends and acquaintances. Instead, the deciding factors were their own personalities and reactions to those crucial identity-forming times, and their family relationships.

Myth 2: A good way to tell if very young twins are developing identity problems is to hold one up to a mirror. If that twin can't tell whether the reflection is herself or her twin, she is probably in trouble.

Truth: Moms and dads, grandmas and grandpas are always holding babies up to mirrors and teaching them to say hello to themselves. When a twin looks in the mirror and says hello to her twin instead of herself, everyone assumes she doesn't know the difference between herself and her twin. Not necessarily so, say psychologists, who of course have studied the mirror phenomenon. Single-born children under the age of two don't know who they're looking at either. In fact, slightly more than one-third of single-borns *at* age two still don't recognize their own image in a mirror. Psychologists believe the development of a concept of self accompanies the ability to identify oneself in a mirror. And they say that self-concept is a stage in development that many children simply haven't reached yet, even at age two.

Myth 3: If, in the course of forming their identities, one twin becomes more submissive than the other, that twin will most likely have a weaker sense of self.

Truth: Not necessarily. It's important to remember that single-born children don't all end up with similar personalities; each develops according to his or her own abilities and preferences. Twins, too, will show a wide range of behaviors. One study illustrated that range, and the effect of differences in dominance. It showed that clear-cut dominance was very rare among the teenage twins it studied, and it showed that where there was dominance, the less dominant twin showed no problems with ego development. In fact, the twins studied represented a range of relationships from fairly closely identified with one another to fairly independent from one another.

Myth 4: The well-publicized studies on how similar twins are who are raised apart prove that our behavior and identity formation are determined only by our genetic makeup, and what we do as parents has little to do with how our children turn out.

Truth: Those who have conducted the studies on twins raised apart would never say the jury is in on the role of genetics in behavior. The well-publicized Minneapolis study originally involved only sixteen pairs of twins who were raised apart, and researchers there continue to study the results of those interviews and look for more twins to study. So far, the results do point to a greater genetic influence than was previously acknowledged, and most behavioral scientists now believe that *both* environment and genetics play a part in how we all develop.

From the viewpoint of identity formation, it is interesting to note that twins raised apart generally display more similarities than twins raised together. Some psychologists who study twins raised together believe that sharing an environment—the same family—contributes to the development of *differences* in twins, as they carve out their unique place in the family. Some of these psychologists have gone so far as to question the twin method of research that assumes twins in the same family have exactly the same environment.

Even the results of the Minneapolis study have been questioned. Editor and clinical psychologist Peter Watson believes that similarities between twins raised apart may be largely attributable to predictable coincidence rather than to some unknown genetic link that causes two women to wear the same color sweater to a party. He bases his argument primarily on the fact that researchers in that study collected a list of personality traits and habits from the twins studied and then matched them. Watson believes you could do that nearly as successfully for any given segment of the population, and that to get a true test of similarities, researchers need to set up the list of traits ahead of time and apply that test to the twins.

Obviously, much is left to be studied in the area of twin similarities and identity formation.

WHAT DOES ALL THIS HAVE TO DO WITH SEPARATION?

Back to the original question: Do twins need to be separated in order to successfully develop separate identities?

The answer is: Maybe. And there are two more ideas to consider before you make a decision:

• First, psychologists have found that *psychological* separation is much more important than *physical* separation. Just because you put them in separate classrooms doesn't mean your twins will automatically have strong separate identities. Conversely, being in the same classroom isn't an identity disaster for some twins. And to make matters even more confusing, each situation could be right for the same twin pair in different years.

The bottom line is that multiples will pick up on your perception of them as parts of a unit or as separate individuals. Active, sensitive parents can set the stage for identity development, and can go a long way to defuse twin mythology your children will hear from others all their lives. According to the most recent behavioral research, you needn't assume the worst about your multiples. They are as capable of forming healthy identities as are single-born children.

• Second, and perhaps most important, you, as a parent, are the best judge of how to respond to each stage of identity development in your multiples.

10 | What's Good About Twins

"There are days when it seems my two-year-old boys just have it in for me all day. Those are the days when it is *really* hard to tolerate, much less appreciate, my twins."

Some days it's hard to remember what *is* good about these twins or triplets you've been handed. When your toddlers have collaborated to destroy the kitchen you just cleaned; when you've changed the fourteenth diaper of the day and it's only noon; when it's four in the afternoon and you're so tired you want to scream at your screaming babies to leave you alone—those are the times you wonder how you got into all this—and more important, how you can get out of it.

You know you can't really get out of it—short of running away from home, which even in the worst of times may seem a bit drastic. But if you can remember what's good about it all, maybe you can feel a little better about the fact that you have multiples, and about how all this will change you.

You might want to copy the list that appears on the last page of this chapter and keep it on your refrigerator, or tape it to your bathroom mirror, or keep it anywhere else you'll see it every day. It comes from information that appears in other chapters in this book, and it might help remind you of what is good about your special children, what is good about all of this for you, and what you can do as a parent of multiples.

HERE'S WHAT'S GOOD ABOUT BEING TWINS

Twins Can Be More:

1. Confident. Even as youngsters, twins and triplets often have a higher level of confidence than do some single-born children, maybe because they have always had an extra base of security (their co-twin) from which to act.

2. Supportive. All their lives, twins can provide support and empathy for each other in times of stress, and many learn well how to provide that loving support to others in their lives, too.

3. Innovative. Most twins take turns competing and collaborating —the very skills that can serve them well in a competitive adult world. Single-born children don't always have a partner with whom they can experiment in these roles.

4. Substantial. Instead of feeling like "half a person," many adult twins report that they feel like "more than one" because of the strong relationship with their co-twin, coupled with the strong sense of self that most twins develop.

5. Self-knowing. By the time they are adults, many twins believe they have a deeper level of self-knowledge than many single-born adults, because their twinship has required that they explore aspects of their individuality more closely.

6. Sought-after. Many adult twins feel they have always been sought after as friends by single-borns, who see them as loyal confidants because of their twinship. Some even feel that twins make the best spouses.

7. Giving. Giving of themselves in a close relationship isn't often as difficult for some twins as it may be for single-borns. They can learn from their earliest days how to share themselves without fear of losing themselves.

HERE'S WHAT IS GOOD ABOUT HAVING TWINS

1. Creative living. You can learn to live your life more creatively than you might ever have done if you had one baby at a time. With two or more babies, you can ignore the rules, traditions, and expectations that often come with parenthood. And you can use your unique situation as an opportunity to understand your needs with more clarity than you ever have, and figure out how to fulfill them with more creativity than you've ever had.

2. Family cohesion. Studies have shown that families with multiples tend to see themselves as special and as a unit that works together to learn how to cope.

FIVE THINGS YOU CAN DO AS A PARENT OF MULTIPLES

1. Respond to differences you see in your children. You don't have to create them—the differences are already there.

2. Encourage independent decision making. Choosing their own clothes when they are three years old is the first tiny step toward choosing their own college when they are eighteen.

3. Discard cultural stereotypes about twins. You know all twins don't have ESP, a secret language, and matching emotions. You can help demolish the myths by pointing out to others how your children don't fit the mold.

4. Trust your children and their relationship. Allow them to change within it. Believe that they will adjust their relationship as they need to, to maintain balance within themselves and with each other.

5. Surround yourself with people who think as you do. Loving support will create a climate in which your family and your multiples will blossom.

WHAT'S GOOD ABOUT TWINS

Twins can be especially:

Confident	*Supportive*	*Innovative*
Substantial	*Self-knowing*	*Sought-after*
	Giving	

They can teach you the meaning of:

Creative living. You can throw out all the old rules and invent the ones that fit your special situation as parents of multiples.

Family Cohesion. Some studies show that familes with multiples feel they all learn how to work together more skillfully than families who have babies one at a time.

You can help your multiples if you:

Respond to the differences they already have.
Encourage independent decision making.
Discard cultural stereotypes about twins and triplets.
Trust that your multiples will change and adjust their relationship with each other as they need to.
Surround yourself with loving support from people who agree with your viewpoint about multiples.

READER QUESTIONNAIRE

You are invited to complete this questionnaire. You can either photocopy this page and answer the question, or use a fresh sheet of paper with questions and answers. You are welcome to include or omit your name and address, as you wish. I am primarily interested in whether you found this book helpful or not, and why. Send completed questionnaires to Pam Novotny, P.O. Box 1125, Boulder, Colorado, 80306.

1. How old are your multiples? Are they twins, triplets, or more? What are their genders? Are they identical or fraternal?

2. Were these your first birth? If not, how old are your other children?

3. Why do you think you had multiples? (Age, drugs, heredity?)

4. What was the biggest help to you after your multiples were born? (Equipment, person, attitude, etc.?) If you have other children, was the biggest help the same when you had one baby, or different?

5. What was the most difficult for you after your babies were born? (Isolation, your emotions, family adjustment, baby care, etc.?) If you have other children, was the most difficult thing with two babies the same as the most difficult thing with one?

6. What was the best thing about having multiples?

7. If you had multiples again, what would you do differently? If you are planning to have more children, how will having had multiples change what you do when you have one baby?

8. What parts of this book did you find particularly useful? What parts were not helpful, or were not believable?

9. If you were writing this book, what would you add that wasn't covered?

RESOURCES

This is a list of some organizations you might find helpful. When you write to one of them, be sure to enclose a stamped, self-addressed envelope. In addition to these groups, you might find others listed in the white or yellow pages of your local telephone book. Many states also have clearinghouses for self-help groups listed in the white pages under the state name: Connecticut Self-Help/Mutual Support Network or Michigan Self-Help Clearinghouse, for example. Clearinghouses such as these can give you a list of all the self-help groups in your area.

Organizations for parents and multiples:

NATIONAL ORGANIZATION OF MOTHERS OF TWINS CLUBS
Mothers of multiples share information, concerns, and advice. Information sheets, quarterly newspaper, chapter development kit. 12404 Princess Jeanne NE, Albuquerque, NM 87112-4640.
(505) 275-0955

TRIPLET CONNECTION
Information and support for parents and expectant parents of triplets or more. Pregnancy and parenting information and support. Newsletter and telephone support in forming local groups or organizing workshops. 2618 Lucile Ave., Stockton, CA 95209.   (209) 474-3073

INTERNATIONAL TWINS ASSOCIATION
Organization for twins or members of any multiple set, of any age. P.O. Box 77386, Station C, Atlanta, GA 30357.

PARENTS OF MULTIPLE BIRTHS ASSOCIATION OF CANADA
Information and support for parents of twins and more. Booklets, leaflets, and reports of interest to parents of multiples, and a quarterly news magazine. 283 7th Ave. S, Lethbridge, Alberta, Canada T1J 1H6.   (403) 328-9165

SOUTH AUSTRALIA MULTIPLE BIRTH ASSOCIATION
Information and support for parents of multiples. Advice for professionals dealing with families of multiples. Leaflets on language development, reading disability, social development, and physical growth. Contact the S.A. Multiple Birth Association, or the Australian Multiple Birth Association through the La Trobe Twin Study, La Trobe University, Bundoora, Vic. 3083, Australia.

TWINLINE

A private, nonprofit agency, funded by the California Department of Health, serving to develop ways of supporting families with twins and other multiples. Services include: Twinline Warmline (telephone counseling), family meetings, family network, handouts, and research reports. P.O. Box 10066, Berkeley, CA 94709.   (415) 644-0861

CENTER FOR STUDY OF MULTIPLE BIRTH

Mail-order publications on twins. Call or write for current list. Suite 463-5, 333 E. Superior St., Chicago, IL 60611.   (312) 266-9093

THE TWINS FOUNDATION

An international nonprofit organization established by twins to collect, preserve, and communicate information about twins and twin research. They are establishing a research library, museum, traveling exhibits, and a twins hall of fame. Quarterly newsletter. P.O. Box 9487, Providence, RI 02940-9487.

Childbirth, infant care, and new mother care:

INTERNATIONAL CHILDBIRTH EDUCATION ASSOCIATION, INC.

Organization committed to family-centered maternity care and the philosophy of freedom of choice based on knowledge of alternatives. ICEA network locates classes and birthing options. Newsletter, books, and pamphlets. P.O. Box 20048, Minneapolis, MN 55420-0048.
(612) 854-8660

ASPO/LAMAZE (AMERICAN SOCIETY FOR PSYCHOPROPHYLAXIS IN OBSTETRICS)

Lamaze childbirth and prepared parenthood classes, with professional, physician, and parent coalitions. Newsletter, publications, national directory for referrals. 1840 Wilson Blvd., Suite 204, Arlington, VA 22201.   (703) 524-7802

AMERICAN ACADEMY OF HUSBAND-COACHED CHILDBIRTH

Classes in the Bradley method of prepared childbirth. P.O. Box 5224, Sherman Oaks, CA 91413.

NAPSAC (NATIONAL ASSOCIATION OF PARENTS AND PROFESSIONALS FOR SAFE ALTERNATIVES IN CHILDBIRTH)

Promotes education on safe childbirth alternatives and personal responsibility of parents. Assists in establishment of family-centered maternity facilities. Quarterly newsletter, handbook, directory. P.O. Box 428, Marble Hill, MO 63764.   (314) 238-2010

CESAREAN SUPPORT EDUCATION AND CONCERN
Information and referral on cesarean birth, cesarean prevention, and vaginal delivery after cesarean. Listing of cesarean support groups nationwide. Quarterly newsletter. 22 Forest Road, Framingham, MA 01701.   (617) 877-8266

CESAREAN PREVENTION MOVEMENT, INC.
Support network for those healing from cesarean birth. Encouragement and information for those wanting vaginal birth after cesarean. Quarterly newsletter. P.O. Box 152, Syracuse, NY 13210.
(315) 424-1942

POSTPARTUM EDUCATION FOR PARENTS
Groups led by trained volunteers offer emotional support for new parents. Guide for starting parent support group. Newsletter, telephone counseling. Write c/o Jane Honikman, 927 N. Kellogg Ave., Santa Barbara, CA 93111.

NATIONAL ASSOCIATION FOR HOME CARE
Can provide a list of home health-care agencies near you for qualified medical help in your home. 519 C St. NE, Washington, DC 20002.   (202) 547-7424

LA LECHE LEAGUE INTERNATIONAL
Mother-to-mother help and encouragement for those who want to breastfeed their babies. Bimonthly magazine. Pen-pal and telephone networks within local chapters. P.O. Box 1209, Franklin Park, IL 60131.   (312) 455-7730

NURSING MOTHERS COUNSEL, INC.
Telephone counseling for questions on breastfeeding, with medical advisory board. Offers publications like *Maintaining a Milk Supply While Separated from the Infant*. P.O. Box 50063, Palo Alto, CA 94303.

AFTER BABY'S ARRIVAL
Doula service. (Care for the mother). 4825 Roland Ave., San Carlos, CA 94070.

MOM SERVICES
Doula service. 78 Elm Rd., Briarcliff Manor, NY 10510.

DOULA, INC.
Doula service. PR 7, So. Ferry Farm, Narrangansett, RI 02882.

MOTHERCARE SERVICES
Doula service. 83 Franklin Ave., Watertown, MA 02172.

MOMS
Doula service. 121 Summit, St. Louis, MO 63119.

MOTHER'S HELPERS
Doula service. 3326 Cambridge, St. Louis, MO 63143.

MOTHERING THE MOTHER
Doula service. 535 Clifton Rd. NE, Atlanta, GA 30307.

WARM WELCOME
Doula service. 3978 Fuller Court, Boulder, CO 80303.

AMERICAN INSTITUTE FOR FOREIGN STUDY SCHOLARSHIP FOUNDATION AU
PAIR PROGRAM
Links families seeking young European girls to work legally as mother's
helpers, with suitable girls who also take a class while in this country.
Write 100 Greenwich Ave., Greenwich, CT 06830.
(203) 869-9090 or toll-free (800) 243-4567

Parent support groups:

THE MOTHERS' CENTER DEVELOPMENT PROJECT
Research, advocacy, and support for parents during pregnancy, childbirth, and child rearing. Yearly newsletter and annual conference. 129
Jackson St., Hempstead, NY 11550.
(800) 645-3828 or (516) 486-6614

THE NATIONAL PARENT CENTER
Helps parents become actively involved in their children's education.
Monthly newsletter, handbook. 1314 14th St. NW, Suite #6, Washing-
ton, DC 20005.   (202) 483-8822

PARENTS' RESOURCES, INC.
Parents help parents in small local support groups. Quarterly newsletter, speakers, reprints. P.O. Box 107, Planetarium Station, NY, NY
10024.   (212) 866-4776

Parent groups for those with premature, handicapped, or hospitalized children:

PARENTS FOR PARENTS, INC.
Emotional support and practical information to parents or guardians with
a hospitalized child. Semiannual newsletter, telephone support, monthly
meetings. 125 Northmore Dr., Yorktown Heights, NY 10598.
(914) 962-3326

CHILDREN IN HOSPITALS

Information and education for children and parents during hospitalization of either. Quarterly newsletter, book and film bibliography, lists of educational materials. Barbara Popper, 31 Wilshire Park, Needham, MA 02192.   (617) 369-4467

PARENTS OF PREMATURES

Emotional and educational support for parents who have experienced the birth and hospitalization of a premature or sick infant. Monthly newsletter, clothing bank, library, parent support group packet. 13613 NE 26th Place, Bellevue, WA 98005.   (206) 883-6040

NATIONAL COUNCIL OF GUILDS FOR INFANT SURVIVAL

Support and education for parents who experience sudden infant death syndrome (SIDS) and for families using in-home monitors for high-risk infants. Quarterly newsletter, group development guidelines, correspondence. P.O. Box 3586, Davenport, IA 52808.   (319) 326-4653

PARENT CARE

Information, referrals, and support to parent groups, families, and professionals concerned with infants who required special care at birth. Quarterly newsletter, resource directory, annual international conference, seminars. University of Utah Medical Center, 50 N. Medical Dr., Rm. 2A210, Salt Lake City, UT 84132.   (801) 581-5323

LET'S PLAY TO GROW

Develops small clubs for families of children with special needs. Parent training, education for child through recreation. Newsletter, guidelines, and technical assistance in starting clubs. 1250 York Ave. NW, Suite 500, Washington, DC 20005.   (202) 393-1250

PARENTELE

Information and support for parents of handicapped children. Quarterly newsletter, resource guide, bibliography. 5538 N. Pennsylvania St., Indianapolis, IN 46220.   (317) 259-1654

PARENTS HELPING PARENTS

Support and information to help families cope with having a special child —with mental or physical disabilities. Newsletter, how-to manuals, telephone support. 535 Race St., #220, San Jose, CA 95126.
(408) 288-5010

PILOT PARENTS PROGRAM

Support to parents of children with developmental disabilities (mental retardation, cerebral palsy, epilepsy, autism, and others). Handbook to develop chapters, pen-pal program. Est. 1971. 3610 Dodge St., Omaha, NE 68131.   (402) 346-5220

PARENTS ANONYMOUS
Mutual help for parents who are, or fear they may be, physically and/or emotionally abusing their children. Semiannual newsletter, information, and referral. Guidelines for developing groups. 7120 Franklin Ave., Los Angeles, CA 90046.   (800) 421-0353

Marriage and family groups:

WORLDWIDE MARRIAGE ENCOUNTER
Multifaith group aims to renew couple relationships through improved communication. National magazine, local informal telephone networking, monthly renewal group, neighborhood sharing groups. 1025 W. 3rd Ave., Columbus, OH 43212.   (614) 294-3774 or 882-4121

ASSOCIATION OF COUPLES FOR MARRIAGE ENRICHMENT
Network of couples who want to enhance their own relationships and help strengthen marriages of other couples. Local support groups, retreats, workshops. Monthly newsletter. P.O. Box 10596. Winston-Salem, NC 27108.   (919) 724-1526

Women at work and at home:

NATIONAL ALLIANCE OF HOME-BASED BUSINESSWOMEN
For women who work from their homes. Helps eliminate isolation, encourages and stimulates personal, professional, and economic growth. Quarterly newsletter, annual national meeting, local chapters, chapter manual with start-up guidelines. P.O. Box 306, Midland Park, NJ 07432.   (201) 423-9131 after 2 P.M.

MOTHERS' HOME BUSINESS NETWORK
Information, advice, and moral support for mothers who want to establish or continue a business at home. Quarterly newsletter, classified ads, *Mothers' Money-Making Manual,* annual directory of members, fact sheets about common business problems, listings of business opportunities. P.O. Box 423, East Meadow, NY 11554.
(516) 997-7394

MOTHERS AT HOME
Support for mothers who want to stay home. Monthly newsletter, local groups. P.O. Box 2208, Merrifield, VA 22116.   (703) 352-2292

ASSOCIATION OF PART-TIME PROFESSIONALS
Information on federal part-time employment, job sharing, benefits for those working part time. Newsletter, publication list. P.O. Box 3419, Alexandria, VA 22303.

NEW WAYS TO WORK
Specific information on a variety of nontraditional work options including job sharing, and more general information on trends and issues. Publication list. 149 Ninth St., San Francisco, CA 84103.   (415) 552-1000

FOCUS ON ALTERNATIVE WORK PATTERNS
Written and telephone advice and counseling for job seekers (donation requested); clearinghouse for part-time and shared jobs in the Seattle area. Conducts workshops, maintains reference library, monthly and quarterly publications. 509 Tenth Ave. East, Seattle, WA 98102. (206) 329-7918

MESSIES ANONYMOUS
Motivation, support, and a program of change for disorganized home-makers who want to improve the quality of their lives and their self-image by taking control of house and life. Quarterly newsletter. 5025 SW 114th Ave., Miami, FL 33165.   (305) 271-8404

SIDETRACKED HOME EXECUTIVES, INC.
Program for organizing housework, laundry, personal life, happiness, and just about everything else with specialized card-file systems. Books, cassette tapes, newsletter. P.O. Box 5364, Vancouver, WA 98668.

Baby equipment and mail-order sources:

KIDPOWER UNLIMITED
Makers of the Twin Matey, a baby carrier that allows you to carry two babies in front, one front and one back, or to separate the carrier to carry them singly. P.O. Box 12045, Overland Park, KS 66212. (416) 533-3697 or (716) 856-4485, Visa and Mastercard accepted.

KID-KUFFS™
Makes leash systems for children, including the Kid-Kuff Single, Kid-Kuff Double, and Kart-Kuff™ safety belt for shopping carts. Zelex Inc., 507 S. Federal Blvd., Dept. T-11, Riverton, WY 82501. (307) 856-7048

A BABY CARRIAGE
Five models of twin strollers: side by side, front-rear, and triplet models included. For brochure: 5935 W. Irving Park Road, Chicago, IL 60634.   (312) 794-CRIB

BLUE SKY CYCLE CARTS
Covered bicycle carts big enough for two babies or children. For brochure, send $1 to: 29976 Enid Road E., Eugene, OR 97402.
(503) 689-3091

TWIN VIEW MIRRORS
Special rearview mirror for your car combines two mirrors to help you keep an eye on your twins while traveling. Perfectly Safe, Dept. 401, P.O. Box 988, Stevens Point, WI 54481.

CONSUMER PRODUCT SAFETY COMMISSION
Information on latest safety rules and regulations concerning baby gear and equipment. Washington, DC 20207.

JUVENILE PRODUCT MANUFACTURERS ASSOCIATION
Information on safety of baby products. 66 E. Main St., Moorestown, NJ 08057.

Periodicals:

TWINS Magazine
P.O. Box 12045, Overland Park, KS 66212.   (913) 722-1090

DOUBLETALK
Newsletter, reprints, mail-order children's books on multiples, specialty items, books, and pamphlets. P.O. Box 412, Amelia, OH 45102.
(513) 753-7117

BIBLIOGRAPHY

Books

Adebonojo, Festus, M.D., Eleanor Sherman, and Linda Carlen Jones. *How Baby Grows*. New York: Arbor House, 1985.

Ainslie, Ricardo C. *The Psychology of Twinship*. Lincoln: University of Nebraska Press, 1985.

Bau, Stephen, and Michael Kahn. *The Sibling Bond*. New York: Basic Books, 1982.

Bellin, Howard, M.D., and Peter Steinberg. *Dr. Bellin's Beautiful You Book*. Englewood Cliffs, N.J.: Prentice-Hall, 1981.

Benson, Herbert, M.D., And William Proctor. *Beyond the Relaxation Response*. New York: Times Books, 1984.

Bollinger, Taree, and Patricia Cramer. *Baby Gear Guide*. Reading, Mass.: Addison-Wesley, 1985.

Botwin, Carol. *Is There Sex After Marriage?* Boston: Little, Brown, 1985.

Brazelton, T. Berry, M.D. *Working and Caring*. Reading, Mass.: Addison-Wesley, 1985.

Brazelton, T. Berry, M.D. *On Becoming a Family*. New York: Dell, 1981.

Brewster, Dorothy Patricia. *You Can Breastfeed Your Baby—Even in Special Situations*. Emmaus, Pa.: Rodale Press, 1979.

Brody, Jane. *Jane Brody's Nutrition Book*. New York: Bantam Books, 1981.

Bulmer, M. G. *The Biology of Twinning in Man*. Oxford: Oxford University Press, 1970.

Calladine, Andrew, and Carole Calladine. *Raising Siblings*. New York: Delacorte Press, 1979.

Carper, Jean. *Jean Carper's Total Nutrition Guide*. New York: Bantam Books, 1987.

Ciaramitaro, Barbara. *Help for Depressed Mothers*. Edmonds, Wash.: The Charles Franklin Press, 1982.

Colbin, Annemarie. *Food and Healing*. New York: Ballantine Books, 1986.

Daddy! Daddy! A Guide for Fathers of Twins. Pamphlet published by Parents of Multiple Births Association, 1987.

Dalton, Katharina, M.D. *Depression After Childbirth*. Oxford: Oxford University Press, 1980.

Davis, Adelle. *Let's Have Healthy Children*. New York: Harcourt Brace Jovanovich, 1972.

Day Care Guidelines. American Academy of Pediatrics publication, March 1987.

DelliQuadri, Lyn, and Kati Breckenridge. *Mothercare*. Los Angeles: J. P. Tarcher, 1977.

Dix, Carol. *The New Mother Syndrome*. New York: Doubleday, 1985.

Dodson, Fitzhugh, M.D. *How to Father*. Los Angeles: Nash Publications, 1974.

Dunn, Judy. *Comfort and Distress*. Cambridge, Mass.: Harvard University Press, 1977.

Dunn, Judy, and Carol Kendrick. *Siblings: Love, Envy and Understanding*. Cambridge, Mass.: Harvard University Press, 1982.

Especially for Fathers. California Department of Health Services, 1986.

Eysenck, H. J., and Leon Kamin. *The Intelligence Controversy*. New York: John Wiley and Sons, 1981.

Fathers' Guide. Parents of Multiple Birth Association of Canada, 1986.

Fathers' Survey. Parents of Multiple Birth Association of Canada, 1982.

Fomon, Samuel J., M.D. *Infant Nutrition*, 2d ed. Toronto: W. B. Saunder Co., 1974.

Fraiberg, Selma. *Every Child's Birthright: In Defense of Mothering*. New York: Bantam Books, 1977.

Gershwin, M. Eric, Richard S. Back, and Lucille S. Hurley. *Nutrition and Immunity*. New York: Academic Press, 1985.

Glover, John A. *A Parent's Guide to Intelligence Testing: How to Help Your Children's Intellectual Development*. Chicago: Nelson Hall, 1979.

Goldsmith, Judith. *Childbirth Wisdom*. New York: Congdon & Weed, 1984.

Goulart, Frances Sheridan. *Nutritional Self-Defense*.

New York: Dodd Mead & Co., 1984.

Guilford, J. P., and Ralph Hoepfner. *The Analysis of Intelligence.* New York: McGraw-Hill, 1971.

Halpern, Steven. *Sound Health: The Music and Sounds That Make Us Whole.* New York: Harper & Row, 1985.

Harrison, Helen. *The Premature Baby Book.* New York: St. Martin's Press, 1983.

Kamen, Betty, Ph.D, and Si Kamen. *Total Nutrition for Breastfeeding Mothers.* Boston: Little, Brown & Co., 1986.

Kaye, Kenneth. *The Mental and Social Life of Babies.* Chicago: University of Chicago Press, 1982.

Klaus, M. H., M.D., and Martha Robertson. *Birth, Interaction and Attachment.* Pamphlet published by Johnson & Johnson, 1982.

Klaus, Marshall H., M.D., and John H. Kennell, M.D. *Bonding: The Beginnings of Parent-Infant Attachment.* St Louis: C. V. Mosby, 1983.

Klaus, Marshall H., M.D., and Phyllis H. Klaus, M.Ed., C.S.W. *The Amazing Newborn: Making the Most of the First Weeks of Life.* Reading, Mass.: Addison-Wesley, 1985.

Kornhaber, Arthur, M.D. *Between Parents and Grandparents.* New York: St. Martin's Press, 1985.

Korte, Diana, and Roberta Scaer. *A Good Birth, a Safe Birth.* New York: Bantam Books, 1984.

LaGace, Louise Lambert. *Feeding Your Child.* Toronto: Beaufort Books, 1982.

Lowman, Kaye. *Of Cradles and Careers.* New York: New American Library, 1984.

Lytton, Hugh, Ph.D. *Parent-Child Interaction: The Social Process Observed in Twin and Singleton Families.* New York: Plenum Press, 1980.

McDermott, J. F., Jr., M.D. *Raising Cain and Able Too.* New York: Wyden Books, 1980.

Nance, Walter E., ed. *Progress in Clinical and Biological Research,* vol. 24A. New York: Alan R. Liss, 1978.

Nassif, Janet Zhun. *The Home Healthcare Solution.* New York: Harper & Row, 1985.

Newman, H. H. *Multiple Human Births: Twins, Triplets, Quadruplets and Quintuplets.* New York: Doubleday, 1940.

Noble, Elizabeth. *Having Twins.* Boston: Houghton Mifflin, 1980.

Panuthos, Claudia. *Transformation Through Birth.* South Hadley, Mass.: Bergin & Garvey Publishing, 1984.

Parke, Ross D. *Father-Infant Interaction.* Pamphlet published by Johnson & Johnson, 1975.

Price, Anne, and Nancy Bamford. *Breastfeeding Guide for the Working Woman.* New York: Simon & Schuster, 1983.

Procaccini, Joseph, M.D., and Mark Kiefaber. *Parent Burnout.* New York: Doubleday, 1983.

Pryor, Karen. *Nursing Your Baby.* New York: Pocket Books, 1973.

The Rainbow Connection. Berkeley, Cal.: Center for Attitudinal Healing, 1978.

Raphael, Dana. *The Tender Gift: Breastfeeding.* New York: Schocken Books, 1976.

Rosner, Joseph, Ph.D. *Myths of Childrearing.* New York: Dembner Books, 1983.

Sammons, William A. H., M.D., and Jennifer M. Lewis, M.D. *Premature Babies: A Different Beginning.* St. Louis: C. V. Mosby, 1985.

Satter, E., R.D. *Child of Mine.* New York: Bell Publishing, 1983.

Saunders, Antoinette, Ph.D., and Bonnie Remsbert. *The Stress-Proof Child.* New York: Holt Rinehart & Winston, 1984.

Scarr, Sandra. *Mothercare/Othercare.* New York: Basic Books, 1984.

Schaffer, Rudolph. *Mothering.* Cambridge, Mass.: Harvard University Press, 1977.

Schave, Barbara, and Janet Ciriello. *Identity and Intimacy in Twins.* New York: Praeger Publications, 1983.

Schreiber, Linda, and JoAnne Stang. *Marathon Mom.* New York: Houghton Mifflin, 1980.

Segal, Jeanne, Ph.D. *Feeling Great.* Santa Cruz, Cal.: Unity Press, 1981.

Simonton, Carl, M.D., Stephanie Matthews-Simonton, and James Creighton. *Getting Well Again.* Los Angeles: J. P. Tarcher, 1978.

Singer, Wenda Goodhart, Stephen Schechtman, and Mark Singer. *Real Men Enjoy Their Kids.* Nashville: Abingdon Press, 1983.

Stautberg, Susan Schiffer. *Pregnancy 9–5: Career Woman's Guide to Pregnancy and Motherhood.* New York: Fireside Books, 1985.

Stern, Loraine, M.D., and Kathleen MacKay. *Off to a Great Start—How to Relax and Enjoy Your Baby.* New York: W. W. Norton, 1986.

Tips for Your Baby's Safety. U.S. Consumer Product Safety Commission, 1985.

U.S. Department of Labor. *Time of Change: 1983 Handbook on Women Workers.* Women's Bureau Bulletin 298. Washington D.C., 1983.

Watson, Peter. *Twins: An Uncanny Relationship?* New York: Viking Press, 1981.

Winnicott, D. W. *The Family and Individual Development.* New York: Basic Books, 1984.

Winnicott, D. W. *The Maturational Processes and the Facilitating Environment, Studies in the Theory of Emotional Development.* New York: International University Press, 1965.

Journals and Articles

Abbink, Charlotte, R.N., et al. "Bonding as Perceived by Mothers of Twins." *Pediatric Nursing* (Nov./Dec. 1982).

"Accidents in Infant Walkers Cited." *Rocky Mountain News* (April 30, 1982).

"Advance Report of Final Natality Statistics, 1984." *National Center for Health Statistics Monthly Vital Statistics Report,* vol. 35, no. 4 (1986).

"Advance Report of Final Natality Statistics 1985." *Monthly Vital Statistics Report,* vol. 36, no. 4 (July 1987).

Affonso, Dyanne E., and Jaynelle F. Stichler. "Cesarean Birth; Women's Reactions." *American Journal of Nursing* (March 1980).

Akmakjian, Hiag. "A Crying Need." *Family Health* (December 1981).

Alexander, Terry. "Diagnosing Plural Pregnancy." *MOTC Notebook* (Spring 1986).

Allen, Alison, R.N. "Preoperative Teaching for Cesarean Birth." *AORN Journal,* vol. 34, no. 5 (November 1981).

Allen, Gordon. "The Twinning and Fertility Paradox." *Proceedings of the Third International Congress on Twin Studies* (1981).

Allen, Martin G., et al. "The Effect of Parental Perceptions on Early Development in Twins." *Psychiatry,* vol. 39 (February 1976.)

Amsterdam, Beulah. "Mirror Self-Image Reactions Before Age Two." *Developmental Psychobiology,* vol. 5. (1972).

Applebaum, Richard. "Breastfeeding and Drugs in Human Milk." *Keeping Abreast Journal,* vol. 2. (Oct.–Dec. 1977).

Asch, Stuart S., M.D., and Lowell J. Rubin, M.D. "Postpartum Reactions: Some Unrecognized Variations." *Journal of Psychiatry,* vol. 131, no. 8 (August 1974).

Avery, Gordon B. "The Newborn." *Human Nutrition, A Comprehensive Treatise,* vol. 2. (1979).

"Baby Products Tracking Study." *American Baby,* 1984.

"Babysitting Cooperative Has Feeling of Extended Family." *Rocky Mountain News,* January 1982.

Balking, Rick. "Dads Who Won't Help." *McCall's,* February 1985.

"Bed Rest May Be Hazardous." *Childbirth Alternatives Quarterly,* vol. 7, no. 3. (Spring 1986).

"Beer and the Breastfeeding Mom." *Journal of the American Medical Association,* vol. 258, no. 15 (October 16, 1987).

Beit-Hallahmi, Benjamin, and Maria Paluszny. "Twinship in Mythology and Science: Ambivalence, Differentiation and the Magical Bond." *Comprehensive Psychiatry,* vol. 15, no. 4 (1974).

Begley, Sharon, and John Carey. "The Wisdom of Babies." *Newsweek,* January 12, 1981.

Belmont, Lillian, and Francis A. Marolla. "Birth Order, Family Size and Intelligence." *Science,* vol. 182 (December 1973).

Benirschke, Kurt, M.D., and Chung Kim. "Multiple Pregnancy." *The New England Journal of Medicine* (June 14, 1973).

Berglas, Steven. "Why Did This Happen to Me?" *Psychology Today,* February 1985.

Berkowitz, R., M.D., et al. "Delivering Twins with the Help of Ultrasound." *Contemporary Ob/Gyn,* vol. 19 (February 1982).

Bernbaum, Judy, and Marsha Hoffman-Williamson. "The Pre-Term Infant Goes Home: Preparing the Primary Care Physician." *Children's Hospital of Philadelphia Neonatal Follow-up Program,* November 1986.

Bernstein, Beth A. "Siblings of Twins." *Psychoanalytic Study of the Child,* vol. 35 (1980).

Beuttler, Bill. "Tuned in for Surgery." *American Health,* November 1986.

Bracken, Michael B., Ph.D. "Oral Contraception and Twinning: An Epidemiologic Study." *The New England Journal of Medicine,* vol. 133, no. 4 (September 1979).

Brazelton, T. Berry, M.D. "It's Twins!" *Redbook,* February 1980.

Brazelton, T. Berry, M.D. *"The Importance of Mothering the Mother." Redbook,* October 1980.

Brazelton, T. Berry, M.D. "What Makes a Good Dad?" *Redbook,* September 1984.

Brazelton, T. Berry, M.D. "Grandparents: How they Make a Child Feel Loved." *Family Circle,* June 17, 1986.

"Breastfeeding: An International Priority." *La Leche League International Conference* magazine, 1985.

"Breastfeeding Twins." *Nursing Times,* vol. 76, no. 34 (August 21, 1980).

Breastfeeding Update: Business and Babies Do Mix." *Better Homes and Gardens,* February 1987.

"Breast Reduction, Breast Lift, Breast Augmentation, and Abdominoplasty." *American Society of Plastic and Reconstructive Surgeons, Inc.,* 1984.

"Breathe for Better Health." *American Health,* November 1986.

Brenner, William, M.D. "Twin Pregnancy: Reducing the Risks." *The Female Patient,* vol. 7 (November 1982).

Brown, Kim. "Do Working Mothers Cheat Their Kids?" *Redbook,* April 1985.

Burlingham, Dorothy T. "The Relationship of Twins to Each Other." *The Psychoanalytic Study of the Child*, vols. 3, 4 (1949).

Butera, Jay. "Mom's Milk: Key to Premie Survival?" *American Health*, May 1984.

Chandra, R. K. "Immunological Aspects of Human Milk." *Nutrition Reviews*, vol. 36, no. 9 (September 1978).

"Child Care Strongly Affects Productivity." *Rocky Mountain News*, January 30, 1987.

Cohen, Donald J., Eleanor Dibble, and Jane M. Grawe. "Fathers' and Mothers' Perceptions of Children's Personality." *Archives of General Psychiatry*, vol. 34 (April 1977).

Collier, Herbert L., Ph.D. "A Pilot Survey of ESP Experiences in Twins." Letter to author, 1986.

"Commentary on Breast-Feeding and Infant Formulas, Including Proposed Standards for Formulas." *Pediatrics*, vol. 57, no. 2 (February 1976).

Cranley, Mecca S., et al. "Women's Perceptions of Vaginal and Cesarean Deliveries." *Nursing Research*, vol. 32, no. 11 (Jan./Feb. 1983).

Crohn, Helen. "You Can Hire Successfully." *Mothers Today*, Jan./Feb. 1983.

Cunningham, Allan S. "Morbidity in Breast-Fed and Artificially Fed Infants, II." *Journal of Pediatrics*, vol. 95, no. 5 (November 1979).

Curtis, Richard. "Do Daddies Make the Best Mommies?" *McCall's*, August 1986.

Curzi-Dascalova, Lilia, and Emilia Christove-Gueorguiva. "Respiratory Pauses in Normal Prematurely Born Infants." *Biology of the Neonate*, vol. 44 (1983).

Davis, Elinor, and Patricia Malmstron. "School Placement: Giving Twins a Good Start." *Double Feature*, vol. 10, no. 1 (Spring 1987).

Davis, Flora, and Julia Orange. "The Strange Case of the Children Who Invented Their Own Language." *Redbook*, March 1978.

Dawson, Peter, et al. "Informal Social Support as an Intervention." *Zero to Three: Bulletin of the National Center for Clinical Infant Programs*, vol. 3, no. 2 (December 1982).

Day, Ella J. "The Development of Language in Twins: A Comparison of Twins and Single Children." *Child Development*, vol. 3, no. 3 (1935).

Diamond, Jon. "Honey: Not So Sweet for Infants." *McCall's*, April 1979.

Dick, Shirley K. "New Parenthood Initiation." *Mothers Today*, Jan./Feb. 1983.

"Diet and Iron Absorption in the First Year of Life." *Nutrition Reviews*, vol. 37, no. 6 (June 1979).

Early, Maureen. "Two by Two." *Newsday*, May 5, 1981.

Eisenberg, Leon, M.D. "Caring for Children and Working: Dilemmas of Contemporary Womanhood." *Pediatrics*, vol. 56, no. 1 (July 1975).

Elias, Marilyn. "Dear Diary: You Help My Immune System." *American Health*, Jan./Feb. 1987.

Elias, Marilyn. "To Raise Friendly Children . . ." *American Health*, March 1987.

Elias, Marilyn. "Happiest Marriage: 2 Jobs, Shared Chores." *USA Today*, September 11, 1984.

Englebardt, Stanley L. "What You Should Know About Cosmetic Surgery." *Reader's Digest*, April 1979.

"Exercise Ease-Up." *Redbook*, November 1986.

"Family Cohesion in Families with Twins." *National Mothers of Twins Clubs Newsletter*, Winter 1984.

"Fathers Birthing." *Parents*, June 1981.

Fawcett, Jacqueline, R.N. "Needs of Cesarean Birth Parents." *JOGN Nursing*, vol. 10, no. 10 (Sept./Oct. 1981).

Feldman, Silvia. "Cesarean Delivery." *Self*, May 1979.

Fergusson, D. M., et al. "Relationship of Family Life Event, Maternal Depression and Child-Rearing Problems." *Pediatrics*, vol. 73, no 6 (June 1984).

Fomon, Samuel J., et al. "Cow Milk Feeding in Infancy: Gastrointestinal Blood Loss and Iron Nutritional Status." *Journal of Pediatrics*, vol. 98, no. 4 (April 1981).

Fomon, Samuel J., et al. "Recommendations for Feeding Normal Infants." *Pediatrics*, vol. 63, no 1. (January 1979).

Fomon, Samuel J., et al. "Human Milk and the Small Premature Infant." *American Journal of the Disabled Child*, vol. 131 (April 1977).

Forman, Michele R., et al. "Sociodemographic Factors Associated with Breastfeeding in the United States: 1969 and 1980." Centers for Disease Control and National Institute for Child Health and Human Development, 1983.

Fuchs, Frances, et al. "Sibling Deidentification Judged by Mothers: Cross-Validation and Developmental Studies." *Child Development*, vol. 49 (1978).

Gartner, Lawrence M., M.D., and Kathleen G. Auerbach, Ph.D. "Jaundice and Breastfeeding." *Mothering*, Fall 1986.

Glenn, Jules, M.D. "Opposite Sex Twins." *Psychoanalytic Quarterly*, vol. 34 (1965).

Goldstein, Kenneth M., et al. "The Effects of Prenatal and Perinatal Complications on Development at One Year of Age." *Child Development*, vol. 47 (1976).

Goleman, Daniel. "Mother and Child: Crucial Interaction." *New York Times*, October 1986.

Goshen-Gottstein, Esther. "The Mothering of Twins, Triplets and Quadruplets." *Psychiatry*, vol. 43 (August 1980).

Gray, Donald K., et al. "Duration of Breast Feeding." *Pediatrics.* vol. 75, no. 3 (March 1985).

Greenberg, Marin, M.D., and Norman Morris, M.D. "Engrossment: The Newborn's Impact Upon the Father." *American Journal of Orthopsychiatry,* vol. 44, no. 4 (July 1974).

Greenwood, Sadja. "Women's Health." *Medical Self-Care,* no. 33 (March/April 1986).

Gromada, Karen, R.N. "Maternal-Infants Attachment: The First Step Toward Individualizing Twins." *Maternal Child Nursing,* vol. 11, no. 1 (Spring 1982).

Groothius, Jessie R., "Twins and Twin Families: A Practical Guide to Outpatient Management." *Clinics in Perinatology,* vol. 12, no. 2 (June 1985).

Grunwaldt, Edgar, et al. "The Onset of Sleeping Through the Night in Infancy." *Pediatrics,* vol. 26, no. 4 (October 1960).

Hales, Dianne, and Robert Hales, M.D. "Search for the New Self." *American Health,* June 1984.

Hall, Barbara. "Changing Composition of Human Milk and Early Development of an Appetite Control." *The Lancet,* April 5, 1975.

Halpern, Steven. "Sound Affects." *Mothering,* Spring 1987.

Hanna, Pat. "Dear Journal." *Rocky Mountain News,* Nov. 6, 1986.

Harlap, Susan, and Joseph Eldor, M.D. "Births Following Oral Contraceptive Failures." *Obstetrics & Gynecology,* vol. 55, no. 4 (1980).

Hart, Georgiana, R.N. "Maternal Attitudes in Prepared and Unprepared Cesarean Deliveries." *Journal of Obstetrical and Gynecological Nursing,* vol. 9, no. 4 (July/August 1980).

Hay, David, et al. "Reading Ability and Twins." La Trobe University Twin Study, 1984.

Hay, David, et al. "Zygosity Determination and Blood-Grouping in the La Trobe Twin Study." La Trobe University Twin Study, 1984.

Hay, David, Ph.D., et al. "Twins in School." La Trobe Twin Study, 1984.

Hay, David, Ph.D., et al. "Language Development in Young Twins." La Trobe University Twin Study, 1984.

Heath, Helen A. "Three Eight Year Olds." *Child Development,* vol. 38, no. 3 (September 1967).

Heird, William C. "Feeding the Premature Infant." *American Journal of the Disabled Child,* vol. 131 (1977).

"Help Wanted." *Ladies' Home Journal,* August 1986.

Hernandez, Jacinto, M.D., et al. "Growth Inhibiting Activity of Human Breast Milk." *Pediatrics,* vol. 63, no. 4 (April 1979).

Hift, Josephine, Ph.D. "An Experimental Study of the Twinning Reaction and Ego Development." Adelphi University. *Dissertation Abstracts International* (1980).

Holahan, Carole, K., and Lucia A. Gilbert. "Interrole Conflict for Working Women: Careers Versus Jobs." *Journal of Applied Psychology,* vol. 64, no. 1 (1979).

Howell, Mary C., Ph.D. "Effects of Maternal Employment on the Child." *Pediatrics,* vol. 52, no. 3 (1973).

Howell, Mary C., Ph.D. "Employed Mothers and Their Families." *Pediatrics,* vol. 52, no. 2 (1973).

Howell, Mary C., Ph.D. "The Impact of Working on Mother and Child: What are the Facts?" *Journal of the American Medical Women's Association,* vol. 40, no. 3 (May/June 1985).

"Identical Twins Are Not Identical Where Teeth Are Concerned." American Dental Association news release, September 10, 1982.

"Infant Feeding." *Canadian Journal of Public Health,* vol. 70 (Nov./Dec. 1979).

Joseph, Edward D., M.D., and Jack H. Tabor, M.D. "The Simultaneous Analysis of a Pair of Identical Twins and the Twinning Reaction." *The Psychoanalytic Study of the Child,* vol. 16 (1961).

Jackson, Donald Dale. "Reunion of Identical Twins, Raised Apart, Reveals Some Astonishing Similarities." *Smithsonian,* October 1980.

Jones, Verna. "Illegal Au Pair Girls," *Rocky Mountain News,* October 5, 1986.

Jelliffe, D. B., and E. F. P. Jelliffe, eds. "The Uniqueness of Human Milk." Symposium by the American Society for Clinical Nutrition 1975.

Jelliffe, D. B., and E. F. P. Jelliffe. "Breast is Best: Modern Meanings." *New England Journal of Medicine,* vol. 297, no. 17 (October 27, 1977).

Jakobsson, Irene, and Tor Lindberg. "Cow's Milk as a Cause of Infantile Colic in Breast-Fed Infants." *The Lancet,* August 26, 1978.

Judy, Stephanie A. "Traveling with Baby." *Mothering,* Fall 1984.

Jeffers, Susan, Ph.D. "Change What You Can Change." *Redbook,* February 1987.

Kabara, Jon J. "Lipids as Host-Resistance Factors of Human Milk." *Nutrition Reviews,* vol. 38, no. 2 (February 1980).

Keating, Kate. "Are Working Mothers Attempting Too Much?" *Better Homes and Gardens,* October 1978.

Klein, Arnold W., M.D., and David C. Rish, M.D. "Plastic Surgery: Out of the Closet." *Shape,* May 1984.

Kohen-Raz, Rueven. "The Impact of Twin Research in Developmental Studies on Models of Human Development." *Progress in Clinical Biology Research,* vol. 69B (1981).

"Lactation and Composition of Milk in Undernourished Women." *Nutrition Review,* vol. 33, no. 2 (February 1975).

Larsen, Spencer A., Jr., and Daryl R. Homer. "Relation of Breast versus Bottle Feeding to Hospitalization for Gastroenteritis in a Middle-Class U.S. Population." *The Journal of Pediatrics,* vol. 92, no. 3 (1978).

Lassers, Elisabeth, and Robert Nordan. "Separation and Individuation of an Identical Twin." *Adolescent Psychiatry,* vol. 6 (1978).

Lazar, Philippe. "Preconceptional Prediction of Twin Pregnancies." *Proceedings of the Third International Congress on Twin Studies.* (1981).

Lee, Robert E., Ph.D. "Returning to Work: Potential Problems for Mid-Career Mothers." *Journal of Sex & Marital Therapy,* vol. 9, no. 3 (1983).

LeLeiko, Neal S., M.D., and Marvin S. Eiger, M.D. "State of the Art Breast and Formula Feeding." Paper presented at the American Academy of Pediatrics Conference, September 1986.

Leo, John, and Arthur White. "A Sad, Baffling Dependency." *Time,* April 6, 1981.

Leonard, Marjorie R. "Problems in Identification and Ego Development in Twins." *The Psychoanalytic Study of the Child,* vol. 16 (1961).

"Less is Enough for Swimmers." *American Health,* August 1986.

Liebhaber, Myron, M.D., et al. "Comparison of Bacterial Contamination with Two Methods of Human Milk Collection." *The Journal of Pediatrics,* vol. 92, no. 2 (February 1978).

Lipson, Juliene G., R.N., et al. "Psychological Integration of the Cesarean Birth Experience." *American Journal of Orthopsychiatry,* vol. 50, no. 4 (October 1980).

"Live Births by Birth Weight and Age of Mother, United States 1984." National Center for Health Statistics, January 1986.

Lund, Carolyn, and Linda Lefrak. "Discharge Planning for Infants in the Intensive Care Nursery." *Pediatric Nursing,* vol. 8, no. 2 (March/April 1982).

Lytton, Hugh. "Do Parents Create, or Respond to, Differences in Twins?" *Developmental Psychology,* vol. 13, no. 5 (1977).

Lytton, Hugh, et al. "The Impact of Twinship on Parent-Child Interaction." *Journal of Personality and Social Psychology,* vol. 35, no. 2 (1977).

Lytton, Hugh, and Dorice Conway. "Twin-Singleton Language Differences." *Canadian Journal of Behavioural Science,* vol. 12 (1980).

Mahler, Margaret S., M.D. "Thoughts About Development and Individuation." *The Pyschoanalytic Study of the Child,* vol. 18 (1963).

"The Market for Diapering Products." *American Baby: Baby Products Tracking Study,* 1984.*

Martin, Thomas O., and Ruth B. Gross, Ph.D. "A Comparison of Twins for Degree of Closeness and Field Dependency." *Adolescence,* vol. 14, no. 56 (Winter 1979).

Martin, N. G., et al. "Gonadotropin Levels in Mothers Who Have Had Two Sets of DZ Twins." *Acta Genetica Medica Gemellolgica,* vol. 33 (1984).

Martinez, Gilbert, and John Naelzienski. "1980 Update: The Recent Trend in Breastfeeding." *Pediatrics,* vol. 67, no. 2 (February 1981).

Martinez, Gilbert, and Fritz W. Krieger. "1984 Milk-Feeding Patterns in the United States." *Pediatrics,* vol. 76, no. 6 (December 1985).

Martinez, Gilbert, Fritz W. Krieger, and Alan Ryan. "Factors Affecting Mothers' Decision to Breast Feed or Bottle Feed." Paper presented to the 1985 Annual Meeting of the American Statistical Association.

Matheny, Adam P., Jr. "Chaos: Is It the Only Cause of Injury to Twins?" *Twins,* Sept./Oct. 1986.

Michlewitz, H., M.D. "Triplet Pregnancies." *Journal of Reproductive Medicine,* vol. 26, no. 5 (1981).

Mitchell, Karen, R.N., and Nancy Mills, R.N. "Is the Sensitive Period in Parent-Infant Bonding Overrated?" *Pediatric Nursing,* vol. 9, no. 2 (March/April 1983).

Mittler, Peter. "Biological and Social Aspects of Language Development in Twins." *Developmental Medicine and Child Neurology,* vol. 12 (1970).

"Mother Knows Best: Human Milk Nutrient Joins Formula." *Medical World News,* September 24, 1984.

"Mothers of Premature Babies Have Special Milk." *Rocky Mountain News,* September 19, 1985.

Mosteller, Michael, et al. "Twinning Rates in Virginia: Secular Trends and the Effects of Maternal Age and Parity." *Proceedings of the Third International Congress on Twin Studies,* 1981.

Neifert, Marianne R. "Returning to Breast-Feeding." *Clinical Obstetrics and Gynecology,* vol. 23, no. 4 (December 1980).

Newton, Niles. "Psychological Differences Between Breast and Bottle Feeding." *The American Journal of Clinical Nutrition,* vol. 24 (August 1971).

Nichols, R. C., and W. C. Bilbro, Jr. "The Diagnosis of Twin Zygosity." *Acta Genetica: Switzerland,* 1966.

Nilsen, Stein Tore, et al. "Male Twins at Birth and 18 Years Later." *British Journal of Obstetrics and Gynaecology,* vol. 91 (February 1984).

Notzon, Francis C., et al. "Cross-National Comparisons of Cesarean Section Rates." Paper presented at the 1985 Annual Meeting of the American Public Health Association.

"Nutrition and Lactation." *Pediatrics,* vol. 68, no. 3 (September 1981).

"Nutritional Composition of Milk Produced by Mothers Delivering Preterm." *Journal of Pediatrics,* vol. 96, no. 4 (April 1980).

O'Brien, Diane. "The Twins Who Made Their Own Language." *Family Health,* vol. 10, no. 9 (September 1978).

O'Conner, P. A. "Failure to Thrive with Breastfeeding." *Clinical Pediatrics,* vol. 17, no. 11 (November 1978).

Ogra, S. S., and P. L. Ogra. "Immunologic Aspects of Human Colostrum and Milk." *Journal of Pediatrics,* vol. 92, no. 4 (April 1978).

Oski, Frank A. "Iron-Fortified Formulas and Gastrointestinal Symptoms in Infants: A Controlled Study." *Pediatrics,* vol. 66, no. 2 (August 1980).

Ortmeyer, Dale H. "The We-Self of Identical Twins." *Contemporary Psychoanalysis,* vol. 6 (1969–70).

Paluszny, Maria, M.D. "Queries that Mothers of Twins Put to Their Doctors." *Clinical Pediatrics,* vol. 14, no. 7 (July 1975).

Paluszny, Maria, M.D., and Benjamin Beit-Hallahmi, Ph.D. "An Assessment of Monozygotic Twin Relationships by the Semantic Differential." *Archives of General Psychiatry,* vol. 31 (July 1974).

Pederson, Frank A., et al. "Father Participation in Infancy." *American Journal of Orthopsychiatry,* vol. 3, no. 39 (April 1969).

Peterson, Gail H., M.S.S.W., et al. "The Role of Some Birth-Related Variables in Father Attachment." *American Journal of Orthopsychiatry,* vol. 49, no. 2 (April 1979).

Philippe, Pierre. "Twinning and the Changing Pattern of Breast-Feeding: A Possible Relationship in a Small Rural Population." *Social Biology,* vol. 28, nos. 3–4 (1981).

Picciano, Mary Frances, and Helen A. Guthrie. "Copper, Iron and Zinc Contents of Mature Human Milk." *American Journal of Clinical Nutrition,* vol. 29 (March 1976).

"Postpartum Depression." *International Childbirth Education Association Review,* August 1980.

"Primary Biases in Twin Studies: A Review of Prenatal and Natal Difference-Producing Factors in Monozygotic Pairs." *The American Journal of Human Genetics,* vol. 2, no. 4 (December 1950).

"Quick Stress-Beater." *Ladies' Home Journal,* October 1986.

"Quick Workouts." *American Health,* February 1987.

"Quintuplets and Other Multiples Have Built-In Advantages, Reese Doctors Find." Press release, Michael Reese Hospital and Medical Center, March 23, 1982.

"Racial and Educational Factors Associated with Breast-Feeding; United States 1969 and 1980." *Morbidity and Mortality Weekly Report; Centers for Disease Control,* vol. 33, no. 11 (March 23, 1984).

Record, R. G., et al. "An Investigation of the Difference in Measured Intelligence Between Twins and Single Births." *Annals of Human Genetics,* vol. 34 (1970).

Ricks, Thomas E. "Reseachers Say Day-Care Centers Are Implicated in Spread of Disease." *The Wall Street Journal,* September 5, 1984.

Rodriguez, Johnette Frick. "Mothering the New Mother." *Ms.,* May 1986.

Rose, Richard, et al. "Data from Kinships of Monozygotic Twins Indicate Maternal Effects on Verbal Intelligence." *Nature,* vol. 283 (1980).

Saarinen, Ulla M., et al. "Iron Absorption in Infants." *The Journal of Pediatrics,* vol. 91, no. 1 (July 1977).

Saunders, M. C., et al. "The Effects of Hospital Admission for Bed Rest on the Duration of Twin Pregnancy: A Randomised Trial." *The Lancet,* vol. 2, no. 3 (1985).

Scofield, Michael. "Music Zaps Stress." *Woman's Day,* July 29, 1986.

Scott, D. H. "Follow-Up Study from Birth of the Effects of Prenatal Stresses." *Developmental Medicine and Child Neurology,* no. 15 (1973).

Segal, Nancy. "Focus on Language Development." *Twins,* March/April 1985.

"Siblings: Report on Work by Judy Dunn." Release from University of Colorado News Media Relations, 1985.

Silver, Nan. "Do Optimists Live Longer?" *American Health,* November 1986.

Silver, Sandra. "A Mother's Guide to Breastfeeding and Mothering the Premature or Hospitalized Sick Infants." *Clinical Pediatrics,* vol. 17, no. 5 (May 1978).

Shanley, Kathy. "Twice As Much." *American Baby,* October 1985.

"Smell Therapy." *New York Times Magazine,* November 17, 1985.

Smith, Dinita. "All About Twins." *Parents,* January 1984.

"Spouses, Confidants Figure in Prepartum, Postpartum Depression." *Journal of the American Medical Association,* vol. 255, no. 24 (June 27, 1986).

Stahl, Linda. "A Pair-Shaped Project." *Louisville Courier-Journal,* May 19, 1985.

Stukane, Eileen. "Why You're So Tired." *Redbook,* November 1986.

Terry, Grace. "The Separation-Individuation Process in Same-Sex Twins: A Review of the Literature." *Maternal Child Nursing Journal,* vol. 4 (1975).

"Trends in First Births to Older Mothers." *National Center for Health Statistics Supplement,* vol. 31, no. 2 (May 27, 1982).

Trowell, Judith. "Possible Effect of Emergency Caesarian Section on the Mother-Child Relationship." *Early Human Development,* vol. 7 (1982).

Trowell, Judith. "Mother/Child Relationships of a Group of Women Admitted Expecting a Normal Vaginal Delivery." *Child Abuse and Neglect,* vol. 7 (1983).

"Vital Facts About Vitamins." *Family Circle,* March 1987.

"Walk for a Tighter Waist." *American Health,* March 1987.

"Walkshaping." *American Health,* October 1986.

Watts, Denise, and Hugh Lytton. "Twinship as Handicap: Fact or Fiction?" *Twin Research 3: Intelligence, Personality and Development,* 1981.

Weichert, Carol. "Breast-Feeding: First Thoughts." *Pediatrics,* vol. 56, no. 6 (December 1975).

"When Conception Occurs One Month After Discontinuing the Pill, Twins Are More Likely." *The Journal of the American Medical Association,* vol. 239, no. 18 (May 5, 1978).

"Why Women Work." *Medical Self-Care,* no. 17 (July/August 1983).

Wilson, Ronald S. "Twins: Patterns of Cognitive Development as Measured on the Wechsler Preschool and Primary Scale of Intelligence." *Developmental Psychology,* vol. 11, no. 2 (1975).

Wilson, Ronald S. "Twins and Siblings: Concordance for School-Age Mental Development." *Child Development,* vol. 48 (1977).

Wilson, Ronald S. "Twins: Mental Development in the Preschool Years." *Developmental Psychology,* vol. 10, no. 4 (1974).

Wilson, Ronald S. "Synchronized Developmental Pathways for Twins." *Progress in Clinical Biology Research,* vol. 69B (1981).

"Wives Who Work Increase Their HDL Levels." *Journal of the American Medical Association,* vol. 249, no. 6 (February 11, 1983).

Woodruff, Calvin. "The Science of Infant Nutrition and the Art of Infant Feeding." *Journal of the American Medical Association,* vol. 240, no. 7 (August 18, 1978).

Wyshak, Grace. "Health Characteristics for Mothers of Twins." *Acta Genetica Medica Gemellologica,* vol. 33 (1984).

Yalom, Irvin D., M.D., et al. " 'Postpartum Blues' Syndrome." *Archives of General Psychiatry,* vol. 18 (January 1968).

Zuger, Bernard. "Monozygotic Twins Discordant for Homosexuality: Report of a Pair and Significance of the Phenomenon." *Comprehensive Psychiatry,* vol. 17, no. 5 (1976).

INDEX

abdominoplasty, 153–154
adolescence, 144, 241, 261–262, 263
adult twins, 120, 236, 264
Ainslie, Ricardo, 248, 258
allergies, 48, 66, 77, 106
  to cow's milk, 48, 66, 69, 70, 77
  to lactose, 69, 77
  to plastic, 72
  solid foods and, 106
American Academy of Pediatrics, 45,
    46, 105, 106, 115
American Health, 157, 162, 163
American Institute for Foreign Study
    Scholarship Foundation, 26, 277
American Society of Plastic and
    Reconstructive Surgeons, 156
attention, public, 122, 126–127
au pairs, 24, 26–27, 277

Baby Boomers, 3
Baby Gear Guide, The (Bollinger and
    Cramer), 137
Bamford, Nancy, 214
barter arrangement, 32
bathing equipment, 118
Benson, Herbert, 172
bicycle carts, 137, 281
bicycle riding, 161
bilirubin, 62–64
birth-control pills, 5–7
birth order, 263, 264
body care, mothers', 14–16, 17, 149–
    169, 212
  abdomen in, 150–151
  breastfeeding and, 50, 150
  cosmetic surgery and, 153–156
  exercise in, 129, 157–163
  marital relationship and, 192–193
  nutrition in, 55, 163–169
  skin in, 152–153
  weight in, 149–150

Bollinger, Taree, 137
bonding, 21–23, 214, 246–256
  breastfeeding in, 48–49
  engrossment in, 186
  fathers and, 185–187
  twin bond and, 246–253
bottlefeeding, 41, 51, 52, 65–77, 114
  cleaning procedures for, 73–74
  commercial formulas in, 66–70, 107
  convenience of, 65
  equipment for, 71–73
  goat's milk in, 70–71
  growth rate and, 78–79
  homemade formulas in, 70
  keeping track of, 74
  procedures for, 74–77
brain development, 46–47, 50, 64,
    68, 253
Brazelton, T. Berry, 185, 198
breastfeeding, 33, 39–64, 104, 107,
    200–201, 276
  bonding and, 48–49
  child spacing and, 51
  convenience of, 47, 65
  developmental advantages of, 49
  growth rate and, 78–79
  immunological advantages of, 41,
    48
  incidence of, 44, 53
  mother's body and, 50, 150
  nutritional advantages of, 41, 45–
    47
  options offered by, 51–52
  outside support for, 43–46
  physiological process of, 53–55
  post-partum depression and, 49–50
  prematurity and, 50–51, 115
  problems in, 60–64
  procedures for, 55–60
  reasons for, 45–52
  relactation and, 51–52, 71

  resting necessary to, 47
  return to work and, 212, 214
  schedules in, 55–56
  simultaneous, 56–57
  water intake in, 55
*Breastfeeding Guide for the Working
    Woman* (Price and Bamford), 214
breasts:
  infections of, 62, 212
  nipples of, 40, 42, 46, 60–62, 72
  plugged ducts in, 62
  shields for, 61
  surgical repair of, 154–155
breathing techniques, 169–173
burping, 56, 76

caffeine, 167
cardiac failure, congestive, 70
Carper, Jean, 164
carriers, baby, 94–95, 137, 280
cesarean sections, 14, 17, 24, 192,
    276
childbirth, 12, 13–16, 275
  complications in, 15–16, 24, 192
  infant behavior after, 90
  medical interventions in, 14, 17,
    24, 192, 276
  surprises in, 14–17
childbirth education classes, 14, 187,
    190, 275
child spacing, 51
circumcision, 90–91
Clomid (clomiphene), 5
clothing, baby, 117–118
Collier, Herbert, 249–251
colostrum, 48, 53, 61
commercial formulas, 66–70, 107
competition, sibling, 263–265
contact, physical, 20, 21–22, 91, 95,
    193
contact dermatitis, 72

cooking co-ops, 32
cosmetic surgery, 153–156
Costill, David, 159
cow's milk, 45, 48, 66
    allergies to, 48, 66, 69, 70, 77
    formulas based on, 68–69, 70, 77
Cramer, Patricia, 137
cribs, 36, 118–119, 135
crying, 90–98, 113–114
    dealing with, 92–97
    by mothers, 98–99
    reasons for, 90–92
    sleep and, 100

Davis, Adelle, 165–166
daycare, 207–208, 212–213, 217–
    224, 261
depression, 141, 208–209
    post-partum, 13, 18–19, 33, 49–50
development, child, 196–197, 227–
    243, 253–254, 255
    breastfeeding and, 49
    heredity vs. environment in, 92,
        228–229, 231, 232, 266–267
    intelligence in, 64, 227, 228–231
    language in, *see* language
        development
    methods for optimizing, 236–238
    myths about, 227–236, 251–252
    parental gender differences in,
        184–185
    patterns of, 228
    school and, 235–236, 238–243
    social development in, 236
diapers, 35, 91, 115–117
dominance, in twins, 242–243, 248,
    265–266
Don't Shoot the Dog (Pryor), 191
doulas, 25, 27, 276–277
dressing alike, 119–120, 126–127,
    197–198
drugs, nonprescription, 168–169
Dunn, Judy, 90–91, 197, 264

eczema, 48
Enfamil, 66
engrossment, 186
equipment, 115, 135–137, 280–281
    bathing, 118
    bottlefeeding, 71–73
    exercise, 161

nursery, 35–37, 118–119
outing, 125, 135–137
solids-feeding, 109–110, 135
exercise, 129, 157–163
extrasensory perception (ESP), 248–
    251

family members, 13, 179–203
    cohesion of, 271, 272
    fathers, *see* fathers
    grandparents, 31, 182, 197, 198–
        203, 261
    help from, 30, 31, 32–33, 190–
        191, 198, 199–203
    return to work and, 211–212
    siblings, 24, 32, 127, 182, 195–
        199, 202–203, 229
    sleeping arrangements of, 59, 102–
        103
fathers, 141, 179, 195, 198, 202–203
    coping strategies for, 188–190
    marital relationship and, 183, 189,
        192–195
    myths of, 183–188
    positive reinforcement of, 190–191
    return to work by, 211–212
    role of, 181–183
    siblings and, 197, 198
    societal expectations and, 179–181
Feel the Fear and Do It Anyway
    (Jeffers), 145–146
fertility drugs, 3, 5
fighting, 263–265
finger foods, 109, 110–111
first year, 81–137
    clothing needed in, 117–118
    dressing alike and, 119–120
    crying in, 90–98
    diapers and, 35, 91, 115–117
    equipment needed in, 109–110,
        118–119, 135–137
    outings during, 120–130, 135–137
    planning for, 83
    prematurity and, 111–115
    resources for, 275–277
    routines in, 82–90
    safety in, 133–135
    sleep patterns in, 99–104
    solid foods in, 46, 51, 105–111, 115
    traveling during, 130–132
formulas, 45, 65–71, 76, 77, 107, 114

fraternal twins, 6–9, 183, 234, 265
    breastfeeding of, 56
    hereditary factors in birth of, 6–7
    incidence of, 3, 7, 9
    language development by, 233,
        234, 265
    multiple paternity of, 8–9
    opposite-sex, 6, 56, 234–235, 265
    racial factors in birth of, 7–8
fundal height, uterine, 150–151

gates, safety, 134
gender differences, 90–91
    language development and, 234,
        235–236
    parental, developmental effects of,
        184–185
goat's milk, 70–71
"good enough" mothering, 259
grandparents, 31, 182, 197, 198–203,
    261
    adopting of, 202
*Grandparents/Grandchildren: The
    Vital Connection* (Kornhaber and
    Woodward), 199
Gregor Mendel Institute of Medical
    Genetics and Twin Studies, 8
growth charts, 40, 78–79

Halpern, Steven, 174
harnesses, baby, 137, 280
Harrison, Helen, 111
help, 23–34, 110
    asking for, 33–34
    evaluating needs for, 24–25
    family members as, 30, 31, 32–33,
        190–191, 198, 199–203
    non-paid, 30–33
    prematurity and, 113
    types of, 25–33
heredity, 152
    environment vs., 92, 228–229,
        231, 232, 266–267
    identity formation and, 266–267
    intelligence and, 228–229, 231
    multiple births related to, 6–7
highchairs, 109, 110, 135
homecoming, 12, 111–113
home-economics departments, 31
home health care, 25, 28, 276
homemade formulas, 70

homemakers, visiting, 25
hook-on seats, 109–110, 135
housework, 25, 141, 148, 208–209, 211, 224, 225, 280
Howell, Mary C., 211
human milk banks, 71, 77

identical twins, 183
    breastfeeding of, 56
    dressing alike of, 197–198
    incidence of, 2–3, 7, 9
    individuality development in, 180, 252, 265
    language development in, 233, 234, 235
    myths about, 179–180
identity formation, 256–263, 265–267
immune system, 41, 48, 66, 162–163
individual differences, infant, 90
individuality, development of, 180, 245–267
    adolescence and, 144, 241, 261–262, 263
    competition in, 263–265
    dressing alike and, 119–120, 126–127, 197–198
    heredity vs. environment in, 266–267
    identity formation in, 256–263, 265–267
    myths about, 246–252, 265–267
    parental influence on, 252–256, 259–260
    return to work and, 212–213
    separation in, 238–243, 245–248, 267
    social development and, 212–213, 252–254, 264
    twin bond and, 246–253
infant seats, 59, 115
insurance coverage, 24–25, 28, 156
intelligence, 64, 227, 228–231
    heredity vs. environment in, 228–229, 231
    intelligence tests and, 228–229, 230–231
iron, 46–47, 68, 107, 114–115, 165

jaundice, 62–64
Jeffers, Susan, 145–146
job sharing, 216

journal writing, 176
jumping rope, 161

Kamen, Betty, 164
Kennell, John, 21
Klaus, Marshall, 21
Kornhaber, A., 199

lactation centers, 44
lactose, 46, 68, 69, 77
La Leche League International, 30, 43–44, 61, 71, 108, 129, 276
Lancet, The, 15
language development, 228, 231–236, 260, 262
    gender differences in, 234, 235–236
    problems of, 232–236
    secret languages in, 227, 231, 232, 233–234
let-down, milk, 54
Let's Have Healthy Children (Davis), 166
Lewis, Michael, 256
Louisville Twin Study, 133, 231, 248

McDermott, John F., Jr., 264
marital relationships, 20, 183, 189, 192–195, 211–212, 279
Matthews-Simonton, Stephanie, 143, 144, 174–175
meat-based formulas, 69
Medicaid, 24–25
microwave ovens, 111
mind focus, 172–173, 174
mirrors:
    rearview, 137, 281
    self-concept and, 265
Mother Care/Other Care (Scarr), 219
mothers, self-care of, 19–21, 139–177
    body care in, *see* body care, mothers'
    crying and, 98–99
    making changes and, 144–146
    personal responsibility for, 141–144
    planning ahead for, 140–141
    positive attitudes helpful to, 141–144
    recharging techniques in, 173–176
    relaxation techniques in, 169–173

resources for, 275–277
    self-appreciation and, 176–177
    time control in, 146–149
Mother's Home Business Network, 217, 279
multiple births, 1–9, 269–281
    advantages of, 269–272
    birth-control pills and, 5–7
    causes of, 2–9
    fertility drugs and, 3, 5
    fraternal, 6–9
    geographical location and, 8
    hereditary factors in, 6–7
    incidence of, 2, 3, 7, 9
    mothers' age in, 3, 7
    multiple paternity in, 8–9
    myths about, 179–180, 227–236
    prenatally undetected, 3, 14
    previous births and, 7
    psychological factors in, 8
    racial factors in, 3, 6, 7–8
    resources for, 274–281
    rules for parents of, 271
    societal expectations and, 179–181
music, 173–174

National Alliance of Homebased Businesswomen, 217, 279
National Institutes of Health, 185, 187
National Organization of Mothers of Twins Clubs, 44, 202, 249–251, 274
New England Journal of Medicine, 9
New York Times, 22
9 to 5 (The National Association of Working Women), 206
nipples, bottle, 71–73, 114
nipples, breast, 40, 42, 46, 60–62, 72
nursery, 35–37, 118–119
nurses, visiting, 28

obesity, infant, 106–107
outings, 120–130
    destinations for, 127–130
    equipment for, 125, 135–137
    obstacles to, 121–127
oxcytocin, 50

pacifiers, 49, 91, 95–96
packs, carrying, 137
parenting centers, 31

Parents of Multiple Birth Association of Canada, 182, 274
part-time work, 215–216, 279
paternity, multiple, 8–9
paternity leave, 188–189, 211
Pediatrics, 106
Pep-Up, 165–166
Pergonal, 5, 8
Peterson, Christopher, 142
Phillips, Robert H., 170
phototherapy, of newborns, 63–64
picnics, 129
PKU (phenylketonuria), 70
play groups, 130
positive reinforcement, 190–191, 200
predigested formulas, 69–70, 77
pregnancy, 12, 25
Premature Baby Book, The (Harrison), 111
prematurity, 15, 111–115, 134
    bottlefeeding in, 114
    breastfeeding in, 50–51, 115
    equipment for, 115
    growth rate in, 78–79, 113
    help in, 113
    homecoming and, 111–113
    jaundice in, 63
    resources for, 277–279
Price, Anne, 214
prolactin, 50, 51
Pryor, Karen, 191

quadruplets, 2, 5, 202, 252, 254
Quick Relax, 171
Quick Release, 170–171
quintuplets, 5, 202

reading disabilities, 235
reciprocity, 260
relactation, 51–52, 71
Relaxation Response, The (Benson), 172
relaxation techniques, 169–173
retrolental fibroplasia, 114–115
rocking, 94

safety, 35, 133–135, 281
Saunders, Antoinette, 171
Scarr, Sandra, 219, 253, 254
school, 120, 180
    learning problems in, 235–236

separation in, 238–243, 245–247, 267
secret languages, 227, 231, 232, 233–234
self-employment, 217, 279–280
Seligman, Martin E. P., 142–143
separation, 238–243, 245–248, 267
sextuplets, 5
shopping centers, 129–130
siblings, 24, 32, 127, 182, 195–199, 202–203, 229
Siblings: Love, Envy and Understanding (Dunn), 197
Similac, 66
Simonton, Carl, 143, 144, 174–175
sleep, 59, 99–104, 113, 114
    "crying it out" and, 100
    environmental temperature in, 91
    family arrangements for, 59, 102–103
    infant's weight and, 100
    methods for inducing, 101–104
    solid foods and, 99–100, 107
sleep-deprivation studies, 193
smell therapy, 176
smoking, 154, 167–168
social development, 236, 212–213, 252–254, 264
solid foods, 46, 51, 105–111, 115
    allergies to, 106
    equipment for, 109–110, 135
    finger foods in, 109, 110–111
    sleep and, 99–100, 107
sound, soothing, 96–97, 102, 173–174
Sound Health: The Music and Sounds That Make Us Whole (Halpern), 174
soy-based formulas, 69, 77
special formulas, 70
stairs, 134
Stern, Daniel, 22
stimulation, infant, 37, 102, 103–104, 113, 114
stretch marks, 152, 153, 154, 192
strollers, 115, 123, 125, 135–136, 280
sucking, 56, 63, 91, 95–96
sugar, 168–169
supermarkets, 128, 137
support groups, parental, 30, 128–129, 277–279

swaddling, 91, 94–95
swimming, 159
sympathetic pains, 251
synchrony, 260

taurine, 66
thumb sucking, 96
tooth formation:
    bottlefeeding and, 76
    breastfeeding in, 49
    sucking in, 96
toxemia, 15
transitional objects, 258, 260–261
transitions, post-partum, 12–37
    body adjustments in, 14–16
    bonding in, 21–23
    breastfeeding in, 49–50
    coming to terms with, 19–21
    emotional reactions to, 13–14, 16–19, 98–99
    getting help for, 23–34
    planning ahead in, 34–37
traveling, 130–132
triplets, 228–236, 246, 252, 254, 255, 280
    incidence of, 2, 5
    resources for, 274
twins:
    advantages of, 269–272
    developmental myths about, 227–236
    eating schedules of, 56–57
    identity formation in, 246–252, 265–267
    incidence of, 5, 7
    injuries to, 133
    resources for, 274–275
    sleep patterns of, 104
    twin bond in, 246–253
    see also fraternal twins, identical twins

Vaillant, George, 142
visual imagery, 174–175
vitamin E cream, 152
vitamins, 47, 55, 70, 71, 107, 165–166, 167–168

walkers, infant, 134
Walkers Club of America, 158
walking, as exercise, 158

Watson, Peter, 266
whey, 68
white noise, 97, 102
Wilson, Ronald S., 231, 248
Winnicott, D. W., 259
Winston, George, 174
Woodward, K. L., 199

work, return to, 147, 205–225
   backups for, 223–224
   breastfeeding and, 212, 214
   daycare and, 207–208, 212–213,
     217–224
   by fathers, 211–212
   pros and cons of, 207–212

   reasons for, 206–207
   resources for, 217, 279–280
   rules for, 224–225
   timing of, 212–214
   work options in, 214–217, 280

yeast, nutritional, 165–166.